PRAISE FOR *B*

M000118950

"No idea looms larger in ~~the Mormon mind than~~ ...
pure, unspoiled place that gives people refuge and prepares them
for revelation. *Blossom as the Cliffrose* gathers some of Mormonism's most creative voices to testify to the power of wilderness
spaces—in the land, in our faith, and in our lives. The essays and
poems in this volume come from the heart of the wilderness and
are themselves both refuge and revelation."

—Michael Austin, author of *A Voice in the Wilderness:
Conversations with Terry Tempest Williams* and
Vardis Fisher: A Mormon Novelist

"When I ask my Mormon-Jewish daughter when she feels most
Mormon, she tells me, 'When I am outside, in the canyons, in
the mountains, in the West.' The beloved community of writers
assembled here articulates a thousand reasons why so many of
us feel this way. These are rich and complicated feelings—not
just the sublimity of Wordsworth's environmental imagination,
but also feelings of betrayal, reverence, disappointment, pleasure, misunderstanding, and loss appropriate to a place storied
with theft and massacre, failed dams and inland seas, uranium
and abandoned poisons, dried seeps and sacred groves, salt
and gulls, sego lilies, and hordes of crickets. Danielle Beazer
Dubrasky and Karin Anderson are expert guides to this territory. Let them and this book bring you home."

—Joanna Brooks, author of *The Book of Mormon Girl* and
co-editor of *Mormon Feminisms* and
Decolonizing Mormonism

"I feel as if I've just finished a trek in the desert—burned by the
illuminating sun of the Mormon mindset, parched by the thirst
for certainty and hope both in nature and man, and made holy

by the visions and insights one can only glean in the beauty of solitary, windswept places. These poems and essays dig into the caverns and canyons of a Mormon reader's soul in ways that either comfort or disrupt—and sometimes both. Regardless of the effect, the themes are honest, piercing, and thought-provoking in every sense."

—Tanya Mills, The Book Bungalow

BLOSSOM

AS THE

CLIFFROSE

BLOSSOM
AS THE
CLIFFROSE

MORMON LEGACIES AND THE BECKONING WILD

EDITED BY KARIN ANDERSON & DANIELLE BEAZER DUBRASKY

TORREY HOUSE PRESS

Salt Lake City • Torrey

First Torrey House Press Edition, June 2021

Published by Torrey House Press
Salt Lake City, Utah
www.torreyhouse.org

International Standard Book Number: 978-1-948814-42-3
E-book ISBN: 978-1-948814-43-0
Library of Congress Control Number: 2020946734

Cover art by Mary Vaux Walcott, *Cliffrose (Cowania stanshuriana)*, 1934, Smithsonian American Art Museum

Cover design by Kathleen Metcalf
Interior design by Rachel Buck-Cockayne
Distributed to the trade by Consortium Book Sales and Distribution

Torrey House Press offices in Salt Lake City sit on the homelands of Ute, Goshute, Shoshone, and Paiute nations. Offices in Torrey are in homelands of Southern Paiute, Ute, and Navajo nations.

TABLE OF CONTENTS

FATHER

MOTHER

REVEL

INTERCEDE

POISON

ANTICIPATE

COLLECT

(UN)CLAIM

INHERIT

RISE

WANDER

PRELUDE

Danielle Beazer Dubrasky

Leave No Trace

Fifty miles west of Fort Laramie in Wyoming, the faint wagon wheel depressions left by Mormon emigrants have almost disappeared from the grasslands. The Mormon trek, both iconic and disruptive, evinces a *people* displaced from their established communities who would in turn enact further displacement on Indigenous peoples as part of a larger western narrative. But the Mormon narrative begins in a secluded grove of trees outside of Palmyra, New York, where Joseph Smith describes having seen a vision of deity in a pillar of light. As a person of faith I acknowledge that within the Mormon psyche, the interpretation of this encounter by Joseph Smith ranges a vast scale: from beacon of divine origin leading toward eternal salvation to fabrication or possible delusion with questionable merit. Leanings toward both ends of the spectrum have a place within this anthology. In the call for submissions, the co-editors stated: "We use 'Mormon' to name a *cultural network and historical context* that has, until recently, answered to this moniker since the early nineteenth century. We are interested in ways this tradition has engendered worldviews, habits, idiosyncratic histories, familial narratives, and variant communities. How do these aspects converse with a philosophy of environmental stewardship, protection, and conservation?"

3

To grow up Mormon is to always be aware of pioneer footsteps that crossed the land before. Near Horseshoe Creek a steady wind blows over the grassy hills in a landscape that is open but secretive. Here on a hot day in late July, 1852, the Abraham O. Smoot Company stopped at the top of a steep hill to assess how the wagons and handcarts might descend. My ancestor Elizabeth Mainwaring stepped off the wagon and walked down the hill with her four-year-old son, Joshua, to the base thick with currant bushes. She told Joshua she was going to look for blackberries. She held a tin cup in her hands to give him a drink of water from a stream, then told him to return to the wagon at the top of the hill. That was the last time she was seen by anyone from the company with whom she had traveled along the pioneer trail since Kansas City, Missouri.

A devout Methodist who reluctantly followed her converted Mormon husband from their home in Liverpool, Elizabeth had left behind her mother and three buried children back in England, taking with her on the journey her daughter, a son, and a thirteen-month-old baby girl. After her disappearance, her husband and other members of the wagon train searched for her along the creek. They found her tracks in the direction of Fort Laramie and ran across a group of sheepherders who said they saw a woman traveling alone hiding in the bushes; she seemed deranged and they did not approach her. But another version of the story is that the sheepherders saw a woman on a horse in the company of two men. No trace of her was found, and after a few days, the Mormon emigrants had to move on toward Salt Lake City. Elizabeth was forty years old. Her husband Isaac became deathly ill soon after but recovered and eventually remarried five years later.

The family rumors passed down through my great-grandfather, Joshua—the last one to see his mother—speculated that she decided to start back east, having had enough of the barren western landscape and the hardship of the camps, tending to a baby and a toddler while recovering from illness. But her name-sake daughter, Elizabeth, remembered a mother who would never abandon her children—though she had quarreled with her husband more than once on the trail. Their marriage would have represented both sides of the scale regarding Joseph Smith's story. Elizabeth Mainwaring never forgave Isaac for believing that prophet's vision of salvation through a promised land over her own John Wesley's teachings of his one true apostolic church. While still in Liverpool, she once burned all of her husband's Mormon books and papers in their fireplace out of anger; he responded with anger, possibly even a flogging, a legal act for a disobedient wife in nineteenth-century England. Still at a hostile standoff, they boarded the *Ellen Maria* together from the Victoria Dock near East London, the mother sacrificing her homeland and religion to travel to a strange land to be with her children. On visiting the site near her disappearance more than a century later, one of my cousins told a Bureau of Land Management employee the story of her wandering off. "Quicksand," the agent immediately responded. "It's all over this area. She could have gotten trapped and not been able to call for anyone."

In her essay "The Art of Memoir," Mary Clearman Blew writes about her grandmother who homesteaded alone in Montana for over a year and one day became delusional, thinking she saw her dead mother gesturing to her from across the river. The woman backed away from the river, away from the "ghost," and returned to the safety of her home, choosing not to hearken to her hallucinations, what Blew calls "the beckoning shapes." Blew argues that it is the writer's imperative to follow the beckoning shapes that haunt from wild places despite the risk of losing one's way. In creating this anthology, we wished to create a gathering space of writers to whom the experience of being raised in or influenced by the Church of Jesus Christ of Latter-day Saints gave an inherent affinity for the natural world and wild places. Our interest in the use of "Mormon" to name a "cultural network and historical context" acknowledges common motifs in these writers' experiences regardless of religious belief.

In our understanding, this anthology is the first of its kind in which believers and nonbelievers of the Mormon religion share a stage as each voice comes forward to tell their story. Through the lens of their "Mormon experience," we read the intersections of place, landscape, culture, and history that are both familiar in the western narrative and "peculiar." At the forefront is the complex and often troubling legacy left by the intersections of land use between Indigenous people—particularly Shoshone, Ute, Paiute, and Navajo people—and the Mormon immigrants. These stories speak for themselves. The road trip as a modern-day trek, the discovery of sacred places, mothers and their gardens, definitions of homeland versus wilderness, generational layers of land ownership as a result of usurpation, generational illness from poisoned land, plaintive calls to a Mother in Heaven. These motifs emerged organically during the selection process, revealing aspects of a shared psyche even as "believer" and "nonbeliever" stand at each end of the scale from each other, cousins twice removed but cousins still. These voices represent a range of perspectives from believers within the faith, to those on the threshold, to those who have left but still stand at the periphery. However, they all come together with a common affinity for the natural world, for sustainability, and for understanding how the Mormon experience shaped that affinity.

Current environmental practices in predominantly Mormon communities do not demonstrate such a universal affinity. Instead, environmentalism is often seen through a lens suspicious of government interference. Hence, the battles over national monuments, wilderness designations, and the use of resources on federal land. Not to mention the lack of a concerted effort to conserve water in some of the driest states in the nation or a strategy for countering air pollution and overgrazing. Many of these conflicts are endemic to western rural communities in general. So why single out the Mormon ones? One of the most well-known religious documents associated with the Mormon religion is the Word of Wisdom—a series of directives for both physical and spiritual health. Abstinence from tobacco, coffee, and alcohol is a widely identifiable marker for a practicing Mormon. But the following verses from Doctrine and Covenants might as well be invisible: "Yea, flesh also of beasts and of the fowls of the air, I, the Lord, have ordained for the use of man with thanksgiving; nevertheless they are to be used sparingly; And it is pleasing unto me that they should not be used, only in time of winter, or of cold, or famine." The Doctrine and Covenants is recognized by Mormons as the word of God speaking directly to Joseph Smith. The statement that the early members of this faith were to eat meat sparingly contains a preference for sustainability of resources—both land and animals—not exploitation. What would happen to the ranching industries and subsequent over-grazed lands in Utah if devout Mormons were to take this direction to heart? Why is it that eating meat every day is not shunned in Mormon communities the same way as smoking or drinking alcohol? This scripture is but one example of a doctrine that advocates for stewardship but has been ignored in favor of economic and cultural priorities associated with the West. How did the myth of the western cowboy as a symbol of autonomy override a symbiotic relationship with the natural world despite the fact that such a relationship is preferred in "God's own words"? Some of the voices in this anthology bring to light and contextualize these contradictions and dichotomies.

A generation after the mystery of my great-great-grandmother's lost way, the legacy of her descendants was a cabin in a canyon near the Provo River. Each summer in the 1970s my family would take the five-day road trip on I-80 from Virginia to Utah until my siblings and I piled out of the overheated Dodge Dart and scrambled into the coolness of the Brown Cabin bought many years ago by my grandfather, Isaac Jr. We waded over river rocks in the fast-moving creek, cooled watermelons in the crevices, crossed the Monkey Bridge built by my uncle, or took our pennies down the road to an old store to buy Pixy Stix or Red Vines. We spent all summer playing night games with cousins behind neighboring cabins or riding inner tubes down the creek. And every night I would climb the narrow ladder to the loft into one of the wrought-iron beds with squeaky springs and fall asleep to the creek's rushing sound, only slightly louder than my aunts and uncles laughing through their card games at the large oak table in the room below with a stone fireplace, old piano, and a green cabinet full of puzzles and torn cardboard covers for Candy Land and Monopoly.

On Sundays we walked down to church—an outdoor "chapel" of chairs set between cottonwoods presided over by a "called-for-the-summer" branch president. People from all over the region would come to the meeting. My sister and I could wear pants if we wanted to or spread out blankets on the grass for the sacrament. The passing of the sacrament by boys wearing jeans and casual shirts was followed by a Sunday lesson for the adults in the chapel and a primary lesson in one of the other cabins for the younger ones. Fathers would baptize their children in the creek on a Saturday, wrapping white-clad shivering bodies in a towel, while mothers bore testimony beneath the trees the next Sunday. Going to a church without walls or a ceiling for so many summers of my childhood created a dislike for the 1970s enclosed chapels that seemed designed to shut out the sun. The square hanging light fixtures, brown polyester carpet, and opaque windows felt dreary and oppressive. I longed to look up, "to lift up mine eyes," and see the steep banks on the backside of Mount Timpanogos instead of plaster and fluorescent lights.

Solastalgia is a term created by philosopher Glenn Albrecht that means nostalgia for a place that still exists but that has been irrevocably changed, usually because of development—a shopping mall or subdivision built over an open acreage where children once rode bikes. But it can refer to any place that no longer carries the identity it once had. The site of our canyon church still exists, but it is used for other gatherings. Now on Sundays the canyon is vacant as churchgoers drive their Subarus to attend one of the wards in Provo. But those early memories of outdoor church imprinted on me that the God of my Mormon experience existed primarily in the natural world. The opening verses of Genesis that describe the creation of the earth are deeply familiar to anyone who devoutly practices this religion. And yet the love for the earth from those verses does not seem to be graven on many hearts. Why is environmentalism seen as an enemy to many followers of the Mormon Church rather than as a way to honor divine creation?

Even as I ask this question, I am aware of my own hypocrisy. The Timpanogos Tribe lived and fished along the Provo River until Mormon settlers first starved them out, then massacred them, relocating the remaining people to the Uinta Reservation. The cabins in the canyon of my childhood were originally built in the early 1900s by Brigham Young University as a retreat for faculty until the university decided to sell off that property and develop a place further up the mountain. Was my grandmother's cabin and the canyon I still think of as a refuge also a place where the Timpanogos people lived? Displacement, relocation, and the definition of what is wild are complicated terms in the Mormon religion or stories of the West. For many Indigenous people, what the settlers perceived as wild was a cultivated and communal landscape; their grief of solastalgia resonates with usurpation and marks the homeland they were forced to leave. At what cost was the migration of my ancestors? A mother who disappeared. An Indigenous people decimated.

When she was twelve, my daughter joined her stake youth group on the reenactment of the traditional pioneer trek where she was to dress in pioneer clothes and follow the Martin's Cove trail in Wyoming, pushing a handcart over faint historic wagon wheel ruts not too far from where my great-great-grandmother wandered off. At that age she was excited about sewing her own long skirt and going to the Deseret Industries thrift shop for long-sleeved cotton blouses. We borrowed two bonnets from my sister, whose daughters had gone years before. But I couldn't fight my own cynical thoughts as if my ancestors were channeling their pragmatic admonishment: "We did this so you don't have to." Having been raised in Virginia, my experience of Pioneer Day was gathering with our small ward primary on the closest Saturday to July 24, singing "Primary children sang as they walked and walked and walked…" as we pushed cardboard handcarts across the dusty wooden floor in the cultural hall followed by treats from the local Spudnut Shop.

I also sensed that my grandmother, the savvy, strong-willed, adventurous woman who married Isaac Jr., would have found it a wasteful endeavor to return to the hardships of the past when there was so much to embrace and experience in the future unfurling at her feet. Her father had crossed the plains with his family at the age of ten and later wrote that it was the best time for a young boy, seeing different wild animals or birds each day and sleeping under the stars at night. It gave him a lifelong love for nature, believing it to be a sacred manifestation of a divine creation—so different from young Joshua remembering at age four a cool cup of water, a frantic search, and miles of prairie grass separating him forever from his mother.

Aside from my doubts about the spiritual merits of the whole trek excursion, I could not fight waves of anxiety; I was sending my only child to spend a three-day camping trip with a makeshift family and hordes of other people I barely knew. Clearly, I was lacking in faith. Despite having been a practicing Mormon in Utah for almost thirty years, I still perceive an invisible wall between my dreamy sense of spirituality and my neighbors' industry of gardening, canning, food storage, and self-reliance. I am afraid I may never truly belong to my "people" if the stacked cans of black-eyed peas on my pantry shelf, bought during my one attempt to take advantage of Lin's Grocery case-lot sales and nearing expiration, is any indication of my ability to anticipate an apocalypse. (I wrote that sentence prior to the COVID-19 pandemic and have since repented of my errant ways with a collection of tin cans filled with pinto beans, oats, powdered milk, and potato flakes from the local cannery.)

My daughter returned from Wyoming exhausted but in high spirits, complained only of how the days were too hot, the nights too cold, there were no trees, and she hated biscuits and gravy for breakfast. She had little affinity for the sacrifices of what her ancestors and others may have experienced but returned still a child of the twenty-first century where, when I gave her a fierce long hug, I felt she firmly belonged. But as I consider the drying deserts, burning forests, flooding coasts, I wonder where we will ultimately find refuge. I don't buy into the notion that the earth is gradually being scorched toward an apocalyptic renewal as a new world for the "righteous." We are the ones carrying torches and lighting the fires toward our own self-destruction.

When I was eighteen my father died of a heart attack. A year later my mother sold our house in the South and moved to the southern Utah desert. On my last day in the house, I stood in the dining room emptied of all furniture and voices from my family, filled with a grief that comes from knowing that one can never return to a point in time. When I flew over Las Vegas, over land that was either brown or paved, not a hint of green, I sobbed, not caring about the concerned flight attendants nor other passengers. I wonder now about Elizabeth Mainwaring watching the quay at Victoria Dock fade then disappear as a point in time while she stood on the deck of the *Ellen Maria*, the ship charging irrevocably toward the Atlantic, and her fate on an obscure trail in Wyoming. From the Las Vegas airport, my family drove through the Virgin River Gorge, and for the first time, I saw the Milky Way—lights to another path. But there are still nights I wake up startled by dreams of my old house, backyard woods, fireflies, and my family together in a place that will never again exist. *Solastalgia.*

The Irish poet Seamus Heaney described the dilemma of poets from Northern Ireland writing about the challenges of living in a divided country. In their search to portray their sense of place, they experience "the mystery of living in two places at one time...they make do with a constructed destination, an interim place whose foundations straddle the areas of self-division, a place of resolved contradiction, beyond confusion....A place that does not exist...a place that is but a dream, since this promised land of durable coherence and perpetual homecoming is not somewhere that is ultimately attainable....[It is] an elsewhere beyond the frontiers of writing where the imagination presses back against reality" (190). In many of these writings we see the desire to find that "elsewhere" reimagined out of family lore or cultural tradition.

Heaney also addressed another dilemma for writers influenced by the religious conflicts in Ireland. He talks about how the poets of Northern Ireland have the challenge of being "a source of truth and at the same time a vehicle of harmony.... these poets feel with a special force a need to be true to the negative nature of the evidence and at the same time to show an affirming flame, the need to be both socially responsible and creatively free" (193). This is a challenge faced by many writers of religious backgrounds. Often popular writers of their faiths feel obligated to create works that mirror one-dimensional images of the congregants, works that reflect a homogenous experience. However, Heaney argues that it is the poet's or writer's responsibility not to simply reflect back one's culture but to elucidate the less visible narratives.

Credit for the anthology's title goes to Karin Anderson who

beautifully explains how "blossom as the cliffrose" came about in the following passage:

> Mormon colonizers who came to the Great Basin saw allegory in the Israelites searching for Zion. They compared the arid landscapes of the American West to the "wilderness" of Sinai. Old Testament prophecy must have shone verdant in the imaginations of European and Eastern American people reconciling raw sensory shock into beneficence: "And the desert shall rejoice, and blossom as the rose" (Isaiah 35:1). The astonishing angular beauty of the West was largely indiscernible to eyes trained to see "scenery [as] greenery." Nature was framed as an antagonist that must be tamed; landscape as clay to manipulate; aridity as a taunt begging rejoinder.
>
> Growing up desert Mormon means hearing the phrase so ubiquitously it's formative: I can only dimly gauge how implacably visions of roses obscure truer perceptions of a place that has literally created us. The opposition of "desert" and "garden" in Mormon metaphor has produced landscapes of cognitive dissonance: Euro-green stroked like Renaissance tempura over mineral nuance. Stone-fed cattle scrabbling for imaginary Ohio vegetation. Gridded towns, pitched roofs, and not-from-here franchise lots huddled against ageless expanses of mountain and cliff, chasm and canyon, contour and horizon.
>
> The rose is a lush European metaphor, symbol of cultivation and sophistication, of noble estate, temperamental beauty and inexorable death, clan wars and courtly love. By the time Mormon colonizers imported the image to the Great Basin, its Old Testament significations were compounded into fantasies of racial

sophistication, nostalgia for lost origins, disavowals of alienation. Our title, of course, speaks to the desert's answer: to the ironies of cultivating garden roses against a plenitude of native flora, to the delusions of calling the region "empty," to the violent insistence that "Utah" was a barren place that "no one wanted." The cliffrose grows glorious in its ancient home, cream-yellow flowers proliferating on a tough, vertical shrub rising in delicate, paradoxical grace against sky and stone. The cliffrose is the anti-rose, a subtle, antithetical rebuke to an encompassing colonizer paradigm, the shimmering image of doctrinal breakdown, a gorgeous marker of ideological boundary: aporia. Within our title, we name it "wild" in the sense of already home in its natural place, precisely uncultivated, undomesticated, and ever beckoning beyond the imported garden wall.

The essays and poems in this collection attest to both the crossings and the divides between Indigenous people and immigrant descendants that are a legacy of our complex relationships to the "wild" and to heritage. It is through these various lenses that we see how some honor that originating pillar of light through the trees as a holy embrace while others find the legacy of its circling too exclusive and contradictory. Both views have place here. Earlier in Heaney's essay he states that "writing…is a mode of integration, of redistributing the whole field of cultural and political force into a tolerable order" (189). Thus, the range in this anthology as stories coincide to create a larger picture of peripherally shared experiences with landscape and the land.

In the historical account of Joseph Smith's life, *Joseph Smith: Rough Stone Rolling*, Richard Bushman tells of Joseph traveling with some companions through a backcountry when they see three rattlesnakes. The other men's first instinct is to kill the intruders. But Joseph stops them from doing so by arguing, "'When will the Lion lie down with the Lamb…while man seeks to destroy and waste the flesh of beasts, waging a continual war against reptiles, let man first get rid of his destructive propensities and then we may look for a change in the serpents' disposition.' They avoided killing snakes from then on…and shot wild animals only for food" (241). These words by the founder and prophet of the Mormon religion are indicative of an "Edenic" approach to the natural world, one that seemed to recognize shared resources with wildness—a philosophy that was swallowed up by the collusion of manifest destiny with a belief that a promised land had been restored for the wandering remnants of God's chosen people.

My other great-grandfather with fond memories of sleeping beneath the stars as a child on his trek West once left his wool jacket on a fence post while working on his farm as an adult. When he returned near dusk, he saw that a bird had started to build its nest in a coat pocket. Rather than disturb the nest, he left his jacket and bought another one. By that time, he was a prominent judge in his community and had the means to do so, but even if not, it seems he would have been hesitant to interfere with this other creature, whose home he respected almost as much as his own.

What beckoned Elizabeth Mainwaring to follow a strange path away from her family in the Wyoming prairie? Did she return to Fort Laramie, as some relatives speculate, and meet up with a group who could take her back to England? Or did the land itself take her back into its fold? If we are to follow the beckoning shapes as Mary Clearman Blew urges, what will we find in their wildness? A sacred reflection of our divine origins? Or a desolate landscape, a range of mountains and an open sky that call to us from a source deeper even than God?

Albrecht, Glenn; Sartore, Gina-Maree; et. al. "Solastalgia: The distress caused by environmental change." *American Psychology.* Vol. 15 supplement, 2007.

Blew, Mary Clearman. "The Art of Memoir." *The Fourth Genre: Contemporary Writers of/on Creative Nonfiction.* Robert L. Root, Michael J. Steinberg, Eds. Pearson: New York, 2011.

Bushman, Richard. *Joseph Smith: Rough Stone Rolling.* Vintage Books: New York, 2006.

Heaney, Seamus. *The Redress of Poetry.* Noon Day Press: New York, 1996.

EMBRACE

Tacey M. Atsitty

Lacing XIV

From the mountainside we appear
to wear each other deep into the road.
We appear in the braids of slowed
water at our knees, as though prepared

for a ritual among the falls. It breaks
all around us—lace in its final wear.
We nearly swallow ourselves, bare
every blue we have to give, until lakes

settle in with the stars. We came to see
stars wiggle, to wander the unknowing
grays & blues until finally, our flowing
bares our wrists: I wade for you, and see,

the stars wade for you—resting on an altar croquet
we approach land and sky, kneeling together on that day.

Phyllis Barber

The Desert: *Waiting*

I CAN FEEL THE SUN BOILING MY SKIN, EVEN NOW WHEN I think about it. Turning it red. Scalding me from above. Sometimes there was more than the heat over my head and all around my body—something malignant boiling beneath the Mojave Desert, something below the sand and the rocks. Unbearable heat rose from the magma underneath the surface, and then there were the pictures I'd seen—waterfalls of lava splashing and leaping uncontrollably on the inside of the earth.

Was that the hell I'd heard talked about? People were good at throwing around that word, that idea, that place. *H-e*-double toothpicks, the proper people would call it, and some felt constrained never to say the word at all. I'd heard about it, wherever, whatever it was, and this heat certainly felt like the fires of hell at times—Satan, Lucifer, Beelzebub, and the Prince of Darkness reigning in that very hot place. You'd wish you'd never been sent there. Burning in hell. Flames licking at your elbows while the Devil laughs to have you, at last, in his hooks.

That hell, after World War II, 1950, when I was about seven years old, wasn't always a subject in the four walls of that small LDS ward building in Boulder City, Nevada. It wasn't only a religious topic. Trust me. Even the kids at school had something to say about hell. But the talks at church in sacrament meeting (given by whomever from the congregation the bishop asked to speak on a particular Sunday) seemed to be more about the three glories—the Telestial (the lowest of the three kingdoms for liars, sorcerers, adulterers, whoremongers, and whosoever loves and makes a lie), the Terrestrial (the middle degree for those who were blinded by the craftiness of men and thus rejected the fullness of the gospel of Jesus Christ), and, of course, the Celestial—the Mormons' highest heaven. I never heard that much about "hell" when I went to church.

But once in the Boulder City Ward, this old-timer who lived in McKeeversville—the shantytown built around the railroad tracks when Hoover Dam was being built and which is no longer in existence—stood at the pulpit, raised his finger, and talked about Sons of Perdition, eternal fire, and damnation. His words scared me, that's the truth. And the world didn't feel as safe after that. He was big, a giant of a man, I remember. He wore overalls sometimes and liked to clean the wax out of his ears with one finger. He took us children for rides around the park across from our church. We squeezed into the rumble seat in the back of his 1931 Ford coupe where its inverted trunk caused us no end of joy as we rode in the open air, wind blowing our hair every which way, giggling to feel so free and heedless and privileged. But when he was speaking to the congregation on that day, the ceiling fan turning fruitlessly over our heads and our mothers cooling themselves with fold-up paper fans they kept in their purses, he pointed the same finger that cleaned his ear at all of us sitting below the stage where the pulpit was situated. Little pitchers with big ears, you know. I was too young to distinguish between attitude, opinion, truth, and reality, and even now, I'm unsure. Is hell a for-real place? Did that old-timer know what he was talking about?

This is the harder part, though—to tell you that this desert also reminded me of God, who, I was taught, is all-powerful in the heavens and much bigger than all of us. Who, if not He, decided there should be such a thing as the desert? God created all of this. He's the head of everything. And God must have had something to do with the Three Nephites—the three mortals ordained to live forever by Jesus when he appeared in the Book of Mormon (3 Nephi: 28). They "never taste of death...until all things will be fulfilled according to the will of the Father."

So why was the heat so hard on me? Why did I think it would be bad news to be stranded all by myself outside in this barren place, this Mojave Desert, when there were Three Nephites who watched after you? I should have been faithful and trusting and believing that one of them would show up if I was in trouble, just like the stories I'd heard in Primary and Testimony Meeting where anyone who wanted to stood at the pulpit and bore their testimony of the truthfulness of the Gospel. There were some good stories at those once-a-month Testimony Meetings, and who could predict what some people would say? They'd talk about their trips to Provo and Salt Lake, the way their car broke down and was then magically fixed after they prayed over the hood. They'd talk about how their son had been violently ill and had then been blessed by someone in the priesthood and how he'd revived. Sometimes, even men would cry when they talked about their families and what they believed was the truth. I liked that men felt comfortable with tears in their eyes because I always got choked up myself—part and parcel of the process. When I got older, though, I started to feel this moisture in my eyes and my voice was more habitual than something real.

But back to the Three Nephites. I remember one of those stories. A man was wandering in the desert—dazed and confused, thirsty unto total dryness, ready to give up, probably crawling on his hands and knees in torn clothes, his tongue almost hanging out for want of a sip of water. And, voila, he was found by one of those Nephites, who led him back to civilization. There were tons of those miraculous stories flying around when I was young, such as the one about a man who was prompted to get out of bed and move his wagon one night. He followed the prompting, and, the next morning, found a tree toppled over onto the spot where the wagon had been sitting. These stories used to send shivers down my spine, so I must have believed them. But I guess I must not have been full of complete faith at the time because I thought maybe I could melt before anyone would arrive to save me.

I've been caught in the crosshairs of this zenith and nadir, this zone between heaven and hell, this questioning, this probing of what the truth is. This heat and this desert is part of me. It pounded on my shiny black hair and felt like fire when I didn't wear shoes and skittered barefoot across asphalt. I first negotiated those streets named Arizona, Utah, California, New Mexico, etc. (after the seven states where the Colorado River flows) as a young girl in Boulder City, the town built to build Hoover Dam. Later, in Las Vegas, where we moved when I was eleven (before Howard Hughes, the hotel boom on the Strip, and the Mafia—I'd only heard about this organization through the grapevine so don't know that one for sure), I negotiated narrower but still hot streets. Dressed in a T-shirt, short shorts, and bare feet—sometimes on my heels and cramped toes curled to keep my soles from frying—I could feel heat everywhere: on my head, my arms, my hands, my torso, my everything. Bully of all bullies. That heat. It could hard-boil an egg in the shell. It could hard-boil me. Hot, hot, hot, as if there were no other word in the dictionary. Hot, hot, hot, like the hell some people talked about.

On the worst days, I'd retreat to my house—my safe place. I burrowed inside four walls behind a closed door and lay on top of my bed with a book and pinned curls hopeful against limpness. While my mother rattled pans in the kitchen and I settled my neck on the pillow that became increasingly wet, I'd bet she was wishing, as she often did, that she could move back North where things survived, where life seemed more plentiful and generous. Idaho was her heaven, the place where her family worked their fingers to the bone harvesting potatoes, running farms and ranches, and selling RVs. They were a step above the angels with their stiff upper lips, their goodness, and their dedication to the word of the Lord. Somehow they seemed set apart from southern Nevada and the rest of the lone and dreary world that sometimes felt like hell. I think we secretly worshiped the relatives in Idaho and thought they were more stable than we would ever be. We could blow away while they were digging potatoes.

I'd watched my mother plenty of times, coaxing her plants and trying to encourage things in hardscrabble plots—hens-and-chicks and dusty marigolds, sometimes even sweet peas. She stood for hours with a garden hose filling dry rings dug around the base of her two fruit trees, determined to have peaches and apricots she could preserve in jars for her family that wouldn't stop growing. But the desert didn't have much to give in the way of moisture. Only water from the hose saved those trees. Water brought in from somewhere else. Maybe Lake Mead created by Hoover Dam.

I should tell you it wasn't always as hot as I'm saying, though there were plenty of hot days. There were alluring days, in fact, and indelible memories in those summertimes like standing in front of swamp coolers on high with my cheeks feeling the breeze and like me and my siblings turning a Mexican-baked-adobe brown when we ran outside. And, I was certain. I had answers. To everything, even though I was a skinny, scrawny, loosely-pieced-together kid. I wonder why I thought I knew so much? Was it my religion that had all of the answers to everything? THE TRUTH? Was it my father, the proud and humble bishop who stood in front of the congregation every week, the man respected, the man listened to, and the man who cared for his flock of sheep and was as kind as anyone I ever knew? Was I blessed among the children of humans to know where we came from and where we were going, or was I a product of the simple arrogance that came with being in what I considered the top echelon of my ward, of even more than my ward? Was I better because of this? Was I ordained to a bigger life? I think, perhaps, I had a smidge, if not more, of pride, a streak of self-importance. After all, it is a big statement to say that you KNOW, that you KNOW, WITHOUT A DOUBT, the truth, even if it is outlined by the Church of Jesus Christ of Latter-day Saints and verified by the twelve current apostles and the head of the church known as the Prophet.

But the desert tempered all of that, sometimes in a succulent, generous, breathtaking way; sometimes in a frightening, windblown way. The desert was unpredictable. No mind could fathom its wiles, just as, I happen to think, no mind can fathom who and what God was or is. Our minds are fallible. They are finite. Infinity is an entirely different thing. We can only guess at what lies in store. The desert told me that. In no uncertain terms.

On warm nights, my brother, sister, and I slept outside in a double bed and listened to sprinklers and smelled water at work while we basked in the night sky with its scattering of stars. We listened to crickets and pretended we owned it all until other insects discovered the innards of the mattress. But when we moved to Las Vegas, the wind blew almost incessantly and the streetlights and the neon from the Strip changed the number of stars we could see—another unwanted reminder of the Devil and the unfairness of living in such a skimpy habitat where the wind whined and shrieked around corners of our tract home.

We lived on the edge of town facing an empty desert. Our two-story house was covered with yellow stucco and bordered by hard-packed dirt, a clothesline, the hopeful sticks of an apricot and a peach tree, a fence of stacked bricks, and a sad garden. The wind pummeled the bedroom windows with sand. "I'm boss here!" it seemed to shout as it bent shrubs flat—the ones across the street, the creosote, mesquite, the tumbleweeds before they tumbled. It puffed the clouds away, too, swept the valley clean, uncovered the sun, and made the hills and mountains as sharp as the edge of a serrated knife. It was stronger than my thin, skinny body, which would blow away if I stood out in the open without a wall at my back. It was bigger than I was, that's for sure, and it could push me to places I never asked to go. Was this God or Satan? This unmanaged power? This fierceness? These bulging muscles?

During a winter day, the sky could be steel slate with almost no delineation of clouds, wind blowing against the gray cover but not able to make a dent. I could hear the chorus of clouds being crowded into that big one, those commentators, as they expressed themselves from the underbelly of the sky, mumbling what the answer to all of it was though I could never quite understand what they said. What did it all mean? It seemed so pushy. But maybe this was a show to scare tiny mortals. Or, a question, did tiny mortals only dot the landscape with their cars, houses, and dreams of what it was all about? How important were we, are we, I wonder? The desert goes on and on, miles and miles, impersonal. We try, but fail, to own it, to wrestle it to its knees.

Not much water ever made it to the ground. Not much rain. "Oh, please rain today," I'd pray. "If not rain, at least a few clouds please," though even clouds were less than a real threat. Once in a surprising while there was too much rain. Flash floods. Feast or famine. I remember a raging river in front of our house, too swift for swimming, but an awesome sight for my eyes that were hankering for water. I expected to see floating animals being carried by the current. Floating refrigerators. Floating boats, but all I remember was the water, the rush of it, the brown of it. Bigger and starker than I could imagine. A river on East St. Louis Street in Las Vegas, Nevada.

But the sunsets offset this *sturm und drang*. Nothing was or is more beautiful. Nothing. The sky could be vivid, alight, vibrant, on fire, a mass of yellow, orange, reds, purples, you name it, even chartreuse. These colors reflected on our faces as we stared, slack-jawed, at the power of that sky—stunning like a pop-up picture book, mesmerizing, vital, and more intriguing than the land. Mount Charleston, in profile, was like Mount Fuji in triplicate to the tenth power, on steroids. The sunsets, the sunsets, the sunsets. Grand in the grandest sense of that word. Nothing anywhere could ever be as breathtaking as those sunsets. Who could breathe when the sky lit up this way? It seemed as though we lived in heaven when it became so much more than blue and vast. This was the time when I believed that God was in the heavens, smiling, directing this beauty, this pageant, this wondrous scene before my eyes. This was when I felt blessed to be human, to be part of all of this.

The irony is that the desert has captivated me. This bony terrain, this lonely yet wise place, teaching what it is to be left on one's own, subject to wind and sand blowing against one's face. Insulting. Isolating. Vast. A piece in the puzzle of eternity. It is a stretch of geography that explains God, heaven, and hell with no words, no scriptures, no ideologies. This wind has blown away all of my answers after years of considering various and sundry ideas. I'm almost a clean sweep. Just like the desert on a windy day. An empty cow skull on land stretched across the earth's surface. A drum skin unattached to a drum.

What is the desert? Why does it exist?

By all accounts, I seem to be its prisoner, continually drawn back to this skeletal land, to the long distances with no inhabitants except the grassless mountains, an occasional mountain sheep, the red rock and sand, which are altered by the flash floods charging through the gullies, and the acres and acres of repetitive shrubs. I'm glad that some places such as the Lake Mead National Recreation Area have been preserved to remind us of this spaciousness, this expanse, this empty and daunting creation. I am dismayed when I see how the valleys are being filled by thousands, maybe millions, living in sand-colored apartments, attending beige churches, sleeping in caramel houses dropped into the sand by a developer with big bucks in mind, and some living in homes built to look like medieval castles with doors too tall and strong for actual use. It's all staging: "Yes, I live in a castle. See? I'm King of the Desert. King or Queen of Something." And palm trees. There weren't any when I was growing up, and now, they're everywhere, gracing the streets and the boulevards, making the desert more hospitable.

The desert always lies in wait, lapping its dry tongue at anybody's whimsical sense of propriety. It frames the existence and borders of lives there, this blatant, don't-mess-with-me desert with its horned toads, scorpions, rattlesnakes, deep and blowing sand, sage, creosote, and teddy bear cholla. When the wind stops blowing and the hand of providence holds me close and I return to discover the reason why the desert has such a hold on me, I can see it is a quiet, subtle, magical place with its cobbled pavement, its darkly stained desert varnish, its hard pebble faces polished by wind-driven sand. It is a place designed by large hands: alluvial fans spread by flowing water from the mouths of canyons, the spread of gravel by flash floods, large and small pieces of volcanic eruptions called lava. It is ubiquitous, proud, haughty, even hostile, though it responds when I don't expect it to be something other than it is. There is that moment when the sage gives up its scent to the rain, when the paper-thin globe mallow teaches me what vulnerability looks like. Its scaly survivors leave tracks. Whispery. Barely discernible. I can learn something from their darting skills.

When the wind takes time to rest, there is silence. An elongated quiet. An aloneness. This tells me that, against all odds, certain things last. There are the occasional shouts of yucca blossoming, garish slips of Indian sagebrush, and short appearances by one-day bloomers, but, overall, the land is shy and subtle and speaks to those who take their time to wait for its face to show. Why are we all so impatient? Why do we make up answers to give us comfort rather than listen to the land, which has so much to tell us? The land has been here much longer than any of us ever will be, and it is alive. It is speaking if only we could listen.

I don't say much these days—desert dry, shy, or aware I don't know much of anything, who knows—nor do I try to assert my know-it-all personality anymore, maybe because spoken words blew away one day. I watch the position of the sun in the sky— how it rises at dawn and sinks at day's end. How the sky illuminates into something I can't gather into small thoughts. If I had my druthers, I would be the wind or the sand, blowing every which way, settling, then unsettling. Maybe that is the truth of it anyway.

When I listen to the quiet after the wind, this silence, I know I'm a child of this land, an echo of this teacher appointed to give us a glimpse of the large questions and unpredictable answers.

Star Coulbrooke

OVERLOOK

–Southeast Idaho, Twentieth Century

I

We walk on fire and water,
earth's core molten-sheathed—
I learned this in a two-room school
where Miss Swann taught the basics
first-to-third and Mr. Moser
meted out geography, geology
to big kids fourth through sixth.

Cold Spring runs beneath grainfields,
surfaces in plow-rows, carves hollows
through wind-crusted sagebrush terrain
too rocky for planting. Deer tracks
lead off through stands of barren maples,
roots probing the damp underground.

On the way to Cold Spring, Stove Hollow,
once a homestead, now lies cluttered
with stove lids and chimney covers, teapots
and wash tubs, wooden axle and iron wheels,
discards glinting through decades of weeds.

II

From the two-room cinder block school
set down on river bottom, I learned

history on a slant, the western version,
Indians beaten at Battle Creek, pioneer
ancestors reaping the bounty upstream,
passing it down to their children.

Farmland lives on when you leave, in the curve
of your brain, the bend of your back. My sister,
who never attended the two-room school,
begged Mother not to sell when Dad died.
The land held out its arms to her and never
let go. Now we both walk these hills as if
nothing in the world could matter more.

From here we see the influx of houses
on the river bottom, cottonwoods dying,
fences rising around hobby farms,
horse pastures, our childhood farmhouse
dwarfed on its island of acreage, this land
our ancestors took and we can't give back.

III

On south-facing hills, rattlesnakes
drape over rocks and strike
without warning, warm in their sunning,
a lassitude they can afford.

Down the hollow, cool in the shade,
the house of our childhood waits.

REACH

Scott Cameron

SONNET FOR THE DAY AFTER EASTER

Monday, I saw a tree filled with Cedar
Waxwings; the day before, we watched Easter
like apostles shouting at empty tombs.
We wanted faith effortless as Waxwings

rising, but fell like Icarus, asking
how the maze of absence could make your womb
feel pregnant; in our search for perfection
we wonder can "empty" mean resurrection?

But there they were—one day after, Cedar
Waxwings, epiphanic; their breasts holding
pale yellow like sunlight should look over
Jerusalem's walls at dawn, a cover

for the gnarled night before. Their eyes scolding—
some torture has always hidden in Easter.

Michael William Palmer

Parables on Vanishing

1.

I'M ALONE IN THE BACKYARD FOLLOWING A GARTER SNAKE with my eyes. Afternoon light, Utah light: bright enough that I sit in the fringe of the sycamore's shade while I watch the snake cut through the grass. I am used to garter snakes and fear them no more than kittens. I know their den is under the back porch and I've found them sun-napping in the house and carried them outside. They aren't venomous and don't hurt anyone. I watch the snake with a focused, almost religious attention—an ability I am known for as a boy that I'll eventually lose. When it pauses, I move closer. I pick it up and hold it; its gray-green scales gleam in the sun.

The snake bites me in that comma of flesh between my thumb and index finger. I drop it and it speeds out of sight. My eyes water and my chest tightens, but it doesn't hurt all that bad. When I inspect the bite, it looks like I've been stapled. What I really notice is the scent. My hand smells like it's decaying.

Inside, I wash the wound with soap in the sink and think about it. I have absorbed my father's habit of turning everyday occurrences into parables that could work in a church talk. The easy one for a snake bite would be a "you knew what I was when you picked me up" type of message. But being that I've never seen a garter snake bite someone before, it feels more personal than that, as if the snake sensed something in me. I can't make a thesis out of it and scrap the idea. I keep the water running, trying to rinse out the smell and the regret.

2.

My mother is a smiling vegan Mormon who loves inspirational quotes, homemade crafts, and hybrids of the two. She plays piano by ear, cans her own peaches. She is so resolute that I don't think she's ever once feared for her beliefs.

When she feels sadness, she makes herself busy. As often as anything, she works on the yard—watering, weeding, planting, tilling, trimming. Since she and my dad bought their house in 1986, she has transformed the backyard from a field of weeds with a handful of fruit trees into a garden and a lawn as green as a golf course. It takes pathological watering to maintain that level of greenness in July and August, but maintain it she does. The yard is walled by lines of lilac on the east side and poplars on the west. Burning bushes divide the lawn from the garden on the back of the property. The wild hair of the enormous willow tree sways in the middle of the yard, with a blue spruce commemorating her dead mother to the east of it. The same fruit trees that came with the house—two cherry, one peach, one green apple—remain on the periphery of the garden. Grass from the garden to the patio. Bird feeders in all corners. My mother can say without lying that the place is more beautiful now than it was before we moved there.

She gleefully voted for Ronald Reagan twice. She was not as soft-spoken or as vegan back in the '80s, when I was born, but she does not see the Reagan-supporting or bird-watching parts of herself as being at odds. She says, "Reagan made being an American fun again."

3.

I would describe my family, and perhaps my people more broadly, as being achingly nostalgic for the past. Also as being quite literal, with little to no sense of irony. We changed the name of the town from Battlecreek to Pleasant Grove because we didn't want to think about the battle and the grove was pleasant.

I say the past—but not too far back. We don't share any family lore about estates in England; even when we get the classic genealogical revelation that there is some "royal blood" in the family, that holds our attention for about five seconds. Our romanticized history begins only when our ancestors arrive in America in the 1800s as Mormon converts; it really picks up once they get to Utah. As kids, we learn to imagine our ancestors moving west; we picture them picturing the land we know is waiting for them—that they will find for us.

As for the land's pre-pioneer existence, we are told in school and church that the area was untamable and uninhabitable— unwanted by everyone until the arrival of the pioneers who, with some help from the Lord, made it into paradise. This myth puzzles me even at a young age. I would like to say it's because I noticed the people excluded from the story, but the real reason is that it doesn't seem to describe the actual place in which we live. Utah Valley is beautiful enough that there is no way it could have been good for only 150 years. As if the pioneers created the mountains.

As for the Ute, Paiute, and Shoshone people who lived here before the pioneers, in twelve years of public education, I learn probably three paragraphs total about them. Their erasure is necessary to our story if we're going to stay innocent. Things fall apart if the land wasn't promised but stolen, if it wasn't a desert brought to life but a paradise surrounding a freshwater lake brought to ruin. But the innocence comes at a price, even for us—a neurotic insistence in the face of loss that we're actually seeing preservation.

4.

My parents buy a three-bedroom house with an unfinished basement and a half-acre lot for seventy thousand dollars. It's

1986 and I am not yet two years old. The house is the last one on a dead-end street. The across-the-street neighbors have installed a basketball hoop where the pavement ends, with mint growing behind its imaginary baseline. To the east of our house, a small creek lined with cottonwoods winds through a section we call the dirt hills. On the other side of the water is an orchard that extends to Locust Avenue. It sounds like water and smells like apples. In the back of our house, large slanted windows give an open view of the backyard where we watch deer, bats, raccoons, and one time a moose down from the mountains. Chickadees pick from the cylindrical gray feeder in the winter and hummingbirds sip from the ruby feeder in summer. And of course we can always see the mountains. It's paradise, or at least it appears that way in memory.

5.

I am riding with my dad in his truck to fix someone's faucet. He is a property manager and prefers to take care of any job himself if he can. Usually, he can. He pays me twenty dollars plus an ice-cream cone to assist him.

Most of his income comes from managing a block of houses in Orem, all owned by the same millionaire, who lives in California. He calls the block "Rawlinson row" after the man. When Rawlinson's children grow up, he will axe my dad and have one of his sons take over the landlording instead. But by then my dad has invested some of his own money into real estate, and can collect rent on those properties.

His truck is orange with colorful stitched seats. The hood has a Jell-O bounce as the truck moves south on State Street. On the way over, my dad outlines the plan, but I barely listen since I can never picture what he describes. I have to see it in motion before I can help.

~

6.

I have a copy of a letter written by my great-grandmother in 1930—a reflection on her life to that point, intended to be opened in fifty years by her descendants. The letter got lost in someone's filing cabinet and was not found until 2018. She writes about moving from England to the Provo bench at age seven, in 1888, and then moving to Pleasant Grove at age twenty after getting married. Shortly thereafter, they move to the Junction for her husband's job on the railroad. "It was rather a lonesome life out there on the desert with no neighbors, no connection with church or social life." They eventually settle back in Provo and she talks about her church callings, her living children, and the one she lost to drowning in Utah Lake. "And although we tried to feel 'Thy will oh Lord not ours be done' it has been a severe trial, even now after nearly 8 years we sometimes have a longing for him that is almost unbearable." In a turn from there that's a little startling, she wraps up the letter by marveling about the technological changes she's seen in her lifetime—telephones, radio, paved roads opening up places once unpassable. She speculates that airplanes will be as common in fifty years as automobiles have become in her lifetime. She looks to the future to deflect from her grief. At the very end of the letter, she writes that she hopes her family will "…remain true to the church of God and to the principles for which your ancestors sacrificed so much, for my husband's parents as well as my own left all their relatives, their homes, and all that was dear to them for that which was dearer than life itself to them, the Gospel of Jesus Christ."

7.

My mother is teaching me how to identify birds by sight, and by sound. She tells me something that sticks with me, that seems to be missing when I read more about bird-watching later: often praised for being meditative, it may be that, but it's also action-packed. Birds have incredible movements and enact their own narratives. In my mother's view, their narratives are free of ours. They spin and dive and eat and communicate. In my mother's backyard, they're so used to her that they swoop in front of her face to get her attention. She radiates a full laugh at their wild, graceful movement.

8.

Over time, the orchards, dirt hills, basketball hoop, and creek all disappear. The dead end is resurrected and stretches out to Locust. The Apple Grove Ivory Homes replace the orchards and the creek is paved over for an apartment complex, which borders our backyard. As these buildings grow, I start to associate my dad's business with a kind of sorrow.

The backyard plants have grown enough that these changes can be forgotten when among them, an anachronistic, Edenic garden in a neighborhood that's half brand-new. Most of the changes, anyway. A car dealership on State Street installs an enormous American flag that can be seen from the backyard, and at night, it's more noticeable than a full moon.

9.

As a teenager, I avoid my parents as much as possible, except when looking for a fight. My mother's eyes come alive in panic at the sight of me, styling glue-stiffened hair and a short-sleeve white dress shirt worn ironically. One day, she breaks down weeping when she sees me wearing a pink women's coat. "The hair is one thing, but *crossdressing*?" I roll my eyes and say I can't wait to move out, for the thousandth time.

I lob every accusation of hypocrisy I can think of at them. A big one is that they act heartbroken about losses in which they are complicit. I ask my dad what the difference is between the Ivory Homes that have bombed our view of Timpanogos and the houses he owns. I ask him what he expects is going to happen over the course of time when everyone is encouraged to have giant families.

Even the backyard is a point of contention. I was despondent when my parents put in a cement patio that sealed up the snakes' den and I despise the lawn. I want wildness and find none. I blame them.

In response to critiques of this nature, my father asks, "Why don't you complain about something you can actually change?" By this he means fix what's clearly broken. Replace the carpets in a flooded basement. Improve yourself with scripture and prayer. But I feel the most self-pity for those things I don't know how to change.

10.

Many of the things I'm most critical of—for example, white men going on and on about a bird they once saw—are the traits I harbor myself. I used to detest my parents' pained yearning for the long-gone, and it's with some remorse that I acknowledge I'm now the same way. I say it's the same, except that I feel we've contributed to the loss, and my parents don't. We share an unbearable longing for what's vanished, but I'm also crying for myself.

11.

The changes outside our window were microcosmic reflections of the valley's overall refashioning. Fewer than 60,000 people lived in Utah County in 1960, and only around 150,000 when I was born. Now, it's up to 600,000 with a population set to increase 177 percent by 2065. As a teenager, I loathed every development I saw, but I now have more complicated feelings. The style of housing in Utah County may be ostentatious, perhaps it could be called abominable, but it's hard to say the houses shouldn't exist at all, just because our family secured housing first. Who wouldn't want to live below such beautiful mountains? Trying to determine who should and shouldn't be allowed to can devolve into apocalyptic eugenics in about five minutes. But I do feel that we've never accounted for our crimes; never even acknowledged our contribution to what's been lost; never grieved.

12.

There is a painting hanging above the piano in my childhood home. It's based on a photograph of my grandfather on my mother's side, who died before I was born. In the image, Grandpa Thomas is adorned in a cowboy hat and chaps, sitting atop a horse at the base of the mountains. He's surrounded by plants, but they're painted impressionistically—it's impossible to say exactly what kinds of plants they're meant to represent. The concrete images are a man and a horse and a mountain—surrounded by bright swabs of yellow and white and green. If not for the context, you might think it was water.

13.

Eventually my parents and I find peace. Distance helps. I move out of the house, then to Salt Lake City, then Texas, and now I live in Chicago with my wife Katie. When I return home, I notice the things my parents have already grown used to: a new freeway exit, strip mall, explosion of the once-nothing town of Vineyard. Because the past image is still in my mind, I can remember what has vanished, though it's amazing how fast the new images take hold.

14.

One year, my parents announce that they'll be moving to the Midwest, as well, at least temporarily: they've been called to serve a second Mormon mission in Fishers, Indiana.

Katie and I pay them a visit. They live in a white, byzantine apartment complex, speed bumps throughout the massive parking lot. It would be hard to find their apartment if not for the way it's decorated. Pictures of Jesus Christ cover every inch of their front window; it looks like a *Jeopardy!* board where every category and clue is a variation of the same question.

I'm surprised by it; my parents had no more than five photos of Jesus hanging up at home. We learn that they have combative evangelical neighbors upstairs, thus the pictures. We also learn that the apartment complex surrounds a manmade pond. My mother tells us that she walks to the water and feeds the ducks every morning. When she stands up and opens the curtains to show us the water through the glass doors, the ducks are standing there like demons, waiting for her.

Later that night, in the guestroom, Katie and I pull out a bottle of wine we picked up at a store on the way, an "Indiana white" with a picture of a basketball hoop on the label. We talk about the Jesus pictures and the ducks. Something about their motionless staring was distressing to me. For a moment, I hate the Midwest and its off-freeway "ponds." I am home-starved— enough so that I don't notice the taste of the wine.

15.

On my most recent trip home, I sit with my mother in the backyard. She is teaching me how to feed the gray jays by hand. She has named them and knows which ones will come close, and which are more cautious. None of them will approach with my presence. Maybe it's just that I'm new; maybe they sense something in me. I can't help but want them to approach, even if I'm not sure it's in their best interest to do so. My mother patiently waits, knowing hunger will prevail.

She looks up at the mountains. "They say we're in a horrible drought, but they always say that, and things seem to work out." I spare her the rant I would have unleashed twenty years ago. Her parable is always going to be one of optimism (from her perspective) and denial (from mine). She looks to nature for comfort, but outside of her backyard, she has to look higher and higher to see what she needs.

In the backyard it's easier. She watches the birds with focus and waits. Time can't be frozen, but she shows me how to grasp at it and cling for a moment, even knowing it won't last.

Laura Walker

Midway Upon the Journey

Tonight, afraid of this slow dying, I walk the wind
swept streets, straining for something, some
thing to tell me where the owl is nesting, why
snow here melts faster than my tears can dry.
Something to make the earth's burning stop.
The surest way to quench the fear of fire is by
stepping barefoot into desert.

High noon is past and shadows creep back out,
inch their way across promised land, fissures
splitting it apart, dried mud in a lakebed that
doesn't know water. Edges crumble to the touch.
A boulder slumps against the hillside, broken
like a jigsaw puzzle, a human heart, like a covenant.
If stillness had a voice, would it echo in this place?

We only believe what we want to believe and if righteous dominion fits into our narrow vision, nestled
between Ego and Id, we'll craft a theology around it
and dance with our eyes covered. Manmade myopia.
When you hit your 40s, the distant flames sharpen
into sudden view and what's up close becomes
unfamiliar and wrong. This is the curse of age. The gift.

Lee Ann Mortensen

ADOPTION STORIES

M‌Y LOVER AND I SIT OUTSIDE A CHINESE RESTAURANT waiting for our sweet-and-sour shrimp, and as we think of nothing but the winter sky and the sour tang of the food we will soon be eating, a woman comes out, paces along State Street folding and refolding a napkin. A man comes out, throws his keys onto the sidewalk, says, "Damn you," and something in Chinese. My lover and I try not to stare, but being relatively curious people, we have to. They pace together, intertwining in their anger. My lover wonders if the woman is his wife. I wonder if she is his mother. Their noses and chins crease in similar ways.

I don't look like my mixed-race parents, though people think I do. Some say I've got the dark, heavy eyebrows and hair of my Mexican father, or the white, casserole sensitivities of my mother's Utah attitudes. But I'm a girl adopted, my own race unknown, except that my skin goes white in winter, and olive dark in the summer blaze. I'm interbred and waiting for things to happen, my genetics indefinite as my cells erupt with inner surprises, ailments, obsessions no one in the family has seen. Perfect teeth. A craving for heat and the desert. Moodiness. A desire for women and their skin. Kidney stones surprising me last year. The doctors told me I couldn't drink coffee anymore because my genes would turn the oxalates into pebbles that come out rough and bleeding. No one in the family has ever talked about kidney stones.

For what seem to be indeterminate reasons, my parents couldn't have children, and in the '50s, even in the New West morality of Phoenix, this meant the neighbors looked at them a little squinty-eyed every time they went outside to pick up the paper. For eleven years Rudy and Joanne busied themselves with a new optical business and the eternal work-ethic of volunteer Mormonism until one high cloud day in January their doctor called and said, "You've got a daughter." They drove their new '64 Cadillac to the hospital, trying not to hit light poles and old ladies on the way, and while they waited, they walked the sterile halls and ate free maternity cookies. If they had been smokers, they would have fired up two or three packs waiting to see me, to see if I was blond or Navajo, to see if all my fingers were in place. When the nurse finally came out, carrying a puffy, filled blanket, my new parents took hold of me as if I were spun glass and hurried to their car, nervous the biological mother might change her mind, might come running after them, her gown flapping open behind her. Only after they shut the Caddie's doors did they open the blanket and look inside at the hugeness of my baby eyes.

They started telling me this story when I was old enough to understand language.

"Tell me how big my eyes were again," I would say every few months.

Two and a half years later, the doctor called again to tell them they had a son, and on that day we became the statistically correct nuclear family.

In order to avoid the uncomfortable questions that can come up when children don't look like their parents, everyone was always noticing resemblances that were not there. People think my brother with his sandier hair looks like my mother, and that I am darker like my father. My brother and mother's desire to play musical instruments seems logical. My father and I enjoy being devil's advocates, which drives my brother and mother a little insane. People nod and smile and feel relief that our family is pretty much like theirs.

But babies grow up and surprise everyone.

Though they love us without hesitation, I imagine my parents have begun to think adopted children give them more than the usual amount of trouble.

My brother was supposed to take over the family optical business and grow rich like my father, but now he often lives in the tented jails outside Chandler, Arizona, waiting for ice and water and the weekend when he can leave to indulge in girls and meth and fast driving. When he gets thrown out of his apartments, he calls my parents. When in a rage he kicks in the doors on the Saab my parents bought him, he calls. When the girls who are having his babies call, I sometimes wonder if he's gotten AIDS yet. It seems he would have by now.

"Are you having safe sex?" I want to ask him.

"I'm so sure," he would say.

Maybe he's just an adoption anomaly.

But then there are my parents' friends with their two adopted sons who like to shoplift, who sometimes work as hustlers for a little weekend junk money. These are boys who often can't take care of themselves, who live in top floor condos their parents have bought them, who wait for their mother to bring Costco food to them every Saturday, family-sized portions of cubed steak, gallon bottles of orange juice, Twinkies by the fifties.

Of course, parents with biological children get surprised too, like when their own genetic children beat up wives, or beat up gay boys in farm fields, or marry for money, or marry for love, or murder homeless women in Pioneer Park, or vote Republican, or vote Democrat, or drink themselves into blindness each night as they try to forget their dead-end lives. You know these stories. You're related to some of them.

But when you're adopted, everything you do seems much more shocking.

I am that, a surprise waiting.

A few years ago I surprised myself, and my parents, by saying, shaky-voiced, "I'm a lesbian."

It took a while to say this. After ten years of being with women I decided it was time. For four days in November during the traditional Gay Coming Out Season of Thanksgiving, every time my parents and I ate some meal, I sat with sweating knees wondering if this was the moment, if this was the second when my voice might leap and frog out the words that would make my parents look down at their turkey and never see food or adoption the same way again.

I was supposed to be the model child, the one who was polite and went to college and had a good job and had a house, though, granted, still a single girl, and not a very good churchgoer, but successful and decent and nice and relatively stable.

After I told them about the women I always called "friends" who had really been lovers, my parents probably wondered where they went wrong, like many parents do when they find out their children are not like them. But for my parents, the crapshoot that is adoption must have made it all seem harsher.

"What about those boys you dated?" my mother asked. "You were always so excited to go out."

"I like to go out," I said. "It wasn't about the boys."

"It's a hard lifestyle," my father said. "Are you really happy?"

I decided to at least say, "I'm happier than I was before." And I'm certainly as happy as anyone can be who lives neurotically on this planet waiting to disappoint her parents, waiting for lovers to leave, waiting for the unknowns of her body to explode.

I am neurotic, but I don't go around looking for "real" parents. I will never look her up on the Web to see if she has my beautiful lips and a need for tequila, nor will I pay some detective to find him as he sits in his trailer home, retired and arthritic and smoking cigars in Sun City, Arizona. I will not call Oprah or Missing Persons asking for help. It's a nightmare scenario I see too often on those tabloid news shows, the heavy, flowered, biological mother running down her genetic offspring's driveway, cameraman close behind. The genetic daughter running out to hug her biological mother. The tears. The happy sponsors.

To me, this is horrifying.

"I'm your mother," the strange woman at the door would say. The cameraman would hold his lens close to my chin. I would smile a little and step back, pushing my dogs away, smiling calmly at my lover as she sat on the couch. I would close the door down to a slit.

"Okay," I would say. I would look at "my mother's" red hair, the hair the only thing my parents knew about her, and I would look at her nose to see if it had an uplift at the tip. I would look at her eyes trying to see something large. My lover would light a cigarette, looking curious and a little worried.

"What diseases have you had?" I would ask, quickly getting to the point as I often do. "I mean, have you had kidney stones? Are your knees bad? I just want to know what I have to look forward to."

"My little girl," she would say. She would come closer, pushing at the door a little, then look down at my tattoos, her legs stopping short of the door jamb.

"Is there anyone gay in your family?" I would say. "An uncle maybe. Or some lesbian grandma? Perhaps I have a queer twin? They say it might be genetic, but how would I know?"

The camera would shift to her face. The TV audience would hold off going to the fridge for beer.

"I don't know anyone gay," she would say.

Of course not.

One set of shocked parents is enough, I say.

And one set of wayward children is enough, my parents say.

Still, I do wonder. I am the kind of girl who likes to speculate.

Is my biological mother fat? Is my biological father a person of color? Did his dark hair start turning a little salt-and-pepper when he hit thirty-one? Does her skin go white in winter, or does it stay dark and bitter all year? Do they go to bar mitzvahs or celebrate Cinco de Mayo? Do they have relatives who've harvested sugarcane, or died in the Communist uprising in Cuba, or who hid in border town hills to avoid scalping parties? Racially, I feel completely unrooted, and this has begun to bother me lately.

"Why don't you just get a DNA test or something," my lover says.

"You know I don't like needles," I say.

Because of Rudy, I'm a semi-Latina with half my cousins speaking nothing but Spanish, telling stories about Pancho Villa and weeping saints and jealous, gun-toting lovers and cousins kept forever in basements. Because of Joanne, I face German levels of discipline from my uncles, and hear all the Mormon pioneer hardship stories of pushing handcarts for thousands of miles and trying to bury dead children in the hard ground of winter. And yet, I can't claim any of it fully as mine. My biological mother might have been as white as a hospital wall, sent to the desert to have her bastard, Irish child then return to shadier New England streets looking, again, like a virgin. Or she might have been dark, a woman who could only get jobs cleaning toilets or hooking, there in the hospital welfare section having yet another illegitimate child like her mother before her.

But I will never know what I am, and in this biology-wedded, pigeonholing culture, that's a sin. People are supposed to be definable. Lovers are supposed to stay sane and romantic. Children are supposed to play and be happy. And everyone is supposed to be able to check off the appropriate racial and marital boxes on all the forms they fill out at the doctor's office and the DMV. But I can never sit back on my green chaise lounge and claim an easy identity without truly lying.

"Uh, well, I was sort of divorced, but now I'm sort of married, but, you know, not exactly because of the gay thing, and, well, my father's half Mexican, so I'm, uh, well, I don't know what I am, but my skin is rather white, except in summer, and I'm sometimes attracted to men, especially gay men, but not a lot, though sex itself is a different matter, but women are still more interesting, especially tall, nerdy women, and, well, I speak Spanish like a Mexican sometimes, like a city Norteña, or like a Puerto Riqueña someone told me once, but my parents don't know anyone from Puerto Rico, I don't think, nor have I been there, and because my family is upper class, or has been at times, well, they're nouveau riche really, I never really went to school with Mexicans or Puerto Ricans or really anyone who wasn't white. So."

Some postmodern theorists might say no one can really define themselves anyway, at least not for long, so what am I whining about? These poststructuralist pomo-chic types might say lacking an awareness of my biological history gives me more freedom to explore and even play with my own constructedness. I, Lee Mortensen, could be a sort of living diorama of fluidity ready at any minute to perform any identity I might have a yen for. Why not be Chicana today? It could happen. Or tomorrow, a divorced bisexual. On Wednesday I think I'll be oppressed and Irish. Saturday I'll celebrate Shabbat. And Sunday can be my drag hag day. Why not let adoption be a fabulous wild card that allows me to float from one thing to another and back again based merely on will, inventiveness, and mojo?

But sometimes, especially lately as I get closer to forty and wonder what I've been all these years, sometimes when I see a dark-haired woman seventeen or twenty years older than me, I wonder if she pushed me out of her body in 1964, white Cadillac waiting in the parking lot, the desert air chilled enough for the nurses to wear sweaters to work. Some days I wonder if I might be walking right next to someone who could pin my postmodern ass down with a little clarifying narrative.

But no one ever will. And so I invent stories. For instance, where is my biological mother now?

From "Birth"

… I imagine her
outside a Tortilla Flats convenience store
sipping beer. Rowdy, tall, she whispers
broken jokes only to the Mexicans
who could have been my father,
but never were.

I see our eyes, yellow and green.
Brown, curving, desert eyes surrounded by hills
and spiny fatigue. We sweat and breathe,
minds wondering
if I can laugh like she laughs, if I can kiss
all the winking Latinos
like she does
and make them think they feel love.

Or maybe the story could go something more like this:
Linda Ronstadt,
you are the one who birthed me
thirty-six years ago,
the one who pushed me out,
your love child.
And you full of pain and screaming,
with your curses
the nurses looked sideways at.
I have your hair and shortness,
but not your voice.
Still, when you sang your mariachi songs
on Johnny Carson

I thought for sure it was you.

Okay, so I grew up in the '70s. Maybe the "truth" is much less
glamorous.
A night of Latino passion
and 9 months later there I was,
a surprise rising under the
air of Phoenix,
not quite warmed by summer.
A winter mestizo child swimming
in the smallest of Arizona seasons,
scaring my father back to Zacatecas,
back to his corn fields and his horses
and his long evening *paseos*.
He left my mother behind,
barely 17 and only just starting to know
that men sometimes leave
even when the weather's cool

Of course, that's probably not it at all. Maybe it's really more
like this:
After a night of thick and heavy drinking,
he gets up early, and before the mist
stops rising from his mouth,
he bends his aching knees into the sweat lodge
to ask the mud walls to bring more people
to his Tuba City Gas Mart,
to make Debra his lover stop
with all her dusty anxieties and move in with him.
He asks the mud walls to keep his boy in college smart,
to protect his sister wherever she might be.
And then, for the first time in months,
he thinks again of how he kept driving past that hospital
in Phoenix, driving in circles,

driving for hours
hitting his forehead to try and make himself go in
and at least look down at his first child's face,
but now it's just something else he never did.

Of course, I don't know any of this. And I really don't want to know. In spite of my racial confusion, in spite of my kidney stones, I like how the mistiness of my genetic past pushes my imaginings. This way I can feel related to everyone, and no one, and pretend that I am always already where I'm supposed to be.

REPLY

Farina King

HOMELAND

My home is not "wild." My home is warm.
My home is clean. My home shelters and cares.
My home speaks.
I know my Home, Not the Wild.

My home is the land. The land is my home.
HomeLand is my mother.
She listens to me.
I listen to her.
She feeds me. She clothes me.
I roll in her embrace.

When I thirst, her veins of water sustain me.
Her Love, the Sky, rains tears of kisses on her.
From these kisses,
Life is born and cycles from infancy;
Adolescence;
Maturity;
To Old Age.

We walk together
In Beauty
To Old Age
With Family and Loved Ones
Rocks, Trees, Plants, Animals
The People—Diné—With Mother Earth.

What Others Call the "Wild" is my HomeLand—Mother Earth.
Protect and Stand With Our Mother
Our HomeLand.

Darlene Young

Utah Mormon

Half of me
fears you see me as wacko;
half of me knows you don't
see me at all. Look at me:
I'm heavy books, white teeth, organ music
and casseroles, but I crank
up U2 in my car same
as you, scream at God
sometimes, haul myself
bedraggled through awkward
misunderstandings.
Still, I'll smile
my big white teeth. I'm the suit
and the dress, spires and spurs.
I am my people, bonneted,
ancient, dusty as sage,
but tangy. Let me get close
and you'll hear the shiver
of juniper, the cricket's
dry thrum. I carry
a landscape in my blood, brown
haunted by green. Scrub oak
fringes my dreams, and out there,
across a weed-scrabbled
mountain valley, the cottonwood
advertises a riverbed, probably dry.
Always the possibility of a house

sheltered there, always at a distance.
I never arrive. The longing
becomes the destination, sweet
in its way. Without the motion
I'd be bereft: Eve stuck
forever in a garden going
nowhere. Mormon
is the horizontal of the flinty earth,
the vertical of spires. Every year
a camp-out; every year the farm.
We can't escape the land
but it is never an end.
Permanent nostalgia, a home
made of homesickness.

Lyn McCarter

JOURNEY TO KEET SEEL, REDUX

A T THE START OF SUMMER, 1962, MY FATHER PUT THE LAST
touches on the Ford station wagon he had salvaged from
a Salt Lake County auction and took us over the sketchy roads
between the national monuments and parks, historical sites and
trading posts of the desert Southwest for the month of June. We
nearly lost our terrier over a cliff at Dead Horse Point and early
on we were sunburned from midday hikes and had to spray Sol-
arcaine on our necks and arms morning and night, and my father
had to replace the radiator hoses after a boil-over in Kanab, losing a day on the road; but even so, our trip was a grand tour of
sparsely visited places in that slab of the American West that
from then on would claim all the feelings and thoughts I had at
the age of five that could mean, deeply, *here*. On later trips, we
returned, exploring further the places we had not had enough
time to explore, and every time as we turned off the highway and
the curve of the earth nudged up remembered horizons, I anticipated the rocks, the canyons, the skies, the *being* of these places.
It was a reunion to me, never losing its draw. Even before the
McDonald's billboard went up at the bridge just north of Moab I
wished for a return to serenity, to sparsely peopled places I could
find in and around Four Corners, Black Mesa, Comb Ridge,
Bullet Canyon, anywhere a sandstone cliff was not echoing

boom box music or a stream was not churned up by jeeps and four-wheelers. In 1988, that desire became so strong that I drove with my then-partner Linda to Navajo National Monument to see one of the grandest cliff dwellings in North America that I had never visited before: Keet Seel.

~

It is a hot, giardia-prone eight-mile distance to the structures after a steep drop at Tsegi Point to the canyon floor. The duty of the National Park Service includes making visitors aware that getting there can be dangerous. To curb the general dumbassery of tourists today, all visitors must obtain permits and attend a Park Service orientation the day before entry. This twenty-minute gathering is the best shot the Park Service has to guard against the damage of thousands of footsteps in and out of the dwelling, the thousands of hands touching rock art, the thousands of knees and hips and shoulders leaning against tenuous walls that will bring the site and its features to complete ruin. When Linda and I arrived, in June 1988, the Park Service required permits to wander the canyons but the only warning we received was a flyer with a graph of average June temperatures and a recommendation to carry two quarts of water. The day trip to Keet Seel required a thirty-dollar horse rental—with guide—available at the concession operated by a Navajo woman just a short distance from the visitor center. Once there, a very young Navajo man emerged from the log shelter and after taking a count of us brought two bridled horses from the shade of junipers nearby and put their reins in our hands. He returned with a saddle and flung it up and onto the horse I held, then reached beneath the mare's belly and threaded the latigo strap through the cinch. He pushed his shoulder into her side to pressure her to exhale, and when she did he quickly tightened the strap. The mare lifted her head sharply and the reins nearly shot from my grip. "You pay now?" he asked me, his dirt-creased palm open.

I gave him my money and he left to retrieve a saddle for the bigger, black gelding Linda would ride. When he reached for the cinch strap, I warned Linda to hold on. Our guide grinned, cowboy hat shadowing his face, and he added "Hold 'im tight!" At the yank of the strap, the gelding back-pedaled and Linda dug her heels in, skidding up dust clouds until the horse stopped and tossed his head in a final salvo. "You pay now?" his palm out to Linda who, eying the gelding warily, freed up a hand and paid.

Two others arrived, a couple from Los Angeles. They introduced themselves by name—Nancy and Greg—and then by socio-economic status—DINKs, or Double-Income-No-Kids. "I'm Billy," our horseman said as he offered the reins of Greg's horse to him; then, "Billy," he said to Nancy and coaxed the reins into her hand. Billy beamed with satisfaction, seeming to be glad-hearted at catching on to this ritual of introductions, a skill that could be handy with tourists renting his horses for the rest of the summer. "You pay now?" He turned to Greg. We watched as Greg pulled his wallet from a snap-pocket of his L.L. Bean field vest and handed Billy a hundred-dollar bill. When Billy returned, he was mounted, trotting out and pulling his cowboy hat down snug over his forehead. "Mount up. Mount up them horses now."

Greg brought his wallet out again and waggled it, attempting to communicate that he wanted money back. Whether Billy knew what Greg wanted or not, he finally retrieved the bill and Greg traded his hundred to us for twenties then paid out four of them to Billy. To shift the focus from this muddled exchange, Linda and I hucked ourselves into our saddles and then back down to adjust stirrups while Billy helped Nancy onto her horse. Greg managed himself up and searched for a stirrup with his right foot as his horse began a slow clop. Billy expertly backed his horse up to allow us onto the trail ahead of him. We could see Greg using his foot as a divining rod for his right stirrup, while his whole foot in the left stirrup had punched through past his heel. Billy tilted to watch, waiting to see if Greg could sort out his bad start. "Hey, what's my horse's name?" Greg called to Billy.

"Your horse name Flicka," Billy yelled back.

"So, what's my horse's name?" Linda asked as she came even with Billy.

"Your horse name Flicka, too."

~

It was a perfect day, a perfect re-entry into the Southwest. The cloudless blue sky, the bees bobbing in the fuchsia prickly pear blooms, clusters of piñon and juniper green in the red stone and sand of the mesas we could see for miles. My heart, I think, beat out of sheer happiness. At Tsegi Point we dismounted and led the horses down the twists in the trail, letting them manage the drops between the water bar ledges without our weight on their backs. At Laguna Creek in the canyon bottom, Nancy's horse suddenly dropped to roll her off, in protest of saddle and rider. She jumped free without being taken down herself, and shouted, "What's he doing!"

Billy was quick to get Nancy's horse up and pointing the right direction again. He offered the reins to her, but she stood unsure, still wanting an explanation. "Why did he do that?"

Billy shrugged. "He itch."

~

Billy was nineteen. He had herded his uncle's sheep from Globe, Arizona, to Black Mesa on horseback before starting this job. His sister worked in a cannery in California, he said, and when we asked where in California he told us Seattle. He was curious about the four of us and, every now and then, trotted up ahead and asked a question of one or the other of the couple riding ahead of Linda and me. He did not use their names or look at them directly and they stumbled a bit not knowing who the question was intended for. "What work you do?" he asked as he drew closer to Nancy and nudged her horse away from the stinkweed the horse was snatching great mouthfuls of every few strides.

"I don't work," she said. "I'm a basket maker."

"Basket Maker!" Billy whooped.

She was puzzled by his reaction. "Yes, I make sweetgrass baskets and sell them at our natural history museum."

Billy nodded vigorously. "You Basket Maker," he said. "You *old*!" Billy flicked his reins against the flank of Nancy's horse as a sterner message to keep away from the stinkweed. It wasn't clear if Nancy understood that being a Basket Maker made her a woman living between 1500 BCE and 500 CE archaeologically, but she clammed up after that. As the horse moved off, giving up on browsing for the moment, Billy signed off his dialogue with Nancy, "No eat the horses. That weed poison."

Linda and I swayed along in our saddles as our horses stuck to the trail. Horseflies lit in my horse's mane and I swatted them away. She shook her head to clear others from her face. "Atta girl," I coaxed her. "Good Flicka," I said as we neared Billy, hoping he would catch that I was on to his impromptu horse naming. Billy looked down canyon steadily and chuckled; he got it. "Your horse name Rainy," he said, slipping in behind me. The mare's ears flicked up, so it was true.

Seeing the group getting spread out ahead, Billy whipped his reins over his hip to snap his horse into a lope. As he passed he leaned toward me and asked, "You like to hike out?"—which could only mean "bust into a gallop"—and gave Rainy a shock of snapping rein, too. He shot ahead, his stubby-toothed grin wide over his shoulder as Rainy lurched to match the fun. When we caught up, Rainy shook her head and danced it up and down a few times, keeping up a half-trot. When she tucked up near Billy's horse she strained to nip its glossy russet rump; but Billy, uncannily watchful, yanked his reins to quarter-turn his horse away from Rainy's teeth just in time.

"Your horse now name Cannibal." He shook his finger at Rainy.

"You're a funny guy, Billy."

He grinned.

~

At the first and largest waterfall we would see that day, the trademark Park Service sign in brown with yellow notched-out letters pointed the way to Keet Seel. Billy arrived first to make sure the horses didn't bolt or that we didn't pass by the narrow canyon on the right that was Keet Seel Canyon, a hanging valley in this canyon system. One that washed out more dramatically in storms and floods than the open floodplain of the main canyon and left its upper portion "hanging" higher after each incident. What, I wondered, did the people of Keet Seel do when the canyon floor frothed away in the floods? Did they lose crops and animals tended near the water sources they found there? The smell of water had our horses shifting their weight side to side beneath us. The stream jumped and dropped in a dozen exposed steps, ledge to ledge, and swizzled into Laguna Creek so calmly, rolling on.

It was hot now. Billy didn't say why we were stopped. The four of us tourists shared sunscreen and tucked the bottles back into the packs we'd brought. We drank from our canteens. Greg unfolded a brochure and trailed his finger along the greenish map printed on it. "Says here Richard Wetherill discovered the canyon." All but Billy turned to look. Greg read, "His favorite mule Nephi broke its hobbles and wandered up the canyon, where Wetherill found the animal and the second-largest Anasazi ruin in North America."

Amused, Linda mouthed "Nephi," which amused me, too. Hearing the mule's name awakened the cabal in us, a name likely odd-sounding to the Angelenos but familiar to Linda and me. To most people we had grown up with in Salt Lake City, lived among still, or were related to, Nephi was a solemn name of a man—a prophet—from the Book of Mormon. To us, a mule named Nephi was funny. We were used to words and phrases blooming with loaded meaning as we came across them in the regular tick of our lives: words like "revelation," "dispensation," which had their Mormon twists; and phrases heard as easily at a supermarket as in church like "white and delightsome." Until the Mormons were called out in 1981 to explain how Native Americans who embraced their religion would become "white and delightsome" as stated in their scriptures, I knew of only one other public demand for the Mormons to explain their assumed racist views. Church leaders solved that callout with a revelation from God that allowed Black men the powers of priesthood they had ascribed to their own white selves. There was no revelation for the already delightsome Billys of North America. All that was required to address the "white and delightsome" question was a word change, a reprinting of the Book of Mormon exchanging "white" for "pure."

The supremacy of "the Church" in the Salt Lake City where Linda and I grew up made its members simply impervious to criticism. When regular television and radio broadcasts were interrupted to beam out the Church's biannual conference meetings, it was normal to us. When we heard neighbors or classmates attest to "the Church" being true in the course of regular conversation, we were used to it. But the accrued effects on us as we grew up resulted in the development of a sentinel brain cell that nudged us more awake when we'd hear certain words. As the budding apostates we were, and as gay adult women in a relationship with each other and both with membership records in the Mormon Church, we were aware of the duality of ourselves when we encountered a harmless reminder like Nephi the mule: we were members and "fallen away" both. It is not even a pernicious duality. Being Mormon or associated with people who are is pleasant, welcoming; the common good is usually at top of mind. Wise still for us to be vigilant, ready ourselves at the sound of certain speech patterns, take notice of certain clothing and food and drink choices of strangers we *know* in these superficial ways. Defend ourselves against a possible few of these nice people who may want to correct us, teach us, maybe shame us.

"Did I pronounce that name right?" Greg asked, noticing us murmuring the mule's name. We assured him he had and then fell quiet as Billy slid off his horse and motioned us all to do the same. He took each animal separately to the water and let it drink, not too much, and wordlessly returned all but Greg's horse. Billy unbuckled the cinch of Greg's horse and then patted its cheek while he spoke to him in Navajo, taking the horse into his confidence while we waited. It was not unlike a scene in a western movie in which someone has to be left behind to make the trip easier for the others. We weren't sure what was going through Billy's mind. Slowly, still speaking to the blinking horse, Billy grasped the saddle horn and yanked the saddle straight. As he reached for the cinch, the horse sidled away. With a calming, "Aa-nh! Aa-nh!" Billy bewitched the horse long enough to pull the cinch tight and return him to Greg. While the horse stood snorting, Greg thanked Billy then hopped a few times with his toe in the stirrup until he was back in the saddle. My own horse stamped, wanting out of the sun, wanting something to happen.

"Here halfway," Billy said to us.

"Halfway there," I said.

"Funny guy," Billy said, meaning me.

~

Six winding miles to Keet Seel from the waterfall. Creek crossings, muscled pulls of horse and rider up embankments, rumbling slides back down. The canyon walls grew taller, shadowed. Every once in a while, curious, Billy asked more questions.

"You like Tokay?"

"No," I answered.

Crows held place in the air, in updrafts from the canyon, over our heads. Black, wobbly stars in a flag of only blue.

"You get high?"

"No" (But really "yes").

Up in front, Greg and Nancy started to sing. It might have been "Tumbling Tumbleweeds" from the notes I could catch. They stopped after a first try. I daydreamed, recalling that first family trip to Tsegi Canyon when I was five. Images came quickly and clearly. A man with heavy silver bracelets pointed to Navajo Mountain for my father and called it sacred. A snake slept in a metate at the Betatakin site, black bands on yellow. At Tsegi Trading Post my father let us choose a souvenir from among the rubber-capped tom-toms, tumbled turquoise stones, brown-skinned Skookum dolls, or we could pull an ice-cold soda pop from the coin-op chest. Weavers' looms at the side of the road under wooden shelters. Campfire sparks spiraling up. A panel of stars above, the white arm of the Milky Way slung over us like a friend.

Smell of horse sweat and leather. Sagebrush, rabbitbrush, beeweed high as our shins on either side. Billy had no more questions. When I looked at him he was holding a sprig of bee-plant, watching an insect tumble in and out of the purple, finlike racemes of the blossom at its end.

~

When we sighted a ring of oak trees marking the hikers' camp-ground and started toward a fuller stand waving their branches in an upper breeze, Billy whistled to us to stop. Keet Seel lay only a half-mile away. Get off at the picnic table outside the Park Service cabin, he told us. We went the rest of the way necks craned, scanning the canyon walls.

The ranger met us as Billy clucked at the horses to move them into a clearing where they could be riderless and cool for a while. He said he would come back at the end of our time in Keet

Seel but he would not join us in the cliff dwelling.

"Why not?" I asked.

"Chindis." He chucked his chin toward the cliff dwelling and its sweep of pink-brown brick rooms and walls spread across the alcove above the arroyo where we stood.

Minutes later, from my spot on the seventy-foot ladder chained to the sandstone bib beneath the site, I saw Billy moving up the canyon. His back tilted in counter-balance to the motion of his horse whose blond tail swung side to side as the boulder-sized cheeks of its rump tensed right, then left. He was beyond sight by the time I was at the top and our ranger had begun to tell us about the people and architecture of Keet Seel. Nephi turned up again in her story, and out of reverence for all that was in front of and around us, neither Linda nor I sniggered about the mule again. I asked the ranger about Billy's chindis.

Spirits. Evil ones. Or just ghosts. Our ranger explained that the Anasazi people who lived in Keet Seel were "ancient enemies" of the Navajo people. Touching the dwellings or picking up bits of the tools or pots used by the people who had lived there could bring bad luck to Billy. Some of the dim pictographs on the alcove walls—a deer, a snake, a figure standing arms and legs bent outward—matched modern clan symbols of other Native people with whom Navajo groups still clashed. The picto-handprints on the walls of Keet Seel represented long gone clan members whose spirits could harm him. Billy would have to pay a lot of money for a medicine man to heal him.

What I knew of spirits came in the solemnly told stories I'd heard at Sunday School growing up. Encounters with them were described as airy reunions with white-robed angels you used to know on earth as Grandma or Grandpa, their spirit selves aiming their ghostly arms at you in greeting. The thought of those meet-ups, or the video depictions of them at the Temple Square Visitor Center, had made me more fearful of spirits than I was standing among the ghosts of Keet Seel. The notion of an enemy spirit that could change your luck, could fill you with illness that only a holy man, a medicine man, could chant out of you wasn't wholly far off the stories I'd heard in church. The Devil grabs hold of your soul and you need a man with spiritual credentials to pray you free. There went Billy, having moved up canyon enough to appear here and there, looping in and out of the wispy tamarisk and tumbles of cottonwood branches, just going along with no intention of stirring up trouble. His amble in this canyon of unseen, unprovoked enemies mirrored to me in that moment—more nobly, more elementally—the ways that Linda and I had conditioned ourselves to go about our gay lives among the Mormons. We nodded in recognition of the culture and people we lived among but stayed clear.

In the thousands and thousands of square miles of the Navajo Nation, Billy and all Navajo people who had lived there had structured their lives so that spirits in these ancient dwellings would do them no harm. To complicate things, boundaries defining the Navajo Nation drawn up in the Treaty of 1868 lasso Billy's people in among these dwellings, smack dab in the midst of spirits unrelated to them. I tried to sense the ghosts there in Keet Seel. I invited them to brush my arm. I counted the handprints near the Fire Clan symbol and urged all ten to appear. It may be, I decided, that there is evidence of the unseen only in the behaviors we adopt in response to the unseen; the words, the stories, are only true through what we *do* about them. Even though the trip to Keet Seel was just the trip I'd wanted, the sight of Billy and his horse going up canyon stuck with me as much as the magnificence of the tiers of masonry and mortar puzzled together at my back as I continued to watch for him. Going nowhere but on his way. Sure there was the amazing ingenuity in the architecture to revere, the lifeways to imagine in conditions so vulnerable and so austere, and a dusty, pot-sharded sense of sacredness all around. But Billy, he seemed the living proof of all of it, of the ordinary in the sacred. "Funny guy," I thought, but only meant that I'd come all the way to Keet Seel for a return to country I deeply loved; but then, this.

~

Very seldom, in the years since I stood within the alcove of Keet Seel, have the places I've returned to in the Southwest been clear of people and noise and all the other signs of mega-visitation. This isn't news. So many people are love, love, loving the redrock country with their backpacks, their duckies and rafts, their bicycles, belays, and blogs about it all. The Utah Office of Tourism since 2013 has made a bucket list for the world to visit Utah's national parks as if they are game pieces to collect for a free large soft drink. It is enough, enough already. I don't plan the grand trips I did only two decades ago. I don't even plan the less-grand trips from Salt Lake to Moab as often. Call it age, call it more impatience with the six-month-out camping reservation system necessary to mete out campsites to the millions seeking them. Call it nostalgia, or call it the enflamed sense that sputters in the arch of my ribs because I cannot bear to find that all is different, altered, trampled in the old, best places.

The man at Tsegi Canyon in 1962, pointing to Navajo Mountain for my father, he spoke of sacred. The snake sleeping in the metate, black bands on yellow, spoke of ordinary. I cannot count the times since my trip to Keet Seel the pairing of these ideas has brought me to the sublime by simply traveling the rivulets of memory. It's an easy trip to get there now, just start off in the back of an old Ford station wagon, wait until the feathery sand of the dirt roads churns onto the wide rear windows and sifts down with the car's vibrations, and then see the rocks and cliffs and sky shake out again.

FATHER

Matthew James Babcock

Dreams and Visions

In *The Audubon Society Field Guide to North American Birds: Western Region*
I identify the Bullock's Oriole or at least a distant cousin that boomeranged

on the sagebrush-salted wind across our slow career to perch and bob
like a tongue of wildfire on a slick creekside willow swing in a drought year.

Restless suburban regulars, we foray on footpaths thick with the laissez-faire
architecture of wild mint and quack grass, declare ourselves besieged by red ants

as hell-bent as traffic on an L. A. freeway. You: twenty-seven. Mother: late fifties.
Second daughter: two in August. First daughter: three. Following halfway

through the adult male breeding cycle like stinkbug or Western Grebe: me.
In Centennial Park, near golf course and canyon picnic sprees the weather

continues fickle. Overarched by the Perrine Bridge, my mother stoops to snap

asparagus shoots like a woman drafting a precision map of her
family roots,

checks if they're ripe, tells me offhand that last week while reading out loud,
my grandmother, eighty-nine, said she saw standing next to the
couch

the form of her mother in early twentieth-century Canadian
dress.
A sun-bleached Bud Light cup and Ritz Crackers wrapper
rolled up

in horsetail grass, shiny as shed snake hide, mark a propinquant
par four.
Seems I fall left-of-center in a bloodline of family visionaries.

Before he died, my war veteran grandfather lay in a leather
recliner
in his darkened study, behind shaded windows, eyes pulled
four years blind,

and like a sage cosmographer identifying baby supernovas,
with his finger counted what he said were at first twelve children wearing white, floating around

our then beaming newlywed heads, as prolific as this year's
hatch of checkerspot butterflies. *Audubon*'s says that due to the
breakdown of eastern woodland

habitat and suburbs west, the varieties of Baltimore and Bullock's
have interbred freely, creating the Northern Oriole. Gilded in
sun haze

near a bench donated by the local Rotary our oldest daughter
stands
knee-deep in dandelions as numerous as Pharaoh's dreams.

She blows the puffball spores of our hybrid generations into
space
and time galore, as rare and beautiful as she seems.

Jack Harrell

Crossing the Plains
in My Chevy Impala

On a February morning in 1981, I packed my 1964 Chevy Impala with clothes, record albums, and guitars to move 1,300 miles from my hometown of Parkersburg, Illinois, to the oil town of Vernal, Utah. I was nineteen and the baby of the family. As I packed the car, Mom watched from the front step of our little pink house, anxious I'm sure. When our neighbor Ellis Martin came out his door, headed for work, Mom called to him, "Ellis, I'm losing my baby. He's moving to Utah." Never much of a talker, Ellis simply said, "Birds will fly the nest," and wished me luck.

Mom had offered no objections when I said I wanted to move to Utah, where my older brother and sister already lived. Good jobs were hard to find in Southern Illinois, while Vernal was booming. Mom had other reasons on her side. My friends were a little shady and I'd been in trouble with the law a few times—possession of marijuana, vandalism, an open container violation. When Mom said, "There's no future for you here," that had settled it. She waved from the front step as I drove away. I was leaving my childhood behind, a small-town Midwestern life of corn fields, Protestant churches, and old men gossiping at the grain elevator. At the stop sign on the edge of town, I paused a moment before turning onto the two-lane highway that would take me fifty miles to Interstate 70, at Effingham. The national speed limit was fifty-five mph. It was a three-day trip, eight hours a day: 1,100 miles on I-70 to Rifle, Colorado, before exiting onto two-lane highways, north and west into Vernal.

Two hours in, with the busy St. Louis traffic behind me, I-70 streamlined for the long haul. I pulled into a rest stop, took a bag of weed from the Impala's glove box, and rolled myself a joint. Soon I was in a haze of marijuana smoke, cruising with Pink Floyd's *Dark Side of the Moon* on the 8-track. The rolling hills of Missouri were winter-brown and dusted with snow, strewn with bare trees and tiny towns. The four-lane stretched like a double ribbon of gray disappearing into the horizon. The whole world lay before me, full of potential.

I'd been granted my first sight of the Great Plains and the Rocky Mountains three years before. That summer I cruised my sister's Trans Am while she drove her family Oldsmobile to visit our brother Jerry in Vernal. Jerry, eighteen years older than me, had gone west years before, working oil field jobs in Kansas, Colorado, and Wyoming, finally landing in Utah. On that trip, Sharon's two youngest kids rode with her and Mom. Her three oldest, teenagers like me, rode along in the Trans Am. We snuck cigarettes and played Led Zeppelin's *The Song Remains the Same*, Van Halen's debut album, and Cheap Trick's *Heaven Tonight*. We saved the Kansas album *Leftoverture* for the moment we crossed the Missouri-Kansas border, the opening lyrics, "Carry on my wayward son / There'll be peace when you are done," ringing out like an article of faith.

There's a joke about the Sunflower State: "Kansas is so flat you can stand on a tuna fish can, look straight out, and see the back of your own head." My first experiences on the Great Plains were just that jarring. Southern Illinois is a land of small rolling hills and second-growth woods. You can't see far—the best vistas stretch only a mile or so. And the farms are relatively small. Even out in the country, a glance in any direction reveals a house, a barn, or a grain silo amid the corn and soybean fields. In contrast, Kansas was endlessly flat, with vistas stretching far into the horizon, I-70 bisecting amber waves of grain that went on for miles without a building or fence line. In high school I had learned that the Great Plains were once covered by prairie grasses so tall that horsemen sometimes had to stand on their horses' backs to get their bearings. By the time I crossed the plains in my sister's Trans Am, and three years later in my Impala, those wild grasses were gone, replaced by fields of wheat and other crops—beautiful in their own right, I thought—but not the native, not the natural. At nineteen, I gave no thought to what it meant to remake the land in our own image. The world seemed so glorious and fascinating, so full of potential—a destiny laid out before me. God had made the Great Plains, it seemed, as well as the Dwight D. Eisenhower National Interstate System, precisely for a kid like me to cruise across Kansas at a cool fifty-five mph, listening to Led Zeppelin and relishing the last hit on my roach.

After six hundred miles through Kansas and the flatlands of eastern Colorado, I-70 reaches Denver, where the Rockies come into view. I found the contrast between the Great Plains and the Rocky Mountains astonishing. Beginning at the city of Vail, the freeway tracks along the Eagle River and then the Colorado, the mountainous terrain rising and falling on either side. At Glenwood Canyon, I-70 becomes an engineering marvel. Tunnels cut through mountainsides, and the roadway meanders over bridges and around miles of retaining walls. The eastbound lanes sometimes extend over the Colorado River, while the westbound lanes ride on a viaduct several feet above the canyon floor. The freeway hugs the north bank of the Colorado, and the Union Pacific Railroad hugs the south. Cliffs rise as high as five-story buildings. The drive is exhilarating—a mixture of fear for one's life amid the sheer walls and sudden drop-offs, and wonder at the beauty. But for all our effort and skill, here nature grants us only the narrowest thoroughfare. We may pass on our puny road, but the terrain allows nothing more—as if the land itself says, "Gaze you may, but move along."

Three days after I set off in my Chevy Impala, I arrived at my sister Sharon's house in Vernal. The next day, I got a job in a grocery store. I lived with Sharon and her family for a few weeks, saving for an apartment. One day I found a Book of Mormon in a hallway drawer, stuffed there and forgotten. Curious, I went to my bedroom, lit a cigarette, and started reading the Book of Mormon for the first time. I liked what I found in its pages. It read like the Bible and its teachings made sense to me. But it would be nearly two years before I joined the church. I was already making friends with lapsed LDS kids, smoking pot and drinking beer, playing in a rock band, snorting coke and dropping acid. In those two years I met Mormons good and bad, lovers and haters. At a keg party up Dry Fork Canyon, a complete stranger, so drunk he could barely stand, poked me in the chest repeatedly as he swore that Joseph Smith was a prophet of God.

I stayed at the grocery store for a year before taking a job with my brother Jerry, wrangling oil field drill bits and driving all over the West. In the evenings I smoked pot, on Saturdays I got drunk, and Sundays were for hangovers.

As the months passed, I didn't like what I was making of my life. I returned to the Book of Mormon, this time not just curious, but truly searching. When Jerry's business slowed, he took to the road to drum up sales. I spent hours at the shop reading the Book of Mormon and waiting for the phone to ring. I loved the teachings of Jesus I found. Soon I discovered the other LDS standard works and started reading them, too, along with the Bible. In time I met the missionaries and started attending church, where I met good people, ordinary people, people flawed and variously scattered on their own paths. Farmers and ranchers, grocery checkers and homemakers. A few had been to college—the schoolteachers and the occasional geologist or government employee. My stake president was a lawyer and former smoker. I remember him speaking in church once and using the word *indicative*. I considered that for a moment—"Indicative," I thought. "Ah, like *indicate*." Watching him and others, I soon began thinking of going to college, something I had never imagined before.

Becoming a member of the Church of Jesus Christ of Latter-day Saints changed my perspective in many ways. One evening as a new convert, I was in a congregation of young adults singing "Come, Come, Ye Saints," a hymn I'd never heard. The lyrics were written by William Clayton, while he was crossing the plains in 1846. The third verse begins, "And should we die before our journey's through / Happy day! All is well!" As I took in the meaning of those words, I looked around for a moment, wondering if anyone else had felt the gravity of what we were singing—this invitation to face death without flinching. This was not *wanting* to die, nor was it recklessly daring death. The hymn said "should we die," if we happen to die, nothing could spoil our joy. There was no promise of protection here, nor an escape from suffering. Instead, the hymn offered a pathway through to something better, made possible by Jesus Christ alone.

Over the next ten years I crossed the plains between Utah and Illinois several times. After graduating from Brigham Young University, I moved with my wife, Cindy, and our three children to attend grad school at Illinois State University in Normal. Later we moved to Mahomet, Illinois, where I taught English at Parkland College. In 1995, we returned to the West, this time for a teaching job in Rexburg, Idaho. On that trip we took Interstate 80 across the plains. Cindy drove our only car, our four-year-old daughter riding with her, while I drove the U-Haul with our six-year-old son and eight-year-old daughter. The last hours of that trip, we were on a beautiful, winding two-lane highway near Alpine Junction, on the Wyoming-Idaho border. Around one bend, the mountain rose to our right at a forty-five-degree angle.

Opposite of the oncoming lane, the land dropped off at the same slope for hundreds of feet. As I entered the curve, out of the corner of my eye, I saw a bull elk barreling down the slope to my right. It seemed sure that we would collide. I faced traffic in the oncoming lane. Cindy was behind me, more cars following her.

The U-Haul was not nimble. If I sped up, the elk might collide with Cindy's car. If I slowed down, I might hit it head on. As the massive animal approached eye level with me in the cab, I saw it pulling for all it was worth to avoid a collision. And then, maybe twenty feet from the road, it managed the slightest change in direction and began arcing away. It seemed to me that a team of angels joined that elk—beast and angels muscling tremendously as it got its footing and hurtled up the hill at the same angle as it came down. This all happened in a few moments. But I couldn't help thinking that heaven had pulled for that elk as much as it had for my young family and the others on the road.

Seeing God's hand in the natural world had always come easily for me, as did a love for the artistry of his creations. But Mormonism taught me something more. Living in Vernal as a newly converted Latter-day Saint, attending Sunday school with ranchers and farmers, hunters and fishermen, I learned that God had given us this beautiful earth and everything on it with a charge to take good care of it. Appreciation alone wasn't enough. In Genesis, God told Adam and Eve to populate the earth and to "have dominion over the fish of the sea, and over the fowl of the air, and over every living thing that moveth upon the earth" (Gen. 1:28). The Hebrew word for "have dominion" here is *radah*, which other Bible translations render as *reign*, *bring under control*, or *rule*. In other words, Adam and Eve were commanded to *govern* the earth, to *manage* it. Indifference was not an acceptable option before God, nor was neglect.

Modern revelation reinforced and clarified this biblical responsibility. In the Doctrine and Covenants, the Lord told the Saints that "the fulness of the earth is yours," and "it pleaseth

God that he hath given all these things unto man" (D&C 59:16, 20). However, he also warned that natural resources were "to be used, with judgment, not to excess, neither by extortion" (D&C 59:20). An earlier revelation was even sterner: "wo be unto man that sheddeth blood or that wasteth flesh and hath no need" (D&C 49:21).

By these accounts, God had given the earth to be used and cultivated, to blossom as the rose—not to be exploited or abused. But we can't escape our impact on the world. Our very presence and movement through time and space shapes the environment around us. We leave tracks wherever we tread.

One night in February 2020, I was driving home from Utah at two o'clock in the morning in our family minivan, speeding up I-15 at eighty mph. My wife, Rebecca, and three of her children, in their teens and twenties, were asleep as I listened to heavy metal on my iPod to stay awake. It was cold that night, in the low twenties. We were on a lonely stretch between Malad and Pocatello, where deer and other wildlife roam the rangeland at dusk and late into the night. I've seen them before at the edge of my headlight beams, alongside the road or crossing a few hundred yards ahead. I've had to slow suddenly or swerve gradually to avoid hitting a creature. Traveling at that speed, it's anybody's guess what might happen. Vehicles are usually totaled when they hit a deer or elk. Drivers can lose control and run off the road, or swerve into other vehicles. In nearly every case the animal is killed.

That night I was especially vigilant, watching the sides of the road, at the ready with the steering wheel and the brakes. It happened so quickly. I was in the right lane, no other cars in sight, when I saw a coyote sitting on the shoulder of the road, staring out into the snowy sagebrush and darkness. I let off the gas and steered gradually to the left-hand lane, giving as wide a berth as I could. Had the animal stayed where it was, there would have been no incident. But the coyote turned its head toward me and darted right at the front of our car. I gripped the wheel tightly and felt it go under the right front tire and then the rear. The noise and jarring motion woke everyone in the car. Rebecca sat up and called out, "What was that?"

"We hit a coyote," I said. "It was just sitting there, and it ran right at us."

I tested the play of the wheel. It didn't feel like we'd blown a tire. The steering seemed to be handling well. Given the speed of the impact, I knew the animal had to be dead. Only morbid curiosity would have caused me to stop and go back, to see it mangled and lifeless. Perhaps I should have dragged it off the road, but this thought came only later. Twenty miles on, I took the McCammon exit and pulled into a truck stop. I was shocked at what I saw. On the right-front corner of the van, the body-work below the headlight was simply gone, the wheel and steer-ing mechanism exposed. Days later, the man at the body shop told me it was probably the cold that caused the plastic to break rather than bend to the impact. I was rattled for days afterward, but also grateful we hadn't blown a tire and lost control, know-ing we could have rolled the vehicle and come to a stop in that snowy sagebrush desert, dead or injured, waiting in the quiet darkness for help to come.

What had possessed that coyote, in the flash of a second, to turn from the wide-open field and dart toward us? Why hadn't it simply slipped into the darkness as I passed? My imagination goes wild with this. It seems the animal had been waiting there, called by a god or a devil. Waiting for *me*. Charged to present an unforgettable lesson on luck and danger. Or maybe it had made an appointment for itself, a date with its own dramatic annihila-tion. It haunts me still, the picture of that coyote turning back so resolutely toward instant death.

In 1981, I crossed the plains to Utah in my Chevy Impala. The Mormon pioneers brought tobacco on their trek, and so did I—along with a little bit of weed. They played music when they were weary, and so did I. Joining with the Latter-day Saints, I took my place among the lawyers and testifying drunks. I've seen angels muscle with willful beasts to save life, and I've seen lonesome creatures turn toward instant death—mysteries all.

Most of the time, reality offers only the narrowest passage. Most of the time that's all we need. We drive manmade highways over a wondrous and godly land. Our roads are sure to crumble, but the earth is destined to last forever in glory. Crossing the plains as a nineteen-year-old, I knew the amber waves of grain had their own kind of beauty, and I believed those wild grasses a hundred years before had been beautiful too. What I didn't know then was the responsibility we have—to the land, to each other, and ultimately to God. Jesus said, "The kingdom of heaven is like unto treasure hid in a field" (Matthew 13:44). The treasure is there—no doubt. Can we see it? Can we take good care of it? If so, we can keep it.

MOTHER

Dayna Patterson

OUR LADY OF THE GULLS

First the killing frost. And when crickets boiled up
from the ground like an Old Testament plague,
Merciful Lady, we cried out to you. When they
stormed our barns, houses, clothes, cupboards,

we cried out to you. When their black bodies
swarmed our springtime crops, devouring the corn
and small grain, we attacked with sticks, clubs,
brushes, brooms, and willows. We knocked them

from the stalks, we crushed them under boot heels,
we pounded them with mallets.
Still they came. By the thousands. Millions, little
cannibals, consuming their own dead with our food.

We beat our pans and bells to scare them,
and we cried out for you. We dug trenches of water
for them to drown in, and we cried out for you.
We set the sagebrush and forbs on fire, and we

begged your intervention, Lady. At last, you came
in a cloud of wings. When it passed between us
and the sun, a shadow covered the field.
You heard our farmers' prayers and brought

your mile of gulls, oh Lady of Entomophagy.
You commanded them to eat, and they did eat,

and eat, and eat, disgorging along the water ditches
lumps of cricket, pellets of parts, then they flew

to the fields for more. Some may call them
scavengers. Dirty birds. Rats on wings, but we
know better, Lady of the *Larus californicus*.
We hear in their screech the sound of salvation.

Jennifer Champoux

Eternal Maternal

M Y GREAT-GREAT-GRANDMOTHER LOOMED BEFORE ME, her arms curiously crossed in front, bestowing food on her children. I was twelve years old and it was the first time I had seen an image of my grandmother's grandmother, Louisiana Seegmiller Heppler. She appeared to me in a colorful, hand-hooked rug created by another of her descendants, my dad's cousin Becky Knudsen. Louisiana stood before a pear tree, blond children on one side of her, and raven-haired children on the other. Woven around the borders of the rug was an excerpt from a poem by the Mormon pioneer Eliza R. Snow: "All is well, is well in Zion / Zion is the pure in heart / Come along you holy women / And your blessings here impart."

I knew that Louisiana, or Lucy as she was known, had raised nineteen children, which seemed like an impossible feat to me. She had come to Utah as a pioneer after she and her husband, Andrew, joined the Church of Jesus Christ of Latter-day Saints. As I examined the rug in Becky's Provo, Utah, home, she explained that Lucy supported her first six children while Andrew served a three-year mission for the church in Europe. When he came home he brought company: a Swiss-German widow named Katharina whom he desired to marry as a second wife, and her six children who were about the same ages as his own. But Katharina had caught typhoid on the ship, and before she died two weeks later she pleaded in German with Lucy to care for her children. Lucy promised, and adopted the children, and then went on to bear six more herself. She later adopted a grandson whose mother died in childbirth, making nineteen in all.

Becky told me that given the family's limited means, Lucy found herself wanting to dish out larger dinner portions for her biological children and smaller ones for the German children. But as Lucy approached the table carrying the plates, she forced herself to cross her arms so that the larger portions were placed before the adopted children, and the smaller portions ended up in front of her biological children. It was a gesture of unity, a sign that all were alike. This was the moment immortalized in the rug, with Lucy's arms crossed and extended towards her children on both sides of her. In our family's oral history and now in this rug, it was the defining moment of Lucy's legacy. Becky titled the work *Eternal Maternal*.

Standing before that woven monument to my heroic ancestor, I felt far removed from her by time and space and circumstance. I was a twentieth-century girl from a DC suburb. I had only two sisters and we never had to worry about having enough dinner to go around. Several years later I returned to Provo as an undergraduate at Brigham Young University. The Utah terrain was very different from the richly forested rolling hills and meadows of my Virginia childhood, and the Wasatch Front felt imposing. Looking up at those peaks, I often thought about Lucy, who had lived in the shadow of mountains a little further south, crossing her arms to feed her many children. In my mind, Lucy was like one of those mountains—larger than life, immovable, and mythic.

Over the years, I got to know those mountains as I spent time in them hiking and fishing. While I was in college, my grandfather, Glendon Johnson, would often come down from his home in Salt Lake City, pick me up in Provo, and drive us into Spanish Fork Canyon where we'd spend the day fly fishing on Thistle Creek. He loved the land and noticed everything, pointing out to me the vibrant chartreuse of budding leaves in spring or the way the autumn colors covered the foothills like a Persian carpet in the fall. Lucy's town of Glenwood (about one hundred miles south of Provo) is still nestled against the western side of the mountains of the Manti–La Sal National Forest. If you could fly directly over them, on the other side you'd find a ranch tucked into a little valley along the Muddy Creek. My grandfather's parents had also settled in that area and he had been born nearby. Having grown up in that landscape during the Great Depression, he felt such a connection to it that later in life he wanted to return, and so he and my dad, Woody Johnson, bought Castle Valley Ranch.

I've visited the ranch frequently since my youth and the place has always felt full of history and memory. The landscape itself keeps a record of the lives lived there. On one end of the valley, a search among the gravelly slopes often results in the discovery of arrowheads and chipped flint. About two thousand years ago, Native people sat with their backs against the hills for protection as they worked to make these tools. Six miles away on the other end of the narrow valley, a red-tinged rocky outcropping holds a large panel of petroglyph rock art. There are images of deer, snakes, four-legged beasts, footprints, and skinny human figures with insect-like antennae on their heads. One large human figure appears to be a woman giving birth, her body frontal and her legs spread wide and bent up like an M, a teardrop shape between them.

The little wooden house Lucy raised her nineteen children in still stands today and, from a photo, I've seen it now boasts a trampoline and a plastic children's slide out front. At our family's ranch, there is an adobe and stucco house built by Mormon pioneers. It's been refurbished and now has running water and carpet and cable TV. I've slept comfortably in the little bedroom, but have only peeped warily down the dark steep stairs leading from the kitchen into the cool, musty, exposed-brick cellar. My ancestors don't have a history in that house, but another family must have and I often wondered about who had lived there. Last year during our visit, a local man was helping with some repairs. Before he left, we all stood outside chatting in the familiar, friendly way of the people in that country. He pointed to the old adobe house, shaded by tall cottonwoods, and remarked that his ancestors had once occupied it and that his mother had been born inside seventy years earlier. "On the kitchen table," he added matter-of-factly, "'cause that was how they did."

I had nursed my own babies under those cottonwoods on our visits, and over the years I'd learned to love this land and to see it more clearly. The memory of holy women who lived here and consecrated their lives to children, family, and faith is stamped into the geography. But I felt hopelessly unfit to be counted among their saintly numbers. Although I have many great memories with my children at the ranch, I also have memories of days that were difficult, or I made mistakes, or was jealous of my time. I have stood with my children in awe before the petroglyphs, and I have walked with them in the early morning laughing as we flushed out jackrabbits with comically large ears. But I have also been impatient when my children complained they were hot while hiking to the petroglyphs, or have scolded them when they got their shoes caked in mud chasing rabbits around the pond, or felt resentment when they needed my help and all I wanted to do was sit down and read a book. I didn't feel I could live up to the legacy of women like Lucy, who seemed to sacrifice their own wants so easily and in such dramatic ways for the good of others.

As a mother about the same age as Lucy was at the defining, heroic moment of her life memorialized in the rug, I started to wonder if there was more to her story. The legacy of Lucy told in our family centers on her crossed arms. That story is wonderful. It's tidy and comforting. In the end, everyone has a seat at the table and everyone gets fed. We feel good about our matriarch's decision to care for those in need, and we feel proud sharing in that legacy. But it's in the unspoken, uncomfortable parts of the story that I have found even more meaning. Maybe the fact that Lucy initially dished larger portions for her biological children meant that there was a real danger they would not get enough food. Maybe there were nights when her own youngest child hungrily asked for more, and Lucy had to tell him there was none left while she looked with bitterness at the six bowls of food in front of the German kids. And besides her worries over food, I'm sure she lost sleep tending to the new children's fevers or bad dreams. I'm sure she gave up what precious personal time she had in order to teach them English, mend their clothes, knit their socks, and wipe their bottoms. On the other hand, did the orphans, taken from their homeland and kin, feel uncomfortable with the situation—begrudging their reliance on this new foreign family but still desperately needing it? Did they pine for a grandmother across the Atlantic who would have joyously taken them in if they could have afforded to go back? Even lives lived in faith and hope are messy.

And what about the fact that Andrew wanted to marry Katharina? It's not a part of the story our family talks about much. I learned though, that Lucy at first responded to the proposition with bitter disappointment. Her son Edward later said, "Louisiana was stunned when she learned of Andrew's plans and at first could not accept this condition. She went into the bedroom and fell on the floor and pulled at her hair until blood stained her fingers, so great was her anguish."[1] In spite of such grief, Lucy continued to pray for guidance and understanding rather than deciding to throw the whole thing over. And eventually she found some kind of peace or ability to move forward. Lucy's daughter-in-law, Elmira, remembered Lucy recalling "a time in her life when things were very difficult for her and that her burdens seemed more than she could bear. She went out in the orchard and prayed and seemed to hear as it were a choir from Heaven singing the fourth verse of 'How Firm a Foundation': 'When through the deep waters I call thee to go / The cup of thy sorrow shall not thee o'erflow. / For I shall be with thee, thy suffering to bless / And sanctify to thee, thy deepest distress.' As the music swelled around her, she felt peace come into her heart and strength and courage come into her body and she went back into the house feeling that all was well."[2]

This part of the story made Lucy seem much more real to me. She struggled to know what to do, and she didn't just go along easily and willingly with everything. She had her own vision of what her life should look like and she wrestled with God when something different was asked of her. Also, it strikes me that she felt it important to mention that it was in the orchard where she communed with the divine. Perhaps that was the only place a mother of six young children could go to find a moment of quiet reflection. Or perhaps Lucy sensed the spirit of heavenly parents moving through the landscape.

Perhaps she understood that the earth and its marvels are a sign of God's love and a medium through which our souls can be touched and changed, as I have experienced in my own life. Just last summer at the ranch while I was canoeing around the pond, I saw something impossibly suspended over the water. My mind couldn't make sense of what I was seeing. As I got closer I realized it was a small spider hanging from a silken parachute, sailing across the pond. Occasionally he would lower himself to the surface and skim along top looking for a sign, then climb up and paraglide on. I paddled along beside the miracle as long as I could, seeing my own sign. I felt as close to God then as I ever have. Maybe Lucy felt a similar connection to God in her orchard.

I was also surprised to discover that in addition to her

substantial mothering duties, Lucy served as Primary president for decades, wrote for magazines such as *Juvenile Instructor*, and was the founding president of the Glenwood Woman Suffrage Association. This was another piece of the puzzle to who she was, and I was happy to see this parallel with my own efforts to serve, teach, and write outside of my family responsibilities. I feel I'm constantly searching for balance between my love for the life of the mind and my immersion in motherhood. It felt reassuring and empowering to know that Lucy had felt the pull of both callings too.

In my digging I also learned that Lucy and Andrew were part of the United Order in Glenwood, a cooperative community program organized by the church. They deeded over all their property and received back only what the local bishop deemed adequate for their needs. Resources were scarce, and things were tight. But they saw their community as a united effort to create a new kind of existence, what they called Zion. They wanted to build a place where people could worship God and live together in love with no poor among them. This kind of living required an active kind of hope—the kind of hope that doesn't just wish for things to come, but recognizes "that things can begin to be otherwise here and now, and that they will only begin to be otherwise as the faithful begin to take up the work to which God assigns them."[3] This kind of hope has costs. For Lucy, these costs included not only the dramatic dedication of all her property, her painful consent to polygamy, and her sudden adoption of six children, but also the consecration of her time and energy in small ways, every day.

Annie Dillard asks whether the wonders of the natural world are wonders if they are not observed by anyone. She decides, "The answer must be, I think, that beauty and grace are performed whether or not we will or sense them. The least we can do is try to be there."[4] Similarly, I want to know whether the wonder of a consecrated life has meaning if there's no one there to see it. Lucy, for example, in her tiny desert settlement, struggling to cross her arms at the dinner table with only an audience of small children. How do you choose faith in God and care for others, amidst so much uncertainty, even when no one is looking? The answer must be, I think, the cultivation of a hope that through our small, daily acts of love and consecration the world can begin to be changed *right now*. Lucy could only have made the difficult choices she did—to move to the desert, to live in the United Order, to support her children alone while her husband served a mission, to consent to polygamy, to adopt a stranger's children—if she believed her anxious engagement could transform the world into the Zion that her people longed for. That doesn't mean she did everything perfectly, but she did dedicate her whole life to trying. "I am not sick, I'm only tired," was one of the last things she said before passing away at almost eighty years old.[5]

When I first learned about Lucy in my childhood, I imagined her as a fabled hero, as imposing and steadfast as the Utah mountains. Raising my own children now, I think that actually she lived her life much like I do—tending to mundane daily tasks, wrestling with uncertainty, trying to do a little better each day, and learning to obey the two great commandments: to love God and to love others. Her story is about a real and very mortal woman seeking divine revelation, making promises to God and her fellow beings, and working out for herself how to honor those promises and to live her religion. She didn't have all the answers and her decisions had real consequences for both herself and others. Sometimes I feel I'm crossing my arms like Lucy. Trying to find balance. Trying to juggle my own needs and the needs of others. Trying to feel God's love and to share it with others. I know now that for all of us there are good days and bad days, heroic moments and weak moments, tidy stories and real lives. I still take my children to the family ranch in Utah every summer where they play with cousins, climb the dusty hills, explore the fertile valley by the creek, and let this landscape of faith and family settle into their bones. Like the parachuting spider I saw on the pond, we glide through our days, finding signs of God's love all around and learning to reflect it back to the world.

1. Quoted by Nola Heppler in "Louisiana Seegmiller Heppler," *The Heppler Family Chronicles,* compiled by Rosco Zar Heppler, Jr (Ross Heppler), 2000
2. Ibid.
3. Joseph M. Spencer, *For Zion: A Mormon Theology of Hope* (Greg Kofford Books, Inc., 2014), 27.
4. Annie Dillard, *Pilgrim at Tinker Creek* (Harper Perennial Modern Classics, 2013), 10.
5. "'Grandma' Heppler Called to Reward at Age of Eighty," *Richfield Reaper*, 18 March 1926.

Kathryn Knight Sonntag

THE OLDER COVENANT

The Gospel of Philip
Job 38:33–36

Take me back
before the broken tablets,
back to the secrets of winds
unfurled, constellations rising
in a new horizon, mud
and branch called by name.

I know of the Tree, good
and evil swirling
in its fruit, alive
before the lesser law
became our golden calf.

Lady Wisdom wanders,
knows too well
that nothing transgresses
its appointed order
but we.

Take me back
to the pattern of the heavens
sewn into the lining
of Her dress.

Give me the wisdom
of the ant, she who
needs no instruction
on how to gather
and harvest, on the true
measure of her
creation.

REVEL

Kimberly Johnson

Voluptuary

Fifty-mile Creek in the extravagance
of June, a fullness of flowers: paintbrush
and larkspur, beeflower and attendant bees,

the cedars *sough*, the sunfired pines
forge filigree at the timberline.
My ballerina sister on the riverbank

balances, rod cocked to rearward,
released, and retracted, line tripped
terpsichorean by the weight of the fly.

Her tacklebox cockeyed reveals homemade
damsels: the Emerging Sparkle, the Orange
Sunrise, the Dark Scintillator, and a Green

Butt Skunk. A ridiculous scene, tableau past
cliché, with verdure and soughing
and blah blah blah. She hooks a splake,

flips him to shore, yanks her knife open,
swipes anus to jaw. With a finger inside
she slides guts, gore, and shit in a shining

red pile. She dunks him, lets the stream
clean the gash, chucks him to me
for the icebucket, and here the suckerpunch

of beauty: white vault of ribs in their arch
to the spine, one red vein bulging faithfully
skull to tail, red gills fragile, useless

beneath the operculum, ordered
like layers of vellum. Scales flake off
and stick to my palms like glitter.   Like silver.

Goodfriday

It is true: the thunderhead hoists its wet anvil aloft.
Swifts buckshot out before the downdraft.
The basin gasps, sage exhales, smelling of iron.

Westbound, the hightop two-lane wavers
under early-season heat, asphalt takes
the thinnest shine, first drops hiss.

My truck blows a white wake through roadside
weeds, radio snaps electrically. It is true.
But it is a horror. It is a viper fanged, this verb

that forward thrusts the moment eternal, nails
each thing to its present. Truer still
I should write *the thunderhead converges, lifts, rides*

the steep low, butts the front range, bunches like shoved
fabric, blisters, throws up lightning thirteen miles,
lets down rain in ribs, bubbles under the afternoon...

An endless poem of thunder. But who can dwell
with thunder? The moment's span
would whelm the longest page, its magnitude

of too much weight for me. (*The leader forks, drops,*
attracts the charge from earthward, the molten air
expands, chills, slams shut, a riot of electrons...)

But God, I love the verb. I verb impenitent,
luxuriant, altaring up truth for immortality, for

the pleasure of unlikeness, the prick

of unlikeness! O happy deformation,
spunky verb, I embrace you in my
degradation, my shoddy embodiment

making thunder endless: impossible: sublime.

George B. Handley

Cabin Fever

FAMILIARITY BREEDS CONTEMPT, MAYBE, BUT WITHOUT IT there is little incentive to cherish this world and pass it on to future generations. Perhaps one reason it breeds contempt is that it creates the illusion that we know more than we do. The familiar can be glossed over and neglected. In his remarkable Jefferson lecture of 2012, however, Wendell Berry outlines how familiarity can lead to affection:

> For humans to have a responsible relationship to the world, they must imagine their places in it. To have a place, to live and belong in a place, to live from a place without destroying it, we must imagine it. By imagination we see it illuminated by its own unique character and by our love for it....As imagination enables sympathy, sympathy enables affection. And it is in affection that we find the possibility of a neighborly, kind, and conserving economy.[1]

Imagination saves the familiar by making the commonplace new again. It paradoxically keeps familiarity from being a soporific that lulls us into dull habit. I say paradoxically because imagination implies a self-conscious and reflective distance from what has become familiar through experience and observation. Wordsworth understood a child to be more innately connected to the natural world, but ultimately he argued that the work of memory and imagination in a suffering, alienated adult brings deeper joy and more intimate connection to the world. To maintain a meaningful connection with familiar places, we need virtual as well as physical experience, mind as much as body. Just as faith isn't faith without doubt, to be truly familiar we must also know both proximity and distance, expectation and surprise, intimacy and strangeness.

Absence makes the heart grow fonder, says another aphorism, and it is true that travel has aided my quest to develop a deep and abiding sense of place where I live on the Wasatch Front. But there's the rub. Should I require frequent and distant travel just to love my home more properly? Perhaps literature of place offers a cleaner and more renewable and faithful resource than travel. Literature written by devoted citizens of homes different from mine has certainly taught me how to see my home with new eyes, affirming what Aldo Leopold said a long time ago: what is more important than "building roads into lovely country [is] building receptivity into the still unlovely human mind."[2] And few have taught me more about such receptivity than Leopold himself, Berry, Annie Dillard, John Graves, William Faulkner, Derek Walcott, Elizabeth Bishop, Pablo Neruda, Marilynne Robinson, or Henry David Thoreau. I could go on. The list is long. Great literature, whether or not it could be called "environmental," is inconceivable without great attention to local landscape. All art is a form of what Dillard memorably calls "reconnaissance": our imaginative efforts to understand where we find ourselves on this blue planet.

Over the years, I have had the privilege of hosting at Brigham Young University many great literary critics and readers—but also many great writers, including Walcott and Robinson, Barry Lopez, and W. S. Merwin. It is thrilling to show the region off and watch as their eyes open widely to the wonders of what I have surely underappreciated. You learn a great deal about where you live and what you have when you see your home through the eyes of exceptionally observant visitors. I have marveled that in order to become artists, these writers didn't need the Wasatch mountains with its streams, slopes, and ravines, the great steps that descend from the Colorado Plateau into the Great Basin and its tremendous encircling mountains and the immense sky. They and every great writer I have ever read have made me ashamed that these landscapes haven't, as yet, produced writings that make this place the envy of the world.

As valuable as these visits have been, no one has taught me more about my relationship to where I live than one reader, Alireza Taghdarreh, a man whose knowledge of literature and contact with the world's landscapes have been limited by the political and economic situation of his native Iran. Ali's mother had desired an education, but because she married and started a family very young, she was unable to pursue it. So, she urged her son to become a scholar. Because of the Revolution of 1979, Ali was only able to partially realize her dreams, being forced to stop his formal education after high school.

An autodidact like his mother, he became a lover of great poetry and other literature. He taught himself English by reading magazines and listening to Voice of America. Eventually, he discovered Thoreau's *Walden* and began a ten-year pilgrimage of translating the book into Persian.

Just prior to the release of his translation in Iran, Ali came to America in 2016 to lecture on his experience as Thoreau's translator. Through a mutual friend, I arranged for his visit to BYU where he met with faculty and students over lunch and gave a formal lecture. When we met that morning, I saw before me a middle-aged man of medium height and build, with dark hair and a dashing mustache peppered with gray. His eyes were alive with wonder, his very being radiating love and humility. His speech was fluent but laconic, simple but poetic. He dropped comfortably phrases like, "If you want to be rich, pick up a pebble, throw it in a pond and watch the ripples. You may not know how far they will reach." Or: "Whatever you can find in an ocean you can also find in a drop." A man with no formal education, Ali was nevertheless profoundly insightful in his lecture, which ended with these words:

I found [Thoreau] when he revealed that, like me, he lived in a small cabin. I read *Walden* first when I and my wife and our first daughter lived in a small room. There was little room for a comfortable life or for enough furniture for us but there was enough space to hold a copy of *Walden* and books of Rumi and Hafez with us. Thoreau asks if a greater miracle could take place for us than to look through each other's eyes for an instant, and that instant when you can look through a man like Thoreau is when your small room becomes great. We must be extremely careful not to use our ordinary clocks to measure an instant when it is mentioned in the words of a great soul like Thoreau. I simply picked up *Walden* fifteen years ago and I have been looking through his eyes for an instant for fifteen years. He dedicated his whole life including two million words of writing to people like me, only to add a single, deliberate meaningful moment to our lives and show us that we can be rich in soul, in heart and in mind even if we live in a very small room. One of the sentences that is very interesting to me in *Walden* is this: "I am convinced that if all men were to live as simply as I then did, thievery and robbery would be unknown." And I am convinced from my experience of reading *Walden* with so many American scholars over the course of a decade that hostility, anger and misunderstanding would be unknown between our nations if we picked up books and read them with each other the way that I and my American friends did for ten years. Let us allow Thoreau to sharpen our eyes on the value of love and friendship.[3]

A romantic notion, but in a time when groups and nations stand at odds over stereotypes and communication is polarized, I was inspired to believe again that reading literature introduces us to distinct places and people, one at a time. It mitigates the lazy habit of generalization, of always looking for familiar patterns. Literature's power to defamiliarize reacquaints us with life in its marvelous particulars. In this way, it holds the key to our imagination of community *and* place. As writers from Wendell Berry to Pope Francis have argued, you can't have a meaningful relationship to place without meaningful and healthy community. Our environment is imperiled, in other words, by the same forces that make individuals and nations dangerous to one another.

Before Ali left, I ran to my office and grabbed a copy of my book, *Home Waters*, to give to him. I explained it as a modern account of the challenge of developing a sense of place and connection to the natural world in our distracted and possessive suburban American life. The book even featured a small room in a small cabin. I opened the book to a map of the Provo River watershed, and I told him that, had we time, I would have loved to show him this terrain of my home waters. My book would have to suffice. "Let's talk!" I said, hoping that we could continue our conversations over email.

When our correspondence began in earnest shortly after his visit, he explained why our connection meant so much to him:

> It is a miracle that our poets brought us together despite our politicians. I had an intense thirst for this meeting. I won't forget the moment you approached me and said, "Ali, let's converse!" Your voice filled the whole universe as you said that beautiful sentence to me.
>
> Each time I hold your book in my hand, I feel I am shaking hands with you again....I have been traveling towards you on foot for thousands of miles. I am very glad that I have finally reached you. I value our friendship. Remember. I need you as a friend. I do not think I can find men like you easily. We should be aware of how rare such opportunities are and how to make the best use of them. Literature is not luxury. It should bring our peoples together "to converse." Yes, our nations can read books together. The way Emily says here:
>
>> There is no frigate like a book
>> To take us Lands away
>> Nor any Coursers like a Page
>> Of prancing Poetry—
>>
>> This Traverse may the poorest take
>> Without oppress of Toll—

How frugal is the Chariot
That bears the Human Soul—

Airplanes did not bring me to you. Pages of prancing
poetry did. Let us converse, George. Let us converse.

His emails are effusive about his visit to Utah. The landscape
and the religious culture made him feel more at home as a Muslim than elsewhere in America. We have since picked up books
by Thoreau, Emerson, Dillard and Rumi, all a part of what Ali
described as a "cabin I have built in the air." Especially reward-
ing and surprising is the interest Ali took in the histories I write
about in *Home Waters* of Native American, Mormon pioneer,
and family history, that shaped and were shaped by the story of
the Provo River. He has shared the book with school principals
and teachers and has been reading it with Iranian students of
English. While I hoped to bring these particulars to a wide audience, I never dreamed that among the most extensive conversations I would have about the book would be with readers in Iran.

He and his students have sent me questions about passages
and expressions that they struggle to understand. As he explains:
"We want to see you, listen to your words, hear your sounds. We
want to watch you, understand you....We want to read what you
read, see what you see, listen to what you listen to and ultimately
love the things that you love." As he put it to me on another occasion, "I want them to touch your book in their hands and taste
it with their mind."

So our conversations have become particular to the point
where I have doubted the faith I had in the project. As they
ask for explanations about cultural or geographical references,
I have wondered why I dared to believe that the particulars of
where I live would provide the same meaning to strangers. They
have asked, for example, if I could please explain my description
of the Upper Provo Falls as filled with "tan rocks, slated at angles

and dropped as erratics." "We have been having very long dis-cussions about the exact form and identity of these rocks," Ali wrote. "Would you kindly send us some pictures to save us from the grief?" After more words failed me, I sent them a picture.

Ali asked me to identify the subject and predicate of the following sentence, a simple enough question, but the answer required so much additional explanation that I feared I had lost them altogether: "This is water in its fast cycle, rushing from the pores of rocks seeking the sea or finding its way back again to groundwater or to atmospheric vapor, the attenuated veil of fresh water that sustains life in this corner of the planet." I wrote in response:

> I hope I can clarify. Grammatically the subject is "this"
> but since I use "this is water in its fast cycle," you can
> safely assume the subject is "water in its fast cycle." This
> phrase refers to the flow of mountain water from the
> tops of mountains and from springs that, as the weather
> warms, rushes down from precipitous regions, usually
> creating white water and making a rushing sound. The

predicates are "rushing from" and "finding its way" as descriptions of where this water is going. The final phrase, "the attenuated veil of fresh water" is a reference to the whole system of water exchange that I have been describing that includes atmosphere, rain and snow. This exchange brings the water to the land and then it is returned in the form of evaporation. So the last phrase is probably the one that is confusing to the whole meaning.

When they asked for clarification of my comma usage, I could only explain that it was more particular to my sense of the mountains than grammatical. I was seeking a rhythm true to the feel of mountain water. If that sounds evasive, it is. Rather than blaming their unfamiliarity, I suspected my inadequacy as a writer. They think I am a master of English and yet my explanations only highlighted my failures to grasp the mysterium of mountain water and river rocks, my figurative and literal stumbling stones.

It was both uncomfortable and exhilarating to be examined this closely. Uncomfortable because I could see my linguistic warts but exhilarating because my words, however inadequate, were bringing people from across the planet right up to the edge of my beloved Provo River and my most familiar experience. This felt like new intimacy; it placed me, along with them, as a stranger in a new world and gave me the distance to return home again. Ali exulted: "You can't imagine how many times I have taken 'The drive up the Mirror Lake Highway to the headwaters of the Provo River...' in your book. I wonder if it would have been more beautiful for me if I had taken that road myself." As he also put it, "I would not have enjoyed life in Utah even if I had stayed there as much as I am enjoying it by living through your book and the way you describe it in *Home Waters*. I have almost memorized many parts of your book."

Ali asked me to introduce the ideas of the book to one group of students and I explained:

> I send my greetings to the readers of *Home Waters*. I am very touched and very grateful that there is interest in reading a humble offering I made to help others appreciate the beauty of where I live. I wrote this book too with a desire to describe the ways in which human experience, human suffering, and human memory are embedded in the landscape. I wanted to convey the idea that we can't separate ourselves from our environments, nor can we separate ourselves from the love and compassion of God. Our countries are not only geographically far apart but they are political enemies. I believe that if I were to visit Iran, I would meet not enemies but my fellow brothers and sisters and were I to look upon the environment where your people have lived and suffered, I would feel connected to your home and it would become a part of me. In the same way, I hope you can travel to my land through my words and feel that you have entered into a relationship with people who are familiar to you. And I hope that you can feel some of the love I have for my home. In this small way, I know that we can come to see each other and see each other's home through the eyes of love.

Perhaps because my book argues that human suffering and love of place cannot be separated, it didn't take long for our discussions to get personal. At Ali's encouragement, I have corresponded with students who have suffered tremendous losses. Ali explained why reading in English might be healing for one student: "I told him you have had your own share of sadness and suffering. Your words may bring hopes to a sad and hopeless heart here and encourage him to continue to study English and see the world anew."

Another student, Fatemeh Pakzaban, a single woman of twenty-two who works as a computer engineer and as an English teacher and translator, summarized with exceptional wisdom why our discovered common language and love of literature of place were healing:

> Hello, Professor Handley. Teary-eyed, I listened to your voice message. It's such an honor to have you along, sir. I live among people who had never believed in me and I grew up hearing my parents keep saying I should snap out of my dreams. That's why I'm always scared of making mistakes and losing people's trust.
>
> But somehow, I was lucky enough to feel the essence of literature. I got to know there's a whole different world out there in which every single occurrence can be interpreted in more than one way. Literature taught me even with this shy and uncertain self of mine, I can be seen as a totally different person.
>
> I've learned words have power. They can brighten up your soul and gracefully wrap you in their warmth. They let you see the fabulous hidden world behind the universe and add flavors to the bland life of yours and that's when you finally get to see there's an unknown beauty even beneath the taste of bitter and pain. That's what I love about literature.

She concluded with an argument about why our nations need literature more than ever. To another student, Amin Ghorbani, a twenty-seven-year-old geneticist, who had similar thoughts about nations reading together, I tried to articulate my philosophy:

Dear Amin, Thank you for these lovely and important thoughts. I agree wholeheartedly. Literature is written from within the context of a nation, in a particular language and about particular lives and places. When it is written well, it speaks first to the particularities of human experience, rather than to the universal. And yet, what happens when we read such literature is a miracle of transcendence because when literature is read by those outside of those contexts and particular circumstances, we can begin to see what makes us human, all of us, and what is universal in the particulars of our individual lives and places. As the English author C. S. Lewis said, "Literary experience heals the wound, without undermining the privilege, of individuality. There are mass emotions which heal the wound; but they destroy the privilege. In them our separate selves are pooled and we sink back into sub-individuality. But in reading great literature I become a thousand men and yet remain myself. Like a night sky in the Greek poem, I see with a myriad of eyes, but it is still I who see. Here, as in worship, in love, in moral action, and in knowing, I transcend myself; and am never more myself than when I do."

What he is saying is that through literature we can experience other lives and expand our own sense of ourselves but this doesn't require us to give up our culture or identity. To achieve true communion and understanding between cultures, we must see and respect our differences.

Of course, with limited travel and limited access to books, these chances for communion are scarce. These small groups of students stand in contrast to a national culture that has grown suspicious of reading. Ali noted to me: "People have lost their trust in books because even when they are not censored, people believe they are." I saw a corollary in my society and wrote back:

> This is terrible news. I feel that although books are more available than ever in my own country, we are so large and diverse and there is so much competition for our time and attention, that fewer people know how to read often and to read deeply and so we are ever more vulnerable to misinformation and deception, to shallow thinking, and to utter ignorance.

In this age of "choose-your-own-echo-chamber," we have our own American reasons why connection to place and to others are less likely and less meaningful. Ours is a shrinking and more familiar world, less surprising, less interesting, and less uncommon. While we need affection and familiarity, without imagination familiarity clings too easily to itself, to what is already known and believed. Nothing threatens community and place more than this spirit of tribalism. What Ali says of his nation can be said of mine: "Correct education, critical thinking and a friendship based on love and understanding is the only way to fight hatred and violence in our sad world."

In this new age of COVID-19, Iranians and Americans share more scarcity and immobility than they perhaps did, and this is helping us discover our local landscapes as our true common ground. I like to imagine us all experiencing a more expansive and more precious planet in small cabins of our own, where we rekindle the pleasures of conversations with distant authors who teach us how to see more clearly the treasures of our own neighborhoods. Perhaps cabin fever provides its own cure.

I had never imagined that my work to honor where I live would reach across cultures and landscapes in this way. It hasn't changed the world, but knowing that my love and labor on behalf of my home has planted seeds so far away has given me immense hope in this time of despair. As I wrote to Ali in April of last year:

> Right now, the weather has turned into full springtime, with the fruit trees in pink and white blossoms, and the air as clear as it ever gets. The hills are starting to turn green, as if waking from a deep slumber. I have been on the mountain trails and can see the dead grass matted down from the heavy snows but underneath I see green blades of new grass making their way. As you know from Whitman, leaves of grass teach the lessons of rebirth and the value of democracy and of human diversity.

1. https://www.neh.gov/about/awards/jefferson-lecture/wendell-e-berry-biography
2. Leopold, Aldo. *A Sand County Almanac*, New York: Oxford UP, 1987, p. 176.
3. You can view the lecture here: https://kennedy.byu.edu/events/reading-thoreaus-walden-in-iran/

Lisa Madsen Rubilar

"ALL THE THINGS THE WORLD IS DOING": *MINERVA TEICHERT AND HUMANITY, HISTORY, AND HOPE*

FROM THE TOP OF CEDAR KNOLL, I LOOK SOUTHEAST TOWARD Horseshoe Mountain, its fanned tendons defined by early snow. Beyond the mountain, not visible from here, I know the Manti Temple stands on its own knoll overlooking Sanpete Valley thirty miles away. It's November. I've traveled from Virginia to Utah for a nephew's wedding in Provo, but I couldn't resist traveling an hour south to visit Fairview. My uncle and aunt, Blake and Terry Madsen, have taken me on a drive in the hills west of town where they still run forty head of cattle. The bumpy ride is a ritual I've always reveled in—as a child (visiting from my home in Colorado) when my grandfather, Albert Z. Madsen, would take a crowd of us cousins "over west" in the back of his ancient blue pickup truck; as a college student and as a young married woman, with my grandmother, Ellis Tucker Madsen, who even in great old age loved nothing more than jouncing over those rutted roads; with my father, Albert G. Madsen, emceeing the biannual reunion hayride: *This is Lunch Tree. These are the slopes where we raised wheat. This is where the horse rolled on Dad.* The hills have never been irrigated, but Blake says the spring has gone dry now. He has to haul in water for the cattle.

The Manti–La Sal Mountains that rim the Sanpete Valley on the east are greener, populated with spruce and fir. Their snowmelt feeds the irrigated land on the valley floor, where the native San Pitch (*Sanpit*) people once lived near large marshes, now long gone. The Blackhawk War that ended in 1872 between Mormon settlers and the Indigenous people can be described as a war for water: the settlers obtaining control over the very source of the Ute, Paiute, and San Pitch ways of life. It pierced my soul to learn that Abraham Lincoln signed the order for the removal of Ute people to the Uintah and Ouray Reservation. It seems that even the best of us cannot escape inflicting disaster on those we don't fully *see.* These are facts I'm aware of; yet as I stand under the clear November sun atop Cedar Knoll, the familiar valley and the mountains beyond speak only of peace. Although I've lived on the East Coast now for more than twenty-five years, whenever I travel west, my heart sings, "Home!"

∼

Maybe this is why I've always been drawn to the art of Minerva Kohlhepp Teichert—because her paintings, too, sing of the love she had for the western landscape and its peoples. She never felt at home anywhere else. Years ago, I attended an exhibition of her work at Brigham Young University, and left with a book of her collected letters edited by her daughter, Laurie Teichert Eastwood, which provide a window into the inner life of the artist whose paintings now sell for hundreds of thousands of dollars. Ironically, before her death in 1976, she donated a trove of *Book of Mormon* paintings to BYU because she couldn't find an interested buyer. But that's another story. The saga *she* aimed to tell, throughout her life, was "the great Mormon story" (Gardner 29). Even deeper than that, she felt called to tell the story of her land. She once wrote, "There's too much sagebrush in my blood to forget the beauties of rugged mountains [and] dry plains" (29).

Born in 1888 in Utah and raised in Idaho, Minerva came from a line of independent-minded women who were also devout members of the Church of Jesus Christ of Latter-day Saints. Her grandmother, Minerva Wade Hickman, and mother, Ella Hickman, had traveled unchaperoned by horseback from Ogden, Utah, to Fort Hall Bottoms in Idaho, not exactly conventional behavior in 1880. During that trip, the women made the acquaintance of Chief Pocatello, a Shoshone leader who seventeen years before had led attacks against wagon trains passing through Shoshone homelands. The cattle and sheep that accompanied the pioneers had ravaged the native flora and routed the game, pushing the people to starvation. After one of Pocatello's attacks that killed ten emigrants (memorialized at Massacre Rocks State Park), the US Army retaliated near Bear River, wiping out an entire Shoshone village—including women and children. Pocatello's band reportedly had left the area the day before, escaping the slaughter. Despite this tragic history, Minerva's mother, Ella, told of a friendly encounter with Chief Pocatello, who recited poetry to them, which Ella transcribed. I wonder if anyone has that record now.

In later years, Ella nurtured her daughter Minerva's unconventional spirit and strong will, supporting her decision to study at the Art Institute of Chicago, and then going along with Minerva's determination to homestead by herself in Idaho. But Ella's encouragement only went so far. She offered to help pay for Minerva's studies at the Art Students League of New York if she would *not* marry her Idaho suitor, Herman Teichert—because at the time he didn't share her faith. Minerva eagerly took her mother up on that offer, apparently intending to part with her beau. But in the end, she couldn't resist Herman's down-home charms, and married him anyway.

If Minerva had stayed in the East, if she had accepted opportunities to study abroad, it's likely she would have made a name for herself in posh art circles. Instead, she spent her adult life as a ranch wife, mother of five, grandmother of thirty-five, avid genealogist—and as an artist confident in the value of her vision and the quality of her craft. She said that her greatest artistic preparation was not the Art Institute of Chicago or the Art Students League of New York City, but the months she spent homesteading—all alone—at Indian Warm Springs in Idaho. She slept with a pistol under her pillow, but reveled in the endless hours she could spend outdoors sketching.

It wasn't just the land Minerva learned from. Her daughter describes an event that may have deeply affected how Minerva thought of and related to the Indigenous people she encountered. "As she sat sketching one day, she was startled to discover a large moccasined foot next to her. When she looked up, she saw a tall [Indigenous man] who had quietly walked up behind her to watch her sketch. He told her that he had attended Oxford University, where he had also sometimes sketched" (6). In that moment, her visitor must have become recognizable as someone she could understand, a fellow artist, not a figure in the landscape—a landscape that they both inhabited with love.

~

East of Fairview atop the Wasatch Plateau, the new Mammoth Dam breached in 1917, destroying houses, roads, and the mainline of the Denver & Rio Grande Railroad Company. Coal miners helped repair the line so they could get back to work, but the dam was never rebuilt, replaced instead by several smaller ones. At family reunions, I've camped and picnicked in the shade of aspens near one of them: Gooseberry Reservoir, which lies amid alpine meadows of lupine, larkspur, and bluebells. My grandmother camped there also, from the time she was young, although those earlier reunions lasted a week and involved loading mattresses and feather pillows into the back of a wagon. Grandma had a girlish guffaw, and in her eighties would talk of driving "the elderly" to the Manti Temple. Our family connection to that temple is a long one. In 1883 my great-grandparents, Lois and Amasa Tucker Jr., spent their honeymoon at the temple construction site. He sawed lumber. She cooked for the crew. Grandma told me once of a vision she had while attending the temple. Feeling herself to be awake—while admitting she had a habit of nodding off mid-session—she saw a woman with long red hair, dressed in white, rising gently towards the ceiling.

Minerva Teichert had her own vision in the same temple, but hers is preserved in giant murals on the walls of "the World Room." Painted in 1947 when Minerva was nearing sixty and suffering from lead poisoning from her paints, the murals cover four thousand square feet. Minerva wrote to her daughter, "Pray for me. I need it. I want health, eye-sight, and inspiration" (94). In the Manti Temple, worshipers—who reenact the destiny of Adam and Eve—move through rooms representing Creation, the Garden of Eden, "the Lone and Dreary World," and eventually arrive in "the Celestial Room." While muralists for other temples portrayed the "dreariness" of a fallen world through arid, forbidding landscapes populated only by animals, Minerva envisioned human history as the source and embodiment of the "dreariness" of the world. The east (rear) wall depicts the misguided venture of the Tower of Babel. The south wall portrays the history of "the House of Israel," including a barbaric scene in which a woman is dragged out to be traded for a jug of wine—content the artist had to defend: Minerva searched ten days in her Bible until she located the Old Testament episode she remembered, from the Book of Joel. Near the front of the room is a scene of the Pilgrims embarking on the Mayflower, bent on finding a "promised land."

On the north wall Minerva painted a panoply of rich traders and rulers of various nationalities, all of whom ignore or tread on the poor and dispossessed at their feet. Trained in traditional mural-making—where symbolism reigned—she included the goddess Diana to represent, as scholar Doris Dant wrote, "idolatry in all its various guises, including the exploitation of religion for lucre" (23). The hosts of humankind on the north and south walls converge on the west wall, the only place where landscape plays a role. The dramatic mountains that reach the ceiling cradle a small, idyllic town, symbolic of "Zion." But another astonishing symbol is the focal point of that wall—and of the entire room: a twelve-foot-tall Indigenous man with outstretched arms. According to LDS scholars Richard and Susan Oman (58) and Dant (25), the figure represents North America as a place where the gospel would be restored and nourished before being shared with the rest of the world.

Minerva's use of a Native American man as a symbol is unsettling (to my contemporary eye), and is unlike most of her oeuvre, in which protagonists are individuals engaged in their own particular lives. That said, I believe the meaning of the figure is ambivalent, standing as he does between the approaching hordes and Zion. With his headdress framing him in halo and his arms outstretched, he looks like a Christ-figure, offering healing to the downtrodden and standing in judgment of those consumed by greed, vanity, and heartlessness. And seen from another perspective, in which he represents only himself and his people, the figure tells yet another story, one which opposes the historical lens through which many viewers—heirs to the pioneers who settled in the Sanpete Valley—might consider the scene. From the "dreary" recitation of human history that Minerva portrays on the temple walls, she clearly knew that the arrival of Pilgrims and Conquerors could only end in sorrow for the Native peoples of America. The Indigenous man's unflinching gaze speaks of grit and perseverance in the face of unbearable loss.

~

In 1927, Idaho's Fort Hall Bottoms were flooded to create the American Falls Reservoir. At that time, Minerva and Herman

Teichert and their three small sons were peacefully settled in the Bottoms near the Snake River, on the old Teichert homestead. Forced to sell up and leave their beloved home, Minerva faced the prospect of starting over. Heartbroken, she waited to leave until the water was literally lapping at her doorstep. Then she grabbed an old apron and painted on it her last view of the Bottoms. In 1926, as she prepared for the end, she wrote a small book—out of print but discoverable on the Internet—titled *Drowned Memories*, in which she invokes the names and the stories of people she knew and people she knew *of* through family lore, including Chief Pocatello.

My mother, Laurel McEntire Madsen, still mourns the loss of her own family's homestead thirty-some years ago, not due to rising waters, but to economic conditions that drove her brother—who had inherited the family farm outside Preston, Idaho—from the land. When the bank foreclosed, it did not allow family members to bid on the property. My uncle had tried to convince the powers that be to provide water on a bluff overlooking Cache Valley, hoping to build a home there. His petition was denied. Strangely, water rights were forthcoming after a developer gained possession of that land. The family has always suspected that someone else's greed played a role in the loss of the farm that my grandparents, Ida and Wells McEntire, had purchased back in 1917 and nurtured throughout their lives.

As a child in the '70s, I ran through cornfields there, fell into irrigation ditches, explored abandoned outbuildings that had housed the Navajo families who came from Arizona each summer to work in the beet fields. My mother tells of how my grandmother extended warmth and friendship to those workers, sharing her kitchen with them, giving them home perms, lending them her sewing machine to make clothes from the velvets they bought in town with their wages. The shopkeepers there had no compunction about charging them double the usual price. Ida's open heart was far from the norm. Most of her neighbors viewed the Indigenous laborers with suspicion, and even contempt. I don't know when the Navajo people stopped coming to Preston to work on the farm. The outbuildings I played in over forty years ago were long unoccupied even then. My mother still owns two handmade silver and turquoise rings that the Navajo family sent to Ida from Arizona.

As a child I was unaware that just outside Preston stands the monument to the Bear River Massacre, the largest recorded mass-murder of Indigenous people in the history of the West, called by historian Rod Miller "a bloodbath more extreme than that at Wounded Knee" (xii). Reports described the savage rape of Shoshone women and the murder of children in cold blood. Twenty-three US Army soldiers were killed in the attack on the Shoshone village, compared to between 270 and 400 villagers. The actual number is lost to history, but writer Daysha Eaton tells of farmers who later quit plowing in the area because human bones would continually surface; they decided to graze cattle instead. Easier to leave bones underground, where they require no soul-searching, no acknowledgment, no re-burial. Easier to assume that victors are blameless and brave. Only in 1990 was the killing field at Bear River renamed a "massacre" rather than a "battle."

~

When my uncle lost the farm near Preston, he moved to Logan, Utah, and got a job managing a dry-cleaning business. After a lifetime working amid the smells of mown hay, warm milk, silage, and cow manure, he now went to bed every night with perchloroethylene lingering in his nostrils. For many years, my Aunt June was the only family member left in Preston. When we would visit, she would take us on a tour of the lost farm where she and my mother were born and raised. We'd drive last to the bluff where my grandfather grew dryland wheat, where my uncle had hoped to build a home, and where an upscale development now stands. Neat sidewalks, manicured lawns, immense windows. For me the message is clear: "Keep out. This view is for *us*, not *you*."

Other losses mount or threaten. Whenever I return to my hometown of Fort Collins, Colorado, where Horsetooth Rock gazes down at the ever-expanding city, more farmland has been gobbled by mansions and condominiums. And year after year, the battle to save the Cache la Poudre River goes on. Whenever I travel with my parents to our family cabin near the Wyoming border, they lament that the valley through which Highway 287 passes will be underwater if the powers that be have their way. I've recently discovered that in this case those powers comprise a "regional government dam-building agency" carrying out the Northern Integrated Supply Project (NISP), which aims to divert the Poudre's flow to insatiable Denver suburbs. Most recently, the Colorado Department of Public Health and Environment (CDPHE) issued a water quality certification to NISP, over the vehement opposition of the city of Fort Collins and citizens' organizations. While the Cache la Poudre is now the only "National Wild and Scenic River" in Colorado—a congressional designation—NISP is arguing that the river has no legal standing, because it is a "watershed," not an "entity."

～

In Minerva Teichert's art, the landscape is almost always a backdrop to a human story—as it is in the Manti Temple—but it is also an entity in its own right, shaping and amplifying the action. In a painting of pioneer women and children washing at a river, Minerva filled the bottom third of the image with water, which illuminates and mirrors the people kneeling in a row at river's edge. The reflection of a woman's bright cloak shimmers across the surface. The people's faces are barely hinted at, but their posture speaks of worshipful thanksgiving. Behind them, cattle wander, and on a dry bluff above the river, covered wagons stand against a cloudless sky.

In *Betty and the Seagulls*, a young woman stands, arms stretched skyward to receive the miraculous arrival of birds that descend, according to pioneer lore, in time to save the crops from an invasion of crickets. Everyone else in the painting kneels in gratitude, but Betty's joy is irrepressible, a different kind of prayer. In the background: the knee of a dry hill, the distant wash of the lake, salty as tears.

In *Breaking the Ponies*, a horse plunges forward as if to escape the bounds of the painting; on the animal's back an Indigenous man whose muscles strain to keep him astride. Other riders in the background are subsumed in a swirl of dust, as jagged peaks define the skyline like ravenous teeth.

~

After losing their home in the Fort Hall Bottoms to the American Falls Dam, Minerva and Herman bought a ranch in Cokeville, Wyoming, where they lived the rest of their lives. Minerva's front room was large enough to accommodate mural-size paintings, and was central to all her other activities. She was a multitasker, adding brushstrokes to her paintings while a roast was in the oven or before sanitizing milk bottles for the family dairy. I love these lines from a letter she wrote in 1942: "I mended undies for dad and o'alls [overalls] for Johnny. We went to Kemmerer and I got the board for my painting and some material for Hamilton's shower..." (41). Her art was tightly woven into the fabric of her daily life.

But Minerva was also aware of what was happening beyond her peaceful surroundings. In the midst of World War II, she wrote, "I don't know why I am so *down* but I guess it is all the things the world is doing" (77). Later in the same letter she told of a church party and noted, "Those high priests sure shake hands hard. They broke the blister on my burned hand so it bothers me writing…" Sometimes people commit the horrors of war; sometimes—overzealous and unaware—they cause pain or harm.

~

Looking out from Cedar Knoll on this chilly November afternoon, the Sanpete Valley lies supine below me; the facing mountains have already entered another winter. Uncle Blake tells me that he gave permission for a number of cedars to be removed from the edge of the knoll, and replanted where they'd been lost, along the bank of the San Pitch River. He also tells of the fences he finds cut every year, and trespassers' campfire coals, broken bottles, four-wheeler tracks across fragile desert soil. The endless tug-of-war between loving and abusing the land. I myself am part of—can't help but be part of—both sides of the story.

While Minerva was not an "environmentalist" as we use the word today, in retelling the land's human stories, she hoped to preserve it and its history. Remarkably, she was capable of telling those stories through eyes other than her own. Many of her paintings draw us into the world—perhaps even the worldview— of the people displaced by Mormon pioneers. In *Night Raid*, a cliff face is an implacable white backdrop in front of which the stolen horses gallop, urged on by two Indigenous horsemen. The distant wagons atop the cliff are rimmed blood-red. For all the foreground commotion, who is really stealing from whom? In another painting, five Indigenous horsemen gaze out from a cliff top. Their disconsolate posture and the travois in tow imply the heartache of surveying a beloved land for the last time.

I don't have to be an art critic to recognize that Minerva never painted, never told her stories, in a spirit of contempt. On her canvas, every gesture, every person, every creature, is imbued with deeply imagined life and motivation. We who love the land, who want to save the land, must keep this in mind when telling our stories. How can we hope to influence others if we don't know who they are or what they care about? How can we entice them to listen—to see the beauty we see—if they are merely an obstacle or an adversary? In other words, we can't simply excoriate loggers or ranchers or miners or even developers without finding out what they love and believe in. To use an example from another continent, elephants in Kenya have been protected from poaching only when those living near them were given ways to safeguard their own livelihoods, and were recruited to the cause.

It's high time I recruit myself to help save the land I profess to love. High time I find out more about the powers that be that connive against the Cache la Poudre River. Only then can I say without hypocrisy that every such plan for the use of western land must be examined in the light of day. And if those powers understand only cash value or feel that their privileged needs transcend those of everyone else, we will know it is time to act.

I see in my mind's eye one of my favorite Teichert paintings, *Hole-In-The-Rock.* A cliff face takes up fully two thirds of the frame, while a wagon in the foreground teeters above a precipice. As Wallace Stegner wrote in *Marking the Sparrow's Fall*, raising his own lament to yet another drowned landscape—Glen Canyon, lost to its dam—"The Lake makes the feat of those Mormons look easier than it was, but even now, no one climbing the thousand feet of cliff to the slot will ever understand how they got their wagons down there" (63). The loner-pioneer never existed among Mormon settlers. On the contrary, as Stegner also points out, it is the cooperative spirit that distinguished those hardy souls (62). "Theirs was a group dream, not an individual one."

Unfortunately, the communitarian spirit on which Latter-day Saint culture was founded has been in large measure hijacked by an idea prevalent in the broader culture of western expansion: that of rugged, my-way-or-the-highway individualism. The theme of *mine* not *ours.* Nevertheless, the spirit of cooperation and interdependence still sounds a strong note in a land that has been loved by—cherished by—Latter-day Saints for generations. And it is this communitarian spirit that can help save the West, whose arid landscape is never "dreary," but rather, as Minerva Teichert knew, infinitely precious and beautiful. As she also testified in paint, the land will only be saved by the human beings who inhabit it, by their willingness to look to the dispossessed, to listen to each other's stories, to honor the history, blood, and heartache embedded in its soil, and to rejoice in and conserve the lifeblood of the land: the water that feeds its springs, crops, marshes, and free-flowing rivers.

Dant, Doris R., "Minerva Teichert's Manti Temple Murals" *BYU Studies Quarterly*: Vol. 38: Issue 3, Article 2, 1999.

Eastwood, Laurie Teichert, ed., *Letters of Minerva Teichert*, BYU Studies: Provo, Utah, 1998.

Eaton, Daysha, "Forgotten Shoshone Massacre Story Will Soon Be Told On Grand Scale." January 31, 2019. www.kuer.org/post/forgotten-shoshone-massacre-story-will-soon-be-told-grand-scale#stream/, retrieved 08/14/2020.

Gardner, Peter A. "Painting the Mormon Story." *BYU Magazine*. Winter, 2008.

Miller, Rod. *Massacre at Bear River: First, Worst, Forgotten*. Caxton Press: Caldwell, Idaho, 2008.

Oman, Richard and Susan, "A Passion for Painting: Minerva Kohlhepp Teichert." *Ensign*. December, 1976.

Stegner, Wallace, *Marking the Sparrow's Fall: The Making of the American West*. Henry Holt: New York, 1948, 1998.

Stegner, *Mormon Country*. University of Nebraska Press: Lincoln and London, 1942, 1970, 1981.

INTERCEDE

John Bennion

THE ARID ARCHIPELAGO:
FLOW OF WATER, FLOW OF PEOPLE

WHEN RAIN FALLS ON THE GREAT BASIN, AS IT DOES OCCA-
sionally, flow is determined by slope of the ground, absor-
bency of the soil, density of vegetation, amount of water, and an
element of chance. Drop Mormon pioneers onto the same surface, and they walk or ride or roll in their wagons toward water,
their possessions piled high.

I've felt in my gut and bones this longing for water, and at
times in my life I've engaged in the alchemy of turning water
to grass to beef. However, my father was not only a rancher but
a botanist, and his influence helped me embrace environmentalism. Consequently, I know the climate crisis will transform
the West—both our weather, especially the water cycle, and our
human culture, especially farming, ranching, and other occupa-
tions that depend directly on the water cycle. One result of my
double inheritance is the desire to articulate both sides of the
current opposition between Utah livestock operators—largely
conservative, anti-Fed Mormons, and environmentalists—lib-
erals, often gentiles (which is what Mormons call people not
of their faith), who want the landscape preserved for ecological and esthetic reasons. I've studied how my ancestors' ardent
search for water shaped their lives as they farmed and raised

livestock for five generations on the eastern edge of the Great Basin, in Rush Valley, an arid basin thirty-five miles long and twenty miles wide, just west of the Wasatch Front. Also worth keeping in mind: all the landscapes the Bennions settled on were Goshute homeland. While friendly with the local people, the Bennions and other livestock operators elsewhere weren't influenced much by the Native tradition of adapting to the conditions of the landscape. Still, considering how each generation of my people responded to scarce water and grazing might serve as a case study, hopefully disrupting what have been inflexible ideological oppositions.

Like other ranching families, my twig of the Bennions, a large Utah family who are now mostly city people, located where they found water and pasture. A map of the stream deltas across the Great Basin perfectly matches the map of Mormon settlements. The water sources and settlements form an archipelago—not islands in a sea, but springs and streams in an arid land. Before these Europeans came, the Goshutes had a seasonal pattern of following water and food within a twenty-mile area: greens in the spring, seeds and fruit in the summer, tubers and nuts in the fall, dried fruit and nuts in winter. They ate everything—eighty-one varieties of plants, many kinds of insects, reptiles, small mammals, and sometimes fish and large mammals. Their adaptability enabled them to establish a stable culture that lasted thousands of years. Next to them, we Europeans have a short history in the West.

My ancestors and other European settlers followed a less complex pattern in response to the geography: find a canyon with a stream flowing out, locate grazing nearby, drive their livestock to the new location, dig ditches, plant gardens, and build a cabin or house. When enough people have gathered, build a church and a school. In the past as I've pictured these streams and settlements spread across the eastern part of the Great Basin, I've assumed that the most important relationship might be the hierarchical bond to church headquarters in Salt Lake—a vertical connection. From that city came news, supplies, instructions, and ecclesiastical authority. More recently I've thought how these agricultural settlements were related to each other—a horizontal connection—because both the canyon/stream formation and the pattern of settlement were repeated—parallel fractals, geographical and cultural.

Brigham Young wanted the vertical ties to be strong, his people unified. If they were disobedient, God could "cause the water of every stream in this valley to sink deep into the bowels of the earth…and the clouds would gather no more moisture, and no more rain would fall on the earth" (*Journal of Discourses* 16:113). He also didn't want to rely on gentiles for essential goods, and some of the settlements provided Salt Lake with cotton, wine, iron, beef, wheat, and coal. Finally, he wanted a corridor of settlements from Salt Lake City to the ocean, or at least to the Colorado River for commerce with the West Coast. Consequently, as settlers left Salt Lake and spread across the landscape, they were both pushed by authority and pulled by water and land open for the taking. They believed, and Young supported this idea, that nobody owns water. God provided water for his righteous people—distributed by the religious leaders of the community. Maybe the difference over ownership is subtle, but what it meant in villages is that if someone new moved in, they were supposed to get a share of water. Land also was open for the taking; Mormons didn't understand Native American ways of living on the landscape. My ancestors believed in Manifest Destiny amplified and shouted from the mountaintops. Leaving Salt Lake, they responded to these specific forces, but their outward migration followed universal or biological tendency. Any population in a given environment might expand outward, from a crowded place ruled by a strong central authority and with limited resources, to a place of undeveloped resources and relative independence.

My great-great-grandfather, John Bennion, embraced the

concept of open resources and land, in part due to the poor quality of his father's farm in Flintshire in northern Wales. Plenty of rain watered their crops, but the soil was depleted after centuries of use. Having concluded that farming was "poor prospects," he left his home and joined the Mormon Church in Liverpool. He and his new wife Esther Wainwright, who grew up nearby, sailed to America in 1842 and settled on a farm in Nauvoo, Illinois. Forced out with the other Mormons, they migrated west, arrived in October of 1847 with one sheep and two heifers but plenty of seeds, and established a farm on Parley's Creek. John wrote about "beautiful streams bursting from the mountains" and the opportunity of every man having "as much land set of to him as he wants or can cultivate." He explored other valleys where the Saints could spread if Salt Lake became crowded.

Soon Brigham Young wanted John's homestead for a church farm. Obedient, John disassembled his cabin and hauled and ferried the logs to the far side of the Jordan River, still in the Salt Lake Valley. The next year he moved farther south on the river, where the land was better, more sandy, and low enough that he and other settlers "over Jordan" could more easily take water from the river, which they directed into canals and ditches they had built to irrigate vegetables and wheat and to provide power for a gristmill.

Esther Birch, my ancestor, worked as a maid in John's household until he married her in 1856, when "Ann" was added to her name to distinguish her from the matriarch. The first Esther couldn't abide having another sexual partner to John in the same house and the family needed someone to watch the livestock, so Esther Ann lived for weeks at a time in a shack on the foothills near Bingham Canyon, about fifteen miles west of the main home on the Jordan River.

After only eight years, the foothills were grazed off. John didn't understand the delicate nature of native western grasses, so year after year he allowed his livestock to gnaw the spring growth to nubs, killing what had once been a bounty. He relocated his livestock to Rush Valley, sending Esther Ann and Mary Turpin, whom he had married in 1857, to provide a home for the herders, including the half-dozen children who were old enough to help. The two women thought that being separated from the main family on the Jordan River was personal, but their isolation was also caused by geography, the distance to the next open valley. Their first winter in the foothills they might have died except, according to my uncle, the local Goshute people took them into their willow huts for the worst months.

Esther Ann deflected her frustration by writing poetry about valuing contributions of even the lowly. However, she worried about the faith of her children who herded sheep and cattle for months away from their families and villages. She was especially concerned about bad influences and idle time in the evenings—so she sent her son Israel off to the cattle herd with a Bible in one saddle bag and an edition of Shakespeare in the other. These anchored him, when many herders, isolated from family, village, and church, drifted toward the wild side, weakening what had once been a powerful bond with the church.

In 1868 John was called with other men and women to open a new settlement, this time on the Muddy River to farm and raise sheep in what is now southeastern Nevada. He left his first wife to manage the central home on the Jordan River, and Mary Turpin was not healthy, so he took Esther Ann. This was the most difficult landscape either of them had ever encountered. The land grew thorns better than it grew grass; sheep didn't fatten on the flats and ravines. While living in that area, he and Esther Ann established six new homesteads in succession, trying to find better water and livestock feed. They generally lived in a Sibley tent, which had a wood floor. Another trouble was that the new Nevada state government wanted to tax the settlers after they'd already been taxed by Utah Territory, so after five years in the Mission, John and Esther gave up and went home.

After John and Esther's return, he continued expanding his herds, and by 1875 the native grass in Rush Valley, which had once been in some meadows as high as the belly of a horse, was gone, and he needed to find new grazing land. Because most closer valleys were taken, in the fall he and some of his workforce of children drove about two thousand head of cattle eastward 150 miles to the tangled canyons of the San Rafael Swell. He left his son Israel, who was fifteen, and another teenaged boy to manage the herd. Israel said they branded 700 calves each spring. After John's death two years later, his older sons sold the remaining herd, 1,700 cows, at a loss; according to my grandfather it was a "disastrous adventure." Not just in the San Rafael but everywhere John moved his livestock, he killed native grasses. He hadn't grown up on the landscape and didn't know the destruction that overgrazing would bring—something Goshute people knew by instinct after generation upon generation of rotating through local plant and animal systems.

The second generation in my family also hunted new water sources and grazing range, but had difficulty finding open land. John's son Israel farmed in Vernon, within a few miles of where Esther Ann and Mary had homesteaded in the southern end of Rush Valley. Previous settlers had chosen Vernon because four streams from the Shiprock Range converged and spread there, making the topsoil rich and deep. When in the early 1890s, Israel's farm became "played out" because of continuous use when no manufactured fertilizer was available, he and the bishop decided that the town should open new land, which would require them to take water from a stream that already had too many users. The result was an angry mess that soon divided the whole community. Israel directed his anger against the state legislature, which had dismantled Mormon communal water law; the legislature was composed of gentiles put in because of the desire to secularize Utah Territory and get rid of polygamy, but that body also fiddled with water law. Israel was even more angry with his neighbors. On the Fourth of July the town held two celebrations, "the true one," he wrote, and a "promiscuous gathering." Eventually they came to a tenuous compromise, but wherever water is scarce, farmers will fight—some taking their water turn early or leaving the stream on their land long after their time was up. The results were anger and sometimes violence.

Israel tried to convince his neighbors that, if they were righteous and smart, their water would both increase and go further, but they didn't really listen, and the water didn't increase. Israel was an innovator; he let spring runoff cover his fields with silt, which improved the soil. He also watched water wasted, sinking into the ground as the streams flowed out of the canyons and six miles across a thirsty flat to Vernon, so he decided to move his farm closer to the source of one of the streams—Harker Creek. Not long after that he convinced about a dozen families to follow his dream that righteousness would bring new water, and established Benmore on Bennion Creek, sharing the town name with another founder—Charles Skidmore. They built homes, a school, a church, and a store, planted gardens and wheat, and let their animals graze. They scraped by until the end of World War I when wheat prices dropped, and everyone moved away. For his final home, Israel moved eastward a couple of miles to near one of the former camps of the Goshute leader Green Jacket who liked wintering away from the canyons where snow drifted high. There, I imagine, Israel felt independent from both his neighbors in Vernon and from the gentile state government.

Throughout both John's and Israel's lives, land that nobody specifically owned was open for grazing—a commons that included canyons, mountainsides, and foothills—where no crops could grow, but where cattle could graze. However, Israel became fearful that rich men with the most cattle would take over, crowding out smaller livestock operators. He was also worried about the depletion of grasses. In 1905, he facilitated the process of including the Sheeprock Range in the National Forest

System. Today, across mountain ranges in Utah, the descendants of the original pioneers run their cattle on public land allotments managed by the US government. In facilitating this land transfer, Israel certainly irked the Vernon bishop and other wealthy livestock operators, which probably brought a smile to his face.

During the next three generations, my family followed the two patterns set for them: to leave overgrazed land and less water for new farmsteads or to try to work hard and clever enough that the water would be sufficient. John and Esther Ann's grandson, my grandfather Glynn, operated eight ranches successively, moving on each time for better land and more water, or when the previous place failed because of dishonest partners or natural disaster.

My father, Colin, wrote that, as a boy, he helped his father homestead at Indian Springs. He described the process repeated by every ancestor who moved to new water and land:

> June 21st, 1934. We rented a truck and loaded it with $12 worth of groceries, lumber and fixtures for a cabin, seeds and fruit tree starts, and bedding. We left Salt Lake City in the morning. We traveled over Lookout Pass, Government Wash, Simpson Springs, and finally arrived at our destination—a hollow six miles south of Simpson. We planted a garden before we did anything else…. Then we built our cabin…[and] started to work on our ditch. Shovels and rakes, work that bent backs and gave us aches. When we got the water down, we dragged a harrow, meant for a horse, by 3 boy and one manpower, after we had planted the 10-acre field in alfalfa.

The water came from a spring fifteen miles west of Rush Valley in the Simpson Mountains where the OK Silver Mine had operated. Glynn dragged a hoe to pull the water around the ends of two ridges, judging elevation by looking at the number of riffles in the tiny stream. My father, sixteen years old, was not happy being there: "1934 was the driest year in Utah history. I just remember one rain all summer. I hated the place." The house stood until a decade ago, but the ditch is still marked on the arid landscape.

A few years later Glynn established his final homestead—Riverbed, fifteen miles west of Indian Springs, named for an underground river that in prehistoric times connected two lobes of Lake Bonneville. He finally managed to settle in one place, where he lived from the early fifties to when, incapacitated and senile, he moved into my parents' house in about 1970. Like his grandmother he was a writer, and many of his essays and fiction describe the heroism of settling in a new area and making a go of it. His life consisted of moving his operations farther and farther west, looking for better land, more water, and fewer people, until he was alone in a cabin in the west desert, isolated from his wife, Lucile, most of his family, and his former church. However, my description of him—chasing a failed dream—is not the way he viewed his own life. He shared with his father and grandfather the blood passion of making a livestock enterprise work in an arid county. Early in his marriage he worked in Salt Lake City as a historical journalist. After leaving the city in 1943, he wrote Lucile,

> When I think of the wretched, hopeless misery of the last few years in town, of being constantly reminded and twitted about my failures, of being tacitly regarded and fenced against as a bum, and the miserable little jobs handed me—as charity, and contrast it with the peace of the desert, the happiness of a new hope, and the joy of perfect health and hard, clean work, I realize that I can't and won't go back. And I've worked too hard this summer to throw it away and go back to the hell of the city.

I think he equated the city with his former religion, believing that both city dwellers and those too ardent with their self-righteousness were liable to cheat their fellow man. In his mind his occupation—finding water and using it to irrigate hay for feeding cattle—was an ennobling enterprise.

When Glynn started his last homestead, my father developed one as well, further south in the same ancient river valley. He chose this land because he could claim rights on spring run-off from a nearby canyon, Judd Creek. But his main source of water for irrigating his alfalfa was pumping water from underground with a diesel engine. While much of his act of settlement was similar to that of his ancestors—searching for irrigable land, digging ditches, putting up a tent to establish his claim—technology in the form of a deep well and a diesel-run pump enabled him to settle on land that wasn't a part of the archipelago of streams. My father's main farm was still Greenjacket, which his uncle had deeded to him, and in the 1970s it became his only farm, when diesel prices went from twelve cents per gallon to seventy-five cents and keeping the farm in Riverbed was no longer sustainable. My father was not ambitious like his father and great-grandfather, nor did he want to convince everyone that he had a righteous vision as his grandfather had. He worked closely with government agencies, not only those who oversaw his Forest Service allotments, but also those who helped with his Riverbed homestead, including the Soil Conservation Service and the BLM. He made friends of the officers, and they worked together to improve the land and water. Of course, he still followed the model available to him, adapt the land to his methods of agriculture, not the model of adapting his practice to the needs of the landscape.

The anger over federal control of public lands of the 1970s and '80s—the Sagebrush Rebellion—didn't affect my father's thinking much. He was entering his sixties and set in his ways. However, this movement has affected how my sister Elizabeth, the fifth Bennion to run cattle in the south end of Rush Valley, thinks about her livestock operation. This original movement has transitioned to the wise-use movement and the Public Lands Initiative. My sister's values are the pioneering values, which have been translated and combined with conservative views against the federal government—that families who have lived and grazed their cattle on specific landscapes for many generations shouldn't be restricted and regulated. For contemporary livestock operators, this movement is less a revolution than a return to the previous ideology of open water, open land, and no authority in control over them.

My sister first lived in Oregon on her husband's garlic farm. When my mother decided to sell the Greenjacket ranch after my father's death, Elizabeth and her husband sold the Oregon property and claimed her inheritance in Rush Valley. Instead of searching for new land as every generation did before, they have stayed put on land watered by Bennion creek. They and the descendants of other pioneers are part of an established map of ranches on the archipelago of streams across the Great Basin. Elizabeth and her husband, Alan, experiment with efficient use of the water, having installed wheel sprinkler lines fed from a reservoir, built fences so they can rotate livestock away from grassland before it becomes ruined, buried waterlines and established tanks to pull the cattle toward meadows that had been too far from water. Having learned from the mistakes of her ancestors, my sister believes, as most rural Mormons do, that private owners know better than any government official how to take care of their own land. The same goes for her Forest Service grazing allotment. She doesn't like having a fickle landlord, because local public land policy can change with every election and with the rotation of the local government managers, who might be ardent, anti-cattle environmentalists or (increasingly rare) someone trained in an agricultural school in range management. She would rather the federal government turn the Forest Service land over to individual owners. She watches four-wheeling recreationists tear up the hillsides and mistrusts public land managers.

Unlike our maverick grandfather, my sister remains strong in the church. During our great-great-grandfather's time, obedience in building Zion pushed Mormon livestock operators toward the most piddling streams and sketchiest landscapes, and independence pulled them. Even for the faithful, once a community and ideology were established, not even God nor his prophet could uproot them. Western livestock ranchers have always embraced the idea of open space owned by God where they can pursue water and grazing land, where no government can regulate them. They think environmentalists just want to meddle with what to them is a natural and divine process, more essential than religious authority or doctrine. Consequently, rural Mormons might value their horizontal relationships with each other more than their connection to the central church in Salt Lake City. Repeated geography—water spreading from the mouths of canyons across the Great Basin—resulted in repeated human behavior—a similar process of settlement and a common ideology related to open water and land and independence from authority. This repetition acts like a fractal—a replicated form—and fractals, as natural as the branching of a tree, allow for both similarity and variety. Water in the Great Basin manifests itself as streams, springs, lakes, marshes, and aquifers, and the people formed by their common enterprise are ideologically similar but also varied, especially with regard to religion—active Mormon, active doubter, less active, Jack Mormon, angry apostate.

I borrowed the idea of seeing the Great Basin streams and settlements as an archipelago from oceanic and Caribbean studies—a very different geography than the Great Basin and a very different people than Mormon ranchers. The concept of the "repeating island," described by Antonio Benítez-Rojo, seems useful to me in understanding the resonance between geography and human behavior in the Great Basin. The analyses of archipelagic scholars undercuts the idea that the primary relationship of island communities must be with the mainland—colonizer and colonized. Just as important is the island-to-island relationship, and in the Great Basin, the commonality between settlements. Each of my ancestors had complex relationships with Salt Lake and with government, sometimes obedient, sometimes not. However, all of them had the same driving force as every other livestock operator in Mormon towns on the eastern edge of the Great Basin—making a cattle or sheep operation work in a land of little water. I think it's valuable to mistrust the conventional wisdom that religion and political conservatism alone determine the behavior of Mormon ranchers or that their relationships and ideas are permanent, inflexible, and never evolving. An archipelagic view reveals much about the ways power relations and ideology in Mormon communities and families evolved and continue to evolve.

In addition, an archipelagic view enables us to see more clearly and possibly emulate some parts of the complex patterns the Goshute people used in creating a sustainable culture on the same landscape. Without doubt they had to work all the time to survive, but so did Mormon ranchers, especially at first. One published history of the everyday life of Mormon pioneers is entitled, *Nearly Everything Imaginable*, which is what one pioneer woman answered when asked what they ate when she was a child. However, the Mormon ranchers whose cows guzzled resources soon left starvation behind. Our future must involve sustainability; we have to become more than a people who burn resources to give ourselves prosperity. For example, we could lose the taste for corn-fed beef and reduce the distance food is transported by changing our eating habits.

I hope that we can shift even slightly how we environmentalists view the history of Mormon livestock operations and of Native foraging in the Great Basin, and how those histories might affect contemporary issues and life. The landscape is not a text that can be read separate from human culture, and the relationships are always complex, requiring complex narratives.

Last fall I bought a traditional sheep camp, rectangular with a curved roof, Dutch door, and a wood stove. The camp also has modern features—a propane stove and furnace, solar-powered lights, and a refrigerator. From the doorway of that cabin, I can see my sister and her husband's alfalfa fields, their huge tractor, their grazing cattle. Southward lies the patch of cedars where the Goshute patriarch Green Jacket wintered. Farther west is Bennion Canyon, in the mouth of which my great-great-grandmother and her sister wife kept a home for the boys herding cattle. On the flat below spreads the delta of the stream where my great-grandfather Israel created a town where all would be faithful and water would be sufficient. The curve of the Sheeprock Range lies beyond that, where my family and others have run their cattle, both when it was Mormon Commons and later as Forest Service grazing allotments. Since the first Bennion settled this area the landscape has changed and the people have adapted to those changes, sometimes with sustainable practices, sometimes not. Not just my family but all residents of the arid West face a future complicated by climate disruption. Best land-use practices involve learning from the past, conversing across political and cultural boundaries, cooperating with government agencies, and being intelligently attentive to the condition of water and land.

Natalie Young

Utah Complications

1. Attempting to Explain State History to the Alien

...the white gulls upon the black crickets, like hosts of heaven and hell contending, until the pests were vanquished and the people were saved.
—Orson F. Whitney, Mormon Settler and Apostle

A piece of the truth lies
in the bird's real name: *California gull.*

Early settlers almost starved because of a cricket
invasion, insects as big as a man's thumb.

Divine intervention (or migration)
brought flocks of gulls

who filled the air with white wings and cries,
settled on the fields, feasted and became

Utah's state bird. Oral history is muddled—
Sunday school taught her and She tells the alien

how seagulls saved the pioneers'
crops from grasshoppers. The internet clarifies

and confuses with more truth, claiming
the *Mormon cricket* was likely a *shieldback katydid,*

changing color in mob situations, swarming
fields in a cloak of black.

Whatever the true labels, the bugs came and ate
corn and wheat, squashes and melon.

And no matter if they came for God
or the salt lakes, legions of birds

gorged themselves and saved a people's
right to name a miracle.

2. After Studying State History, the Alien Kills Weeds

Persecution is not uncommon in this state
or its people: Mormons, polygamists.

Massacres less common: Mountain Meadows;
Bear River Shoshone.

And though the alien has second thoughts
about extermination, he's started

spraying unstoppable weeds
in the yard. The poison streams

out, accidentally hitting
an adult grasshopper here, a baby there.

Camouflaged so perfectly
it's always too late to retreat.

The alien takes concern
to the neighbor in a large sunhat.   *Don't worry*

> *they're pests   they'll take*
your garden   your greens   your sage
munch and   pock
> > *they're asking for it.*

The sun is directly overhead and he can hear
a cricket chirping.

Is the insect in trouble or confused
about what is appropriate,

what we do and do not do in the daylight?

The Mormons reached the American West in 1847 and settled in Utah following violent conflicts and religious discrimination in Illinois and Missouri (partially due to their practicing polygamy). The "Miracle of the Gulls" occurred in 1848, when a flock of seagulls flew into the Salt Lake Valley and ate hordes of insects that were demolishing the crops, thus saving the Mormons from starvation. In 1857 at Mountain Meadows in southern Utah, the Baker-Fancher emigrant wagon train was attacked by a militia of Mormon settlers; 120–140 people were killed, mostly families on their way to California. The US Army attacked a Shoshone camp at the Bear River in 1863, after years of clashes and raids on farms in northern Utah and bordering state territories—at least 240 Shoshone men, women, and children were killed.

Darwin Applied
with a Garden Hose

Hand watering a corner of lawn, again—a sad replication
of nature that's anything
but natural

in such dry landscape. 50 days without rain—nearly
the opposite of Noah and the ark.
A moth flutters

out of grass, makes its entrance into the enormous,
cobalt night. And for the first time She worries, or perhaps
just wonders,

what happens to these furry nymphs with the onset of an
     actual storm.
Imagines wings sogged in droplets, antennae hung over
large brown eyes;

earth filled with quick-moving moisture, pounding thunder
     and still
wings thinner than paper flap on. It's a question
of survival

and She, a barefoot woman with a garden hose, deems it a
     miracle in this
open air littered with insects and theories—
theory's insects.

Ronda Walker Weaver

Elements

AFTER WE WERE BAPTIZED IN THE FREEZING WATER IN THE basement of the Rigby Tabernacle, the kids in our Primary class were urged to find our own Sacred Grove. This seemed absolutely impossible to me at eight, and today I shake my head at the weight of this heavy admonishment. And yet, because I was obedient, I began my search in the only world I knew: the harsh, wind-carved landscape of southeastern Idaho, the place that defined my family's livelihood, beliefs, intentions, and actions. But even as a credulous Mormon girl, I had a tough time understanding why Joseph Smith's parents let him go out into the woods to pray.

Air

Stinging Idaho wind blew snow in winter, dust in summer. One of my first memories reels with wind: I'm walking from the red and white family Ford station wagon, up the sidewalk to the front porch of Mrs. James' house for preschool. I'm wearing my new red wool coat. The wind rips it open and sends me flying like a baby bird. I think I will never touch ground. I am scared as the dickens about where the wind might take me, and who will find me when I land.

One winter my father decided that all of us children should

have Christmas trees in our bedrooms. The tree in my sister's and my brand new basement bedroom turned out to be a gigantic white-flocked tumbleweed, rising in splendor above the pink shag carpet. Twinkly pink lights and shiny turquoise balls only added to the breeze and sneezes the "tree" brought with it. Even so, it was as close to the shelter of a Sacred Grove as I would experience that year. Outside, the wind blew so hard we couldn't see out of the six-by-twelve living room windows. The glass froze and cracked, but the snow kept us insulated. Dad dug us a path to the neighbors' house and out to the road. We kids shoveled snow off the flat-roofed house.

I walked the three blocks from home to high school, daily, regardless of the weather. I was skinny as a fence post, long-legged, long blond hair. School dress code required that all girls wear dresses, except on Fridays, when dress pants were allowed. Never jeans. Getting enough sleep was more important to me than getting to school on time. I was always running late. There were no blow-dryers in my era. I walked to school with wet hair, wind whistling up my legs. Five months of the school year, I'd arrive with my hair frozen in clumps.

I have a ridge across my nose; I've heard it called the "allergy ridge." People who have allergies scratch their noses hard enough to crease the bridge. It was the wind—bearing pollen from sunflowers, hay, alfalfa, mustard weed, Johnson grass, willows, and Russian olive trees. The wind brought dust from freshly plowed or newly harvested fields. It picked up sterile dirt from thirst-dry fields and blew it in my face. Farm cats in haystacks, horses and their tack, and Grandpa's trusty companion, Irish Blue Brandy, multiplied the misery. My eyes swelled up, my lungs tightened, and I couldn't scratch my ears, eyes, nose, throat enough to stop the itching.

During the hottest days of summer, when the temperature would reach the eighties, the wind still blew, carrying sand and dust. Grit crept into every crease. I ate sand more than once—

grinding it with my teeth until I could swallow. Idaho wind—brutal, always bringing something with it—gives me chills in the remembering.

Water

When I was thirteen years old, my father hired Franz and Werner Geisan to decorate our home. They plastered straw on the living room wall and then painted over it with avocado green, wiped with a gold accent. We finished the basement at the same time, adding two bedrooms. Brett's was decorated in cowboy, mine and Sheri's with that unforgettable princess-pink shag carpet, contrasting the light blue walls. The campaign against nature sprawled on into the family room, where the Geisans installed a red Formica bar, a library, and a sewing closet. Half of the floor was coated with candy-striped shag carpet; the other half was hand tiled with an embedded shuffleboard. I remember we mixed a tube of my mother's red lipstick into the green paint for the walls.

The new basement bathroom came complete with a lighted vanity and turquoise buttoned chair. And a sump pump, just in case.

The family room was finished by spring. I was excited to have school friends over so we could listen to Cheech and Chong records, watch *Monty Python* on our black and white television (*Rigby! The home of television!*), and drink root beer. It was a modern, glamorous summer, but late that fall, in the wee hours of the night, I woke to the sound of a motor. The water was here. Rigby's farmers required surface water to irrigate, and as it sank into the ground it met the high aquifer. By the end of the season, the ground was saturated. The excess seeped into the basement—through the baseboards and up the sheetrock, soaking the new carpets and anything that touched them.

Dad was away on a church trip; in fact he was in upstate New York, chaperoning a group of teenaged boys from our ward as they visited the Sacred Grove. He came home to a wet carpeted driveway—shag pink, candy-stripe red. He got right to work, mounting our beds on four-inch blocks, and we forged on like pioneers. We went to bed at night with dry feet, knowing full well the morning would bring a shocking wake-up. We tried not to splash as we ran from our bedrooms to the stairway. The sump pump couldn't keep up. Maybe we should never have installed it in the first place—it almost seemed like planning for water was the cause of it. Five autumns later, when my family left Idaho, the sub-water left as well.

Although my family owned a boat, and I took swimming lessons at Heise Hot Springs and Riverside Pool, I didn't learn to swim. My mother was perennially frightened that one of us would drown—I don't know where. In the irrigation ditch that ran along the front of Grandpa's farm? The canal that meandered through town? The dry-farm lake that was only full when the farmers weren't irrigating?

Our own basement?

Mother didn't swim. I'm not sure why she trusted my father to place me all the way under the baptismal water and bring me back up. I wonder how she sat calmly on the bench, near the pool's edge, during lesson time.

My siblings all water-skied, but my mother's fear of losing one of us children kept me from even attempting it. After all, who would take care of her if we all drowned? I stayed in the shallow end of the pool, or near the shore at Quail Lake, or cautiously in the boat, or firmly in a camp chair on the rocks at Palisades Reservoir.

As an adult, I taught water aerobics for seven years. I played in the water with my children. I floated in the Tennessee River on a tube without a life jacket. I kickboarded laps in community pools, but I never let go. Our Alabama home had a pool, and my kids swam like gators. I didn't learn how to swim until I gave myself swimming lessons for my fortieth birthday. I decided this was one phobia I could eliminate. I hired a private swim instructor and took the plunge. That first time on my back, face up, belly up, butt down, was a spiritual experience. I could float! I let go of my kickboard, floorless, and learned to tread water.

Land

On a clear day we could see the Grand Tetons, ninety miles east. They made me think that young Joseph must have walked miles and miles and miles to find privacy. In my world, not even the lodgepole pines of Island Park could have provided cover enough to pray unseen, let alone for three personages to appear. He must have really wanted answers.

Idaho teenagers received their driver's license when they turned fourteen—the same age Joseph was when he first prayed in the grove. We were allowed to drive between dawn and dusk. I had never even turned the ignition in our turquoise station wagon before my first legal day of driving. Farm kids needed this rite of passage in order to help tend the land. Sons, and daughters, played an integral part in farm life—whether it was driving the tractor to plow the fields or running to town for a ball of twine. I wasn't a farm kid, but I was an Idahoan. My folks sent me driving to Idaho Falls to pick up produce and bring baked goods back to our restaurant in town. Driving gave me new respect for the rolling farm fields, the life cycle of crops and farm animals, and the spaces between the places.

We were only one generation beyond farming. My grandfather Jensen was a joker, fisherman, farmer, and rancher. He loved land that could be cultivated or grazed. My grandfather Walker was a smoker, drinker, fisherman, and carpenter. He loved the streams and woods. My memories of both men involve the outdoors. Grandpa Jensen smelled like hay, manure, sweat, and leather. His boots never came in the house, always waiting on the back porch. Mud and manure with pieces of straw and baling twine poked out from under the soles. He wrote poetry on John Deere receipts, or pieces of birch bark, as he waited at the head-gate. He'd put the verses aside to release Snake River water down clean straight rows of potatoes, summer wheat, alfalfa.

Grandpa Jensen grazed his cattle on public lands—the astonishing mountains and streams surrounding Swan Valley. Summers meant visiting Grandpa with a ripe watermelon, a jug of lemonade, cold fried chicken, a potato salad, and chocolate cake. We'd throw a blanket over thistles and weeds, close to a creek, and eat lunch with mosquitoes, deer flies, and cattle. If the cows were content, we'd pull our early morning worm harvest from a moist burlap bag. Grandpa would bait my hook—the worms were too squishy and wiggly for me. Then I'd throw my line into the cold mountain creek and wait. I wasn't nearly as interested in catching the fish as I was in being outside—hot sun, summer breeze, bugs, sneezes, and Grandpa. One autumn Grandpa asked for help to round up the cows and bring them home to Swan Valley. We did that as well as brand them—we made Grandpa proud of his city grandkids.

Grandpa raised sheep for a couple of years. They were not his favorite animal—not independent enough. I fed the bum lambs from a large glass soda bottle, fitted with a rubber nipple. We had to hold on tight, the lambs sucked so hard. One spring, shortly after the lambing season was finished, Grandpa asked us grandchildren to go out to the lambing pens and pick up the tails. I thought he was joking. He wasn't.

Grandpa Walker, a lapsed Mormon, smelled of Camel cigarettes. His kisses tasted like Folger's coffee. Grandpa W. liked to "putter in the yard." With a pair of pliers, a hammer, and a screwdriver he could fix just about anything. He pulled my first tooth with his pliers—I was livid, but the dollar bill I found in my pant pocket later took away the pain. When Grandpa wasn't tinkering with his tools and a pipe or piece of wood, he liked to fish. He'd wake up in the morning, load his creel with worms shocked from the late-night watered lawn, and head up to Palisades or down to the Snake.

Grandpa Walker was made to be a celebrity. He lived in the middle of town and was often outside, so anyone who came by would stop and visit. He was committed to preserving what he called "the old way of life," including the old water traditions. Grand marshal of local parades and rodeos, he rode a borrowed horse, waving his cowboy hat. Early on, when there were only three of us, Mom and Dad furnished my siblings and me with mythic outfits so we could ride in the parade with Grandpa. My brother and sister wore pointed boots. Even better, I wore moccasins. Grandpa Walker thrived on blue sky and legend; he didn't even own a horse. I trace my love of folklore to him. Grandpa helped preserve a section of the Snake River near Roberts. The Mike Walker Boat Dock is named for him. Grandpa made sure there were signs at both highway entrances into town acknowledging that Rigby was the home of the first television.

I didn't know fish had bones until I was a teenager. I can identify the scent of Camel cigarettes upon the slightest whiff. And I can't yet make myself sign an anti-grazing petition.

Fire

An old overgrown apple orchard languished behind our house, beyond the garden. A barbed wire fence marked the boundary. I never wandered into the orchard; I was told the owners weren't kind, and I was afraid of unkind people. But one summer Paul Johnson took a book of matches out to the orchard to smoke. The volunteer fire engine made ruts in our grass trying to get to the fire. The burnt trees still stand, still the closest thing to a "grove" I ever knew.

Grandpa Jensen would burn his ditch banks a couple of times during the planting, growing, and harvesting seasons. The orange arms of the flames would reach up like evil spirits.

Grandpa warned us kids to not get too close. However, just in case we or the fire got out of control, he made sure there were wet gunny sacks to toss onto the flames. The blackened grass around the ditch banks was tough. The smell of fire, burlap, and grass blended and lingered for days.

Dawn and dusk were my favorite times of day. Grandpa Walker told me the skies were on fire. Because of the open landscape, the horizon seemed to burn for miles. Dust in the air made the sunsets rich and smoky. *Red skies in the morning, farmers take warning. Red skies at night, farmers delight.*

When I was in seventh grade, the junior high school burned to the ground. The eighth and ninth grades were junior high grades, so I just missed my chance to be one of the cool kids. I remember the flames crackling, the sirens, the disappointment. When I was older, my father managed the iconic Mack's Inn on the Island Park Highway. One night the old structure went up in heat and smoke; only the old rock fireplace that graced the gathering area remained. Both fires were caused by a random spark.

Fear of fire was almost worse than fire itself. We were taught to vehemently extinguish matches, and then double check. Grandpa stomped out his cigarette butts. Many a farmer saw past, present, and future go up in flames because of combusting hay, exploding wheat dust, or a moment of simple human carelessness.

Potatoes

The schools in southeastern Idaho sat empty for two weeks every October. Potato Harvest. High school kids worked on the combines, sorting potatoes as they came up from the ground and across a conveyor belt. Younger kids earned a dollar for every fifty-pound bag they filled (no rocks!), hand-picked from tilled ground where the potatoes lay bare. Allergy kids, and town kids, worked at our parents' businesses. Walker's Family Restaurant was a hopping place; the Country Diner (we called it the Country

Can) down the street took the overflow. Dad needed all the help he could get during potato harvest. I worked for a dollar an hour peeling carrots, scrubbing potatoes, trimming radishes, cleaning tables, and running the cash register. I tried, oh I tried, over the years to peel those potatoes, but even now my eyes itch, my hands and arms break out in hives, and I sneeze until I cannot breathe.

We were happy to get back to school.

By spring the potato cellars were empty, except for seed potatoes. Our church had a farm, a multi-acre field that yielded a grand community harvest every year. As a project, families would gather at the potato cellar. We brought our own knives to cut the potatoes into pieces, making sure each had at least one eye. We planted the eyes by hand, into the freshly turned dirt. In the late fall, church families would gather again at the farm to pick these potatoes. For some reason, we did it the old-fashioned way, no combines here—did we sense, on some level, that this was our version of sacred ground—an agrarian communion with a higher power? We wore brown jersey gloves, towels, bandanas, or diapers around our faces and necks, and layers and layers of flannel shirts. At lunchtime we gathered at the church to eat a meal made by the women in the ward, then returned to the field to pick spuds until dark. We rose the next morning to do it again. It took a few days to harvest the church farm's potatoes.

There is no downplaying the meaning of an Idaho spud in southeastern Idaho. Potatoes, and the elements that constrain these gems, still anchor regional life. Our seasons revolved around a potato's lifespan. At harvest, daylight savings time allowed the farmers to rise early for the fields as my father rose early to open the restaurant, start the coffee brewing, and cook eggs, pancakes, and breakfast steaks for the multitudes. Dad worked through the evening, with farmers stopping by to drink a cup of coffee and talk crops and cattle before heading home for supper. The workers who had no home-cooked meal to go home to relied on my father's place to supply them with a warm plate, akin to mother's love.

Dad often kept the lights on and the coffee hot until two a.m. It wasn't unusual for the ranchers and farmers to work through mealtime, stop at the bar for a drink or two, and talk the original stock market with anyone who would listen. Then they'd meander down a block to Walker's Family Restaurant for coffee before steering their pickups toward home. Only then would Dad close up shop and hurry home for a few hours' sleep before starting all over again—earlier than the farmers who rose at the crack of dawn to begin their season-specific chores.

While my father ran the restaurant, my mother fed family and neighbors. Often I came home from school to a kettle of potatoes on the stove. We ate them for dinner, fried the leftovers for breakfast, and baked them again the next day. My Idaho mother coated potatoes with shortening, wrapping them in foil before setting them in the oven by four o'clock, ahead of our evening meal. When making bread, she'd add a handful of dried potato flakes for flavor. I could smell potato donuts—spud nuts—frying as I walked into the kitchen, home from school and starving. I can hear Grandma's red-handled peeler flicking off skins before she boiled the naked whites: mashed potatoes in winter, potato salad in summer. Grandma's chipped yellow ceramic bowl is my prized possession; it can only be filled with potato salad. I have eaten potatoes fried, chipped, smashed, scalloped, au gratin, souped, baked, double-stuffed, twice-baked, Dutch-ovened, hashed, candied, and fried—with gravy, ketchup, ranch dressing, sour cream, or my father's secret seasoning.

When I moved to Alabama my grandparents sent me a box of russets, all of them larger than my fist. My neighbors had never seen potatoes so big. They tasted great with fried green tomatoes. I prefer my potatoes home-baked, and no potato on the planet can measure up to the flakiness and versatility of an Idaho Russet. Now, far from my childhood, I call them potatoes, not spuds. That term belongs solely to people whose lives are intertwined with the vines.

Harvest

When I turned sixteen, the elements turned on us. The potato harvest was meager. Farmers paid for this year's loss by hocking next year's yield, but God did not provide: the next harvest was just as dismal. There was no cash for seed potatoes. Farmers begged for loans—another crop, maybe alfalfa this year—but still the land didn't produce. The banks called the loans due. Idaho Farmer's Bank contacted my father, who was paying for this year's services with next year's harvest, just like the rest of the men in the community. Dad lost his restaurant, but the farmers didn't lose their land.

When I turned seventeen, the Teton Dam burst wide open, and the waters flooded the Snake River—rushing from the mountains to the plains. My uncle lost his restaurant, my aunt lost her home and ranch, and the green fields of alfalfa, hay, and potatoes were inundated.

The summer of my eighteenth year, the lodgepole pine forests of southeastern Idaho and Yellowstone turned black. The flames moved rapidly, sparing nothing. The Idaho winds made the fires impossible to control. My family loaded pickups and cattle trailers and headed south to Utah—land of education, Brigham Young, and suburbia.

The landscape changed.

I changed.

Prayer

Whether "Dear Lord" is a curse, or a precursor to prayer, the phrase is common among people who live in the Idaho elements. This land was brutally sacred, each acre fearsome and holy. I realize now there was no reason to search for a grove of trees. Prayer was ever on our tongues, barely distinguishable from profanity. Whether praying for rain, sun, a bountiful harvest, or a late frost—or cursing the very same—there was no call to hike sixty miles to the closest cottonwoods near the lake, and certainly no time to wait around for answer. Pray, curse, act, and be found.

In my late twenties I thought I found my Sacred Grove. I was visiting friends in the rolling hills of western Virginia. Driving a lush side road, I turned off the pavement and the grove rose before me, gentle and inviting—the kind of scenery I imagined God loved best. I knelt in prayer on the mossy ground, accented with wild roses, kudzu vines, and Virginia creeper. Tall scented honey locusts and squat blooming rhododendrons enclosed me. A red cardinal perched in an enormous oak. The prayer was answered in its way: the Sacred Grove I had spent my life searching for was in my heart, where my own truth lay. What I sought was no longer in the lessons from my religious vernacular, but in a place to call my own. My continuous search gave me a new meaning of self and place—one I discovered, defined, and was not compelled to share with anyone else.

Sometimes I long for that young self and the Sacred Groves I appropriated over the years. Occasionally I return to the South, but by now I understand that gentle, lush, fecund, warm, and embracing are not who I am. I had to run away from the place that made me before I could recognize how deeply I am defined by home landscape: I am harsh, tough, brisk, cutting, matter-of-fact, clear, bright, stark, bare, and skeptical. The elements of my making are more sacred to me now than ever. I've claimed my holy ground.

Robert Terashima

Snow Canyon[1]

–for Rachel McMahan

*The flora of this high desert grows
in shallow soil with scant water.*

We strive

to please
others
or ourselves

yet *these
are still–*
blackbrush

yucca
desert scrub…
unless

(and this
is the secret)
stirred

Earlier

today there was
a tarantula
on the road

to the restrooms

(From now
on I'll watch
my step–
not the stars!)

–Must've been
a *"He"*
out looking
for lady friends

Growing up

in California, I saw
all sorts of creatures
at low tide–
sea horses, sea urchins
and shells of course

–but now tourists
have taken everything!

(a pause)

Where would we be
though, if it were not
for more people?

*The Utah Banded Gecko is a sub-
species found in the Borders Area
of Utah, Arizona and Nevada.*

Your eyes
like those of most
Gekkonidae

are large–
unlike others though
you blink!

Better that
than licking dirt off
to see…Ugh!

Datura, or Night Shade, was used
by many of the indigenous peoples [2]
in ceremonies, and as an analgesic.

Above this rim

of rock,
moonlight

–while below

     Look!

flowering

     only now

in the evening

(lush,
though pale)

174

an extravagance–

*May minds
open like these*

*petals
and suffering*

*be over-
shadowed*

by forgetfulness

Up there

by that water
tower they plan

to build a hotel.
Such a shame!

But it's all
privately owned.

Tonight *Joseph*
is playing

at the Tuacahn
Amphitheater– [3]

Come and see!

Footnotes (summarized from Wikipedia)

1. Mormon pioneers came upon Snow Canyon
while searching for lost cattle. It was named
for Lorenzo and Erastus Snow, pioneer leaders.

2. The region was used by ancestral Puebloans
for hunting and gathering from AD 200 to 1250,
and inhabited by Southern Paiutes from AD
1200 to the mid-19th century.

3. Tuacahn initially served as the venue for *Utah!*
a musical depicting early Mormon history. But
lukewarm reviews and audience discomfort
with some subjects depicted led to rewritings,
and, in 1999, showings were discontinued, to be
replaced by Broadway musicals and, beginning
in 2005, Disney Theatricals.

POISON

Michael McLane

IF THEY POLLUTE THEIR INHERITANCES:
NUCLEAR TESTING AND THE ADVENT OF
MORMON ACTIVISM IN THE GREAT BASIN

I HAVE TWO DISTINCT MEMORIES OF SIXTH GRADE. THE FIRST is being forced to learn Billy Joel's "We Didn't Start the Fire" in its entirety, an experience that may well be responsible for my affinity for historical tragedies. The other is my teacher, Ms. Wright, telling the class that she was a Downwinder. This wasn't part of any curriculum, but perhaps that was the point. We didn't know what the word Downwinder meant. She explained it as best she could and I think it mostly just frightened us, or at least me. Why would anyone bomb their own people? Bombs were for enemies. The word became a fixture in my mind.

Four years later, I first read Terry Tempest Williams' *Refuge* and found that word again. I was also reading authors such as Rachel Carson, Wallace Stegner, Juanita Brooks, and Fawn Brodie. My sixteen-year-old brain didn't fully understand what their work offered, but the authority I had taken for granted, be it religious or governmental, was upended a little at a time in those pages. Faith and history shared a similarly scarred landscape. Both wavered in the desert heat. Though I couldn't possibly have articulated it at the time, those books represented a simultaneous rejection of the ideologies I had been raised in and an obsession with the forces that drove, interwove, and endlessly complicated them.

Not long after, my mother began treatment for the first of two aggressive cancers she has had, both of which are types often tied to Downwinder clusters. I once suggested she file for funds from the Radiation Exposure Compensation Act. It was the only time we talked about her cancers within a Downwinder context. After all, she grew up in Salt Lake and governmental culpability is well-defined in space and time. But the Great Basin resists temporal and geographic borders. There were many histories to be found there, as well as a cancer of my own. It became the scar my mother and I share like a hyphen on our throats—a link, a combination, and something missing, all at once. Many others share such marks and scars far worse. They are the embodiment of faith and trust conflated in dangerous ways. It turned out you could bomb your own people, and with the right mix of politics and history, you could even convince some of them to accept it.

Mormons make up a disproportionate number of those most directly affected by American nuclear testing. The present tense is important in that statement because this story, and that of all Downwinders, continues despite the frequent relegation of nuclear testing to the Cold War kitsch bin, alongside "duck and cover" drills and fallout shelters. We are still learning the intergenerational effects of excessive radiation exposure on human beings. It is a newer kind of pioneer legacy, one that was covered up for decades. Meanwhile, the current administration calls for upgrades to the American nuclear arsenal, as well as renewed uranium mining and nuclear testing, all of which reopens wounds for those who know all too well what these actions mean for their families and their lands.

~

On July 6, 1962, the Storax Sedan nuclear test was conducted at the Nevada Test Site an hour north of Las Vegas. Its detonation displaced nearly twelve million tons of soil and left a hole 320 feet deep. Multiple plumes of radioactive debris were blown eastward across nearly the entire nation. Sedan deposited more radionuclides around the US than any other test, with hot spots measured from Utah to North Carolina. The test was part of Operation Plowshares, an ongoing effort to utilize nuclear weapons for "peaceful purposes"—such as mining, earth removal, and even widening the Panama Canal—during a brief de-escalation in Cold War hostilities.

I have stood on the viewing platform of what is the single largest crater ever created by humans. Despite the blistering August heat, rain had pummeled the Great Basin for two days prior, so a small pond gathered in the bottom, a rippling oasis. It was almost impossibly beautiful when stripped of its human context—one more unscalable object in a desert that defies human perception and scale at every turn. Then I noticed, floating in the water far below, old tires, scrap metal, and other debris. The negligence, the obscene violence of it all, came back into focus in that moment. It was as if those involved simply pushed what remained over the rim and hoped the land would swallow up the whole spectacular failure.

One can only try and fail to imagine the twelve million tons of earth torn, vaporized, or otherwise shifted from one place to another in a matter of seconds. Anthropologist Joseph Masco notes that the "mathematical sublime," the overwhelming of "the human sensorium providing that strange mix of pleasure and terror involved in surpassing one's cognitive limit," is an inextricable facet of nuclear weaponry and its legacy. We are at the mercy of unfathomable powers in such efforts and the simultaneous violence—at the cellular and the planetary levels—that they perpetuate.

~

At least 928 nuclear tests took place at the Nevada Test Site (now the Nevada National Security Site, or NNSS) between 1951 and 1992. As such, the mathematical sublime is old suit for those in southern Nevada and Utah, the populations that came to be known as "Downwinders" due to their presence in the path of radioactive clouds. In the early days of NNSS, families watched the tests from their roofs in the early morning. In an interview with Rebecca Solnit, Janet Gordon recalls, *"and then you can look up and you will see the beautiful mushroom cloud as it ascends to the heavens with all the wonderful colors of the rainbow."* This seeming reverence is part of Masco's sublime. Even with all we know now of these tests, I find it just as hard to look away from the slow-motion videos of blasts now as Downwinders did the tests themselves seventy years ago. Bars and casinos in Las Vegas had viewing parties. People were fascinated by the blinding flashes, mushroom clouds, and the pinkish haze that appeared in their wake.

Residents had no reason to fear as Atomic Energy Commission officials and local authorities assured them all was well. They were proud to be on the front lines of America's Cold War efforts. They did not question why the detritus always seemed to drift their way. This, of course, was by design. The area had been designated by officials as "a national sacrifice zone" occupied by "a low-use segment of the population." In less sanitized terms, AEC chair Gordon Dean referred to the area as "a damn good place to dump used razor blades." Authorities carefully chose testing times to align with winds that would carry fallout out over the Great Basin. Sacrifices were made by those downwind, and they were prolonged, severe, and dismissed out of hand for decades as lies.

Throughout the Intermountain West, Mormon communities acted as guinea pigs in the government's ongoing arms race. Mormons were perfect test subjects for the military-industrial complex—faithful, used to rigid, patriarchal authority and unlikely to question its edicts. They were accustomed to sacrifice and eager to prove themselves patriotic, even seventy years after the death of Brigham Young and half a century after the Manifesto decrying polygamy, that facilitated Utah's statehood. The distrust of government so prevalent in nineteenth-century Mormons had been largely left behind with their territorial status. This overcorrection in attitudes toward federal entities would prove lethal, endangering not only the lives of many members, but the land on which they relied.

~

To fully appreciate the degree to which nuclear testing affected Mormon communities and shifted the faith and ideology of many in the area, it is useful to look at the way land stewardship and environmental ethics are portrayed in Mormon scripture and culture. One would be hard-pressed to label contemporary Mormons environmentalists. The majority have long skewed towards conservative, Republican ideologies and that remains true today. Communities in southern Utah and around the Intermountain West remain some of the staunchest supporters of extraction industries, deregulation, and loosening of environmental laws. It is easy to forget that many of those same laws were put in place by Republican administrations in the 1970s, often with the support of the church and its followers.

It is common to lump Mormons in with more millenarian, Evangelical sects of Christianity who believe that, as Christ is soon to return to earth and the planet will be "sanctified," there is little need to worry about the current state of the environment. Such notions resonate with many Mormons, even if they run contrary to teachings both in scripture and in other settings. The backbone of an environmental ethos is present, and is especially prevalent in the Doctrine and Covenants. D&C 103:13-14 discuss the inheritances that shall be the reward for establishing

Zion and the consequences for the pollution of said inheritances:

> 13 Behold, this is the blessing which I have promised after your tribulations, and the tribulations of your brethren—your redemption, and the redemption of your brethren, even their restoration to the land of Zion, to be established, no more to be thrown down.
>
> 14 Nevertheless, if they pollute their inheritances they shall be thrown down; for I will not spare them if they pollute their inheritances.

Likewise, in chapter 104, it is explained that "every man" is a steward of the earth, all of which is part of God's creation, and is therefore imbued with the divine:

> 13 For it is expedient that I, the Lord, should make every man accountable, as a steward *over earthly blessings, which I have made and prepared for my creatures.*
>
> 14 I, the Lord, stretched out the heavens, and built *the earth, my very* handiwork; and all things therein are mine.

This chapter goes on to advocate for altruism in terms of both distribution of the earth's bounty and a general stewardship of the earth, which itself is divine. George Handley, whose essay "The Environmental Ethics of Mormon Belief" provides one of the more comprehensive treatments of this subject, explores the idea of consecration further, noting that it does not require despotic, centralized control over distribution of resources; its power is in its spiritual focus on the human heart and the need to overcome its selfish impulses in the interest of the larger biological community. Handley appeals to contemporary Mormons by replacing a need for regulation, an idea unappealing to more conservative Mormons, with a call for personal action on both an environmental and social justice level. A few decades earlier, in an August 1971 *Ensign* article titled "Our Deteriorating Environment," A. B. Morrison writes, "in our mindless rush toward material prosperity, we have unbalanced powerful biological forces that we do not fully understand, that portions of the environment are now extremely unstable and susceptible to rapid and potentially catastrophic change." Such overt statements regarding the environment are rare today despite the fact that the Book of Mormon repeatedly addresses overconsumption, unsustainable practices, and the wanton killing of animals.

Such themes were discussed often by early leadership, particularly Joseph Smith and Joseph Fielding Smith. Even Brigham Young, whose love of millenarian metaphors was unmatched by any subsequent leader, discussed the divinity in all living beings, arguing "the spirit constitutes the life of everything we see," and spoke of maintaining a purity of environment: "Keep your valleys pure, keep your towns as pure as you can, keep your hearts pure...speaking of the elements and the creation of God, in their nature they are as pure as the heavens." It was Young who led the early Mormons to their new home and it was Young who sent them out throughout the Great Basin to found new settlements. Such notions would have traveled with them and helped see them through the difficult task of founding agricultural communities in largely inhospitable places.

Comparatively speaking, there were very few resources and few people in the Great Basin. It is daunting terrain, hostile to all but the hardiest or most determined of people. What it did have was space and relative isolation, which was crucial to both the Mormon settlers and later the Manhattan Project, which needed both in abundance for its testing program. For the Mormon residents of the region, the land was sacred in and of itself and in what it represented. While they were relative newcomers to the area, the subsequent century in the desert cemented a two-fold sense of place that even radioactive iodine and strontium could not quash.

First, the Mormons saw themselves as a people fleeing persecution, and the Great Basin provided a link to the biblical stories they held dear. While the religion was born in the Burned-over District of New York and the fields of Illinois and Missouri, the Great Basin would shape the new faith into a fundamentally desert one, right alongside its Jewish, Christian, and Muslim predecessors. The setting would allow its mythos to take on a fundamentally Old Testament quality that can be seen in the naming of its features—the Jordan River (which emptied into a "dead" salt sea in the Great Salt Lake), Joshua trees, and towns such as Moab, Goshen, and Hebron. Americans back east were suspect of this odd group fleeing into the desert. Rebecca Solnit writes "early Americans feared that the arid lands would change the national character. The desert gives rise to a more intimate and individual fear…[s]olitude, emptiness and silence, the forbidding climate and scale of the land, the slender margin for survival." Where others saw forbidding wastelands, the Mormons saw opportunity and a challenge to be overcome.

The other facet of the settlers' sense of place was likewise Old Testament in nature—it was Zion and it was theirs. What they had endured to get there, and what they further endured once they decided to call it home, all fed into their notion of being part of a latter-day exodus, with Brigham Young their Moses. With the odds against their success, and the stakes so high, it is not hard to see why a firm attachment to place is so ingrained in multiple generations of residents in places such as Enterprise, St. George, or Cedar City. Unfortunately, federal government officials had no such nuanced understanding of the place they were to stage their test program, and they have to bear few of the burdens or scars their actions would create.

~

Several years of nuclear testing had come and gone before any of those downwind started to openly question what was taking place at the Nevada Test Site. The impetus for all that would follow was the Upshot-Knothole test Harry, aka "Dirty Harry," that took place on May 15, 1953. The radiation levels in the fallout cloud from Harry far exceeded previous tests. It settled over St. George, Utah, lingering for longer than usual. The population in St. George and nearby towns received no warning before or after the test, at least not until it was far too late.

A short press release sent to community officials after the cloud was already over the city protected the interests of the AEC and the military. This release ended "If there is fallout, it will not exceed the non-hazardous levels experienced after the April 25th shot." Despite this optimism, checkpoints were established to warn motorists to roll up their windows and wash vehicles when they got home. Meanwhile, mothers and children went outside to see the unusual "snow" drifting down from the sky, much of which landed in gardens, and nearby fields full of cattle. Meanwhile, the physical effects of the radiation were already felt by residents. Many complained of headaches, nausea, fever, and dizziness, and in the days following the test would complain of other symptoms characteristic of radiation poisoning, such as hair loss and burns. In the fields, sheep and cattle burned from the outside-in as ash landed on them, and from the inside-out as they ate plants coated in radioactive ash. Livestock that didn't die displayed horrendous deformities and stillbirth rates in pregnancies following Harry and subsequent tests.

Ranchers and sheepherders had never seen anything like this. Some began to question whether the tests might be to blame. Locals feared for both their livelihoods and for their own health. AEC officials dismissed the concerns of the locals out of hand, insisting that the livestock had eaten poisonous plants and that the ranchers were uneducated, paranoid yokels. This simultaneously reinforced the scientific "authority" of those employed by the AEC and flatly dismissed a century of working knowledge of the land and livestock that had been gathered and passed on from one generation to the next.

By 1955, multiple lawsuits against the AEC were in the works. Internal memos would later show that there was plenty of evidence that radiation was at least a contributing factor in the deaths and damages to livestock, but risks to the testing program were too great, so information remained classified. Judgements against the government were dismissed due to constraints created by a portion of the Federal Tort Claims Act known as discretionary function exclusions, a relatively obscure rule that was, as Philip Fradkin writes, "the doctrine of sovereign immunity…a holdover from the days of absolute monarchs, when the motto was 'The King Can Do No Wrong.'" These exclusions made it remarkably difficult to sue the government or collect settlements in cases involving complex issues such as national defense and public health.

The fierce, collective efforts of so many ranchers in these cases illustrate one of the stranger dichotomies that evolved in Downwinder communities—the risk posed to commodities (i.e. livestock) was viewed as a far greater threat than similar risks posed to human beings. While lawsuits over dead livestock began immediately after testing started, collective efforts to protest human risks lagged far behind. It was only when significant cancer clusters—childhood leukemia, thyroid cancer, reproductive cancers—appeared in downwind communities, accompanied by increases in significant birth defects and chromosomal disorders, that residents cried foul. This illustrated a cognitive dissonance that both flouted and adhered to Mormon belief—while the protection afforded livestock undermined a traditional environmental stewardship ethic in favor of a more modern, capitalist concern, the patriotism that superseded human health concerns was viewed through a belief in eternal families. Put another way, our bodies are merely earthly comforts; they are ephemeral, expendable. They can be sacrificed for a greater good and victims comforted in the knowledge that they will be together forever with family in the afterlife. However, none of that does any work in explaining why livestock, earthly comforts, to be sure, should receive such fierce advocacy by the same communities.

It is difficult to ignore the role that fear of Communism played in victimization of Mormons at the hands of the US government. This is no small irony, as Mormon communities around the Intermountain West had been some of the more successful experiments in communal living undertaken in the US to that time. Given their initial isolation and their desire to be outside the reach of the federal government, cooperation and pooled resources were imperative, both in practical and doctrinal terms. George Handley lays out the doctrinal precedent for this when he writes, "[e]xcessive consumption at the expense of others or of our environment is therefore never justified since such behavior violates the tenets of Christ's governance that requires strict adherence to the care for the needy, careful resource management, and a profound disavowal of materialism."

Nevertheless, by the 1950s, America's brand of capitalism was growing exponentially and its military-industrial complex was the most potent economic force on the planet. The specter of Soviet Communism loomed as its only potential threat. Even the most far-flung rural communities were firmly invested in all that system had to offer both economically and politically—including a nationalist imperative to give all you could in the fight against Communism. The communal living practiced by Mormons shouldn't be conflated with state-driven Communism as practiced in the USSR, but the irony of early protest efforts being placed on the destruction of commodities and livelihoods rather than the destruction of human lives and communities cannot be ignored and shows how strong the pressure to bend to American nationalism must have been at the time, even in communities whose own histories and scripture suggest a different set of priorities.

That so many of the plaintiffs in these cases were Mormons was remarkable, as they would have been going against the sentiments of both the majority of those in their communities and LDS authorities. As Sarah Fox notes, dissent was equivalent to disloyalty and "propaganda went so far as to imply that questioning the nation's nuclear weapons development program was tantamount to inviting nuclear attacks from the Soviet Union." It was a moot point that residents were already being attacked in exactly the same manner by their own government.

In 1984, Judge Bruce S. Jenkins handed down a judgement in favor of ten plaintiffs in a case against the government. It was the first time that a federal court laid the blame for deaths and damages among Downwinders squarely on the federal government. Regarding that judgement, Fradkin pulls no punches: "In the end, these people were betrayed by their government...a crime of betrayal perpetuated in the name of national security." Of course, by 1984, the damage was done. Ranchers were bankrupt, land had been sold off, and many had died. By the 1980s, the breadth of the damage done to both livestock and human beings across the Great Basin and beyond was visible to anyone willing to look past federal bluster. Cancers, reproductive disorders, diabetes, and other maladies inflicted upon Downwinders often took years to manifest, and risks posed to future generations by genetic damage are still not wholly understood.

The silent, ravaging effect of radiation exposure was the mathematical sublime in reverse. Instead of mushroom clouds, temperatures, and kilo- or mega-ton measurements too large to fathom, it was the invisibility of radiation, its microscopic and insidious wreckage on a cellular level that was impossible to see and nearly as hard to understand. The intangible nature of the crime perpetrated on Downwinders became tangible more often in absence than in presence—stillbirths, amputated limbs, lungs and thyroids removed, cemeteries filling with victims of cancer from families with no cancer history.

The degree to which Mormons in the Great Basin were gaslighted by their government is underscored by the way in which nuclear testing tainted not only doctrinal notions of the sanctity of the body, family, and the land, but also the very mythos that had sprung up around their desert Zion. The body as temple metaphor is immediately undone by the presence of radioactive elements in food supplies, especially as their presence is the direct result of human tampering with nature. But it was not only the milk of cattle that was tainted; mothers' milk was a danger as well. Iodine-131 and Strontium-90 both appeared in human breastmilk, a corporeal betrayal that would be difficult to comprehend and even harder to warn women about in conservative, rural, 1950s Utah. Solnit writes in *Savage Dreams*: "Milk is no ordinary thing to fear...If a mother can't tell if her own milk will strengthen or poison her child, the most intimate act is contaminated and the entire future called into question."

However, nuclear testing did not stop at merely threatening the mother-child bond, it worked to sever that "act of faith in the continuity of things" altogether. Men and women were rendered sterile by disorders and cancers of the reproductive system and by cancer treatments and surgeries. The family, the most sacred unit in Mormon belief, was severed, not by God or chance, but by the direct actions of a secular government to which they were fiercely loyal. At the same time that fallout was unraveling families in Mormon communities, it was poisoning the land, and thereby the sacred bounty the faithful coaxed from it. Mormons spent the previous century believing their efforts had "made the desert bloom" only to discover that their irrigation projects had created what Fox deemed "funnels for contamination."

The breach of trust perpetrated on Mormon Downwinders created emotional and ideological divides as complex as the bureaucracy victims navigated in attempts to protest their victimization. Mormonism has long shunned public acts of protest, particularly if such acts are directed at federal officials. Scripture repeatedly prescribes obedience to secular leaders, as in the Twelfth Article of Faith, which states: "We believe in being subject to kings, presidents, rulers, and magistrates, in obeying, honoring, and sustaining the law." In *Mormon Country*, Wallace Stegner provides a longer examination of the lack of dissent among Mormon ranks, a further hardship for those alienated by nuclear testing: "It takes courage for a Mormon to dissent...Those Mormons obey because their whole habit and training of life predisposes them to obedience...They will defend their system militantly, because by and large it has been good to them. By and large it has been responsible, despite its assumption of power over the individual. Call it a benevolent despotism."

The notion that LDS authorities would sit idly by while members were sacrificed to the testing program and then discourage them from protesting the subsequent cover-ups proved too much for many. Carole Gallagher's *American Ground Zero* engages a wide spectrum of Downwinders through both oral history and photography and provides some of the more candid interviews conducted in the wake of nuclear testing. Jamie Stewart, like many Downwinder children in the '60s, developed diabetes as a child. She worked with Paiute people near St. George and saw the disease ravaging the generation who were exposed to tests. When asked about Mormonism and activism, she replied: "They discourage people from becoming politically active. They use as a guideline what their church officials tell them, and I guess for as long as people can remember the church has been telling them not to get involved in it. I feel a terrible, terrible anger at the struggle that I've had..."

Similarly, Darlene Phillips suffered with a lifelong autoimmune disease caused by fallout. She witnessed numerous nuclear tests while working at Bryce Canyon. When her own health began to fail like that of many friends and family, she asked religious authorities about attending a rally against continued testing, only to be told, "No, you stay away from it, those people are Communists," or, "We're lucky to have these tests near us and we should be honored...this is our chance to prove we are loyal citizens of the United States." It would take years and the deaths of multiple family members before she had a change of heart and left the Mormon Church in order to claim back "the right to make my own decisions." Much of her family and community ostracized her as a result.

Phillips' experience illustrates the two-fold problem that many Mormons encountered in trying to have their concerns heard within the religious hierarchy—the potential ignorance of lay clergy and the far more problematic betrayal of religious authorities who speak of sanctified bodies, land, and agricultural bounty while aligning themselves with a government that views bodies and land as little more than collateral damage. The presence of prominent Mormons such as Ezra Taft Benson within presidential cabinets and prominent anti-communist groups made the silence from higher authorities even more difficult to understand or accept.

Increasing Downwinder stories were poignant and divisive, framed by both dissent and the story of patriotic sacrifice. Much like the ranchers after the sheep die-offs, it was the vigilance and relentlessness of a few individuals who raised the alarm on testing, who coaxed stories out of their neighbors and coworkers, that kept this history alive for decades. There were people like St. George resident Irma Thomas, who maintained a map of her neighborhood where boxes represented each house in a three-block radius. Each time a new diagnosis was received, be it for cancer, birth defects, or other severe medical issues, she'd draw an X on the house. The map was a horrifying reminder of how widespread the suffering was. Thomas would soon draw an X on her own home when her daughter, Michelle, who was a talented dancer, was diagnosed with an autoimmune disease that would rob her of the ability to walk.

However, there were also those for whom religious faith was a comfort, a sign that their sacrifice had meaning. Sheldon and Leatrice Johnson's son, Layne, was born with Down's syndrome in 1956, one of twelve in his small class in St. George who were born with significant disorders or birth defects. When pushed on whether what happened in their community was normal or maliciousness on the part of the government, they told Gallagher: "We are a people who can get on the band wagon and really go. We get feeling strongly about things. Even death isn't going to bother us, we're going to go ahead…There's a philosophy that Latter-day Saints have, that all will be well, no matter what…In spite of all the things that will happen, everything will be okay, the end will be all right. Our challenge is to rise above it."

Likewise, Rulea Brooksby and Alta Brooksby Petty described the losses in their community of Kanab during the testing period. Rulea tells how the "same day as my husband's funeral, there was a funeral of a father of eight children who had the same brain tumors, from the same part of Utah." Nonetheless, both insist that "being members of the LDS church we have been strengthened because we know we will be together forever…[t]he gospel has given us a lot of strength."

The Downwinder movement became more cohesive in the decades ahead, but during the 1950s and 1960s the pressure to suffer in silence was significant. Fox details how obituaries during that era do not describe traumatic deaths in detail and refer to "accidents" or merely to "illnesses." Misinformation and censorship maintained by the government and military created an atmosphere where it was difficult for wider communities to know what was taking place, especially if the stories told implicated authorities. Many residents in downwind communities had no direct experience with, or recollection of, illnesses or unusual deaths in their communities. The lack of newspaper coverage often reinforced their views that such incidents were isolated and unrelated to nuclear testing. For many victims, it wasn't until many years later that chance conversations or increased coverage of Downwinder stories would lead to their piecing together what had happened to their families or to themselves.

The number of people who are aware of their own Downwinder pasts or those in their family histories would no doubt be significantly smaller without the tireless efforts of a core group of individuals, who not only organized those affected by nuclear testing but facilitated research showing the effects weren't felt only in St. George, Enterprise, and Cedar City. "Downwind" included the Wasatch Front, Cache Valley, wide swaths of Idaho and Montana, and locales stretching all the way to the East Coast. These activists include Jay Truman, who grew up in Enterprise, Utah, a community especially traumatized by nuclear testing. Truman lost many family members to cancer and in 1980 founded the Downwinders organization. His group, together with others like HEAL Utah and the Nevada Test Site Workers Victims Association, worked endlessly to secure grassroots and governmental support for victims of testing. In 1990, their efforts helped to create the Radiation Exposure Compensation Act (RECA). It was a victory, to be sure, but one limited in scope as only victims who suffered from a select range of cancers in an equally limited geographic range qualified for compensation. Truman himself calls RECA's funds "blood money" and continues to work for coverage for all Downwinders ("JUSTICE, not JUST US") while refusing the payment for which he qualifies.

Mary Dickson grew up in Northern Utah and had little awareness of the history of nuclear tests nearby. During conversations with Carole Gallagher, she began to suspect that cancers in her family were connected to fallout in milk and other agricultural products she consumed regularly during her child-hood. She battled thyroid cancer as a young woman and her sister developed lupus. While attending a hearing on compensation for Downwinders, she met a woman who had grown up in the same neighborhood Dickson had and kept a list of everyone who had fallen ill. "They're all kids I played with, and the kids I knew," she said, "…the list just keeps growing and growing…it gets up to like forty-five people, just in a five- or six-block area." Dickson went on to be another fierce advocate for Downwinders, using her career as a writer and journalist to bring the story to new populations around the state, including through her play, *EXPOSED.*

The efforts of people like Truman and Dickson have kept this story alive throughout the years, facilitating a whole new generation of activists and scholars who continue to dig deeper and advocate, including historian Sarah Fox and documentary filmmakers Tim Skousen and Tyler Bastian. Even more importantly, the remarkable archives that these individuals created, alongside the oral histories of Gallagher and others, are widely accessible now through online platforms such as the University of Utah's Downwinders of Utah Archive. These crucial stories are available to a whole new generation of Mormons and ex-Mormons alike. More and more people are coming forward with stories or questions about their own pasts or the experiences of their families. It is no longer taboo to talk about the crimes perpetrated on Downwinders. Mormons now protest at the Nevada National Security Site regularly, right alongside all others who were harmed and continue to be harmed.

~

On September 7, 1979, President Jimmy Carter announced that a large section of the Great Basin had been chosen as the site to deploy the massive MX missile defense system. Once again, the federal government assumed that residents would roll over and be grateful for the jobs and development, be proud to do their part in closing the perceived "missile gap" with the Soviet Union. They couldn't have been more wrong. In an important about-face that stunned many people, the First Presidency of the Mormon Church came out with a statement strongly opposed to the proposal, which stated: "Our fathers came to this western area to establish a base from which to carry the gospel of peace to the peoples of the earth. It is ironic, and a denial of the very essence of that gospel, that in this same general area there should be constructed a mammoth weapons system potentially capable of destroying much of civilization."

It was the first time church authorities openly opposed nuclear development in the Great Basin or anywhere. Downwinders, along with other anti-nuclear activists, played a large role in applying pressure to church leadership, but Mormons at large played an equally important role. Opposition in the state was near 70 percent. Lessons had been learned from earlier experiences, and Utahns as a whole were done with being a region of sacrifice. Their opposition, together with that of the Western Shoshone people and other local groups, would prove to be too much public outcry, and the project was shelved. While it would still be another four years before Judge Jenkins would finally place blame for fallout deaths where it belonged, this was still an enormous victory.

One can't help but wonder if a similar statement in the 1950s or 1960s would have had similar effect. It is unlikely, but at least it could have served as a catalyst, a means for people to speak out regarding what they experienced. The outcry over MX seemed a moment when everyone was willing to state that land is more than simply its economic or strategic value, that it transcends human needs or desires. While a testing moratorium went into place in 1992, attempts have still been made to restart them (most recently by the Bush administration in 2006 with the Divine Strike test proposal). The current administration wants uranium mines reopened in the Four Corners region, where Diné and other tribes have long suffered from the toxic legacy of tailings pollution as well as radioactive fallout from testing, to supply a proposed upgrade of the nuclear arsenal. This plan would inevitably involve renewed testing as well. Demographics in Utah are shifting rapidly, and partisan divides are acute. The Mormon Church remains a bellwether for the state and current LDS leadership is as conservative as any in recent memory. If such efforts should escalate, it will prove to be a crucial litmus test of both the validity of Mormon stewardship and Utah's cultural memory.

Stacie Denetsosie-Mitchell

KINDLING

When I woke you this morning
from the bustled covers of our bed,
I tolled the names of the dead.

In my frenzy, I ignored
your wicker expression,
the dry flame in your eyes,
because he was like your brother
and he touched an electrical wire,
that you supposed he mis-
took for cloth.

You called your sister that morning,
I overheard flickering tones,
like a spark
building to flame.

The two of you like twigs,
brittle and shedding your skins,
after seasons of indeterminate
weather. Perfect for kindling.

Because you kept asking
Why was he on the roof?
Why was he holding that cloth?
He was a missionary, supposed to be protected by God.

You pray yourself in little circles,
arranging nests of comfort,
imagining yourself encircled in the
white sleeved arms of your Lord.

Nests waiting to be consumed.

You receive comfort, in knowing
your brother is safe with God.

But I've read your scriptures,
I know God's indeterminate nature.
What it means to be *translated*.

Your brother touched Christ's hem,
and blazing fell, cloth in hand,
into the *firmament*.
I guess that's what it takes to
get into your heaven.

Granddaddy: The Glowing Man

Peeling an apricot, I remember my granddaddy's hand.
His veins glowing a greenish-yellow, the color of uranium,
under his brown skin. My granddaddy, the glowing man.
Granddaddy was a miner. He brought home his work,
and like any man, he left his clothes at the door.
Grandma damned his socks, for never going after him.
She washed his clothes in the same river
they drank from. The first time I heard
Uranium contamination was after my grandmother
urinated in a cup at an Indian Health Services Hospital.
I sat in a blue fiberglass chair, next to my granddaddy,
who came in for trouble breathing.
Long after, in their coffin beds, they lie beside
each other, glowing hot coals.

May Swenson "October" Stanza 2, lines 3 and 25

Heather Holland

My Home Is a Valley: *On Reckoning Grief and Reclaiming a Kind of Faith*

O N THE MORNING AFTER HER EIGHTEENTH BIRTHDAY, JES-
sie White stood alone in the dawn-gray, waiting with hundreds of Scottish, Irish, Welsh, and English Latter-day Saints. A
mist of rainwater glistened on the cobblestones of the Liverpool
docks. Sailors climbed the masts and scurried about the deck of
the *Cynosure*, bound for New York City, the next stop on her trip
to Utah's Zion. She shivered and rubbed her hands together and
stomped her feet, hoping to shake the chill that still gripped the
drizzly May morning.

The trip to Liverpool had already been an undertaking—a
two-day drive with other Scots leaving Paisley, a stop halfway to
stay with other newly converted members of their church. And
Jessie couldn't shake her mother's last words to her as she stood
on the stoop of her family's home to say goodbye.

Jessie had hoped her farewell visit would have been met
with some kind of forgiveness. She thought her going so very
far away, probably forever, might mean her parents and siblings
would want one last chance for a kiss goodbye, a fond farewell.
Lizzie, the family's youngest, flung the door open with a joyful
"Jessie!" But Ma came to the door and shooed Lizzie inside. Pa
refused to leave his chair and someone else, Ellen maybe, parted

the curtains a few inches to watch as her mother stood in the doorway, her face lined stone.

"If you're leaving with those Mormons, don't bother writing, and don't come back."

The last two years had been hard on the White family. Jessie's parents worked in the mills, like so many in Paisley—her mother spinning yarn, her father weaving colorful teardrops into the cloth pattern for which their city was famous. Two years of civil war on the other side of the Atlantic had all but halted American cotton production, which meant precious little cotton for the spinners to spin, precious little yarn for the weavers to weave. In the midst of this economic hardship and family heartache, Jessie met a Mormon missionary. The stories he told about a young man in a grove of trees, a new book of scripture, and a Zion blooming in the desert captured her imagination and touched her heart. She chose to join his church, despite her parents' protest. Her family were Protestant Christians, longstanding members of the Church of Scotland—christenings and communions and marriages and meetings with dear friends among the dark pews and colorful glass of Paisley Abbey. How could Jessie be so disloyal, so foolish, to follow this odd group of religious upstarts? Cultish nonsense, her father had called it.

Two years had done nothing to soften her parents' disgust.

Now, at the docks, Jessie shivered again, even though the sun's rise was rapidly warming the day. She felt a hand on her arm and turned to see Mary Murray—five-year-old Agnes and three-year-old William clinging to her skirts. Mary was heavy with her third child and held one hand beneath her stomach to support the weight. Mary and her husband, James, had joined the Mormons a decade before Jessie and were some of the first to welcome her into the fold. Despite the twenty-two-year age gap, Mary had become one of Jessie's dearest friends.

"Hullo, love. How are you faring this morning?" Mary said. "Do you need anything?"

"I am well, thanks. I have what I need."

"James said he was going to see if the brethren need help," Mary leaned in to whisper, "but I think he just wants to know what's taking so long."

Jessie laughed. James was nine years younger than Mary and full of restless energy. He had to be working, always doing something. The staying still and waiting during this journey might just kill him.

Jessie looked toward the bustle of the *Cynosure*. She didn't want to grumble, but she was eager to get on with things. After long months of agony, mustering the courage to leave her family, she wanted to *go*.

When it came time to give her name for the ship register as she boarded, Jessie cleared her throat and gave the man her mother's name: Jane White. If her mother never wanted to see her again in Scotland, Jessie would take her mother along with her to the new world.

~

Jessie White, later Jessie White Murray, was my great-great-grandmother. The story of Jessie's heartbreaking family farewell, of her mother's parting words, was family legend, told with pride to demonstrate Jessie's commitment to the one true church. Jessie White came alone, carried by her conviction and her desire to build Zion in a foreign land, sure of the rightness of her path. The story carried the implication that all of her family who followed should honor that faith.

The story of Mary McHattie, James Murray's first wife, was told with an ache in the voice, a hint about the bedrock pain from which our family had grown.

Jessie grew closer to Mary and James on the voyage to Utah. She helped them care for their children, especially after Mary gave birth to a daughter in mid-June, a mere thirteen days into their fifty-day journey across the Atlantic. The birth was not easy on Mary, laboring beneath the decks, sick from the rolling of the sea. James convinced Mary to give the tiny girl her name: Mary Marie. The *Cynosure* landed in the busy harbor of New York City, and the company of old-world Saints took a train straight through the middle of the Civil War to Nebraska before beginning the slow trek in covered wagons to Salt Lake City.

She was so close, were the words required of our family's frequent retelling. *She could almost see the Salt Lake Valley when she died.*

I don't know how Mary Murray died. Exhaustion? Heatstroke? Dehydration? Disease? Accident? Postpartum complications? She died in Echo Canyon on August ninth, less than two months after baby Mary was born, and was buried in an unmarked grave beneath the soaring, red sandstone cliffs in Echo Canyon before the company moved on. Mary's faith and hope carried her to the edge of everything she knew, but she died just one day's ride away from the top of Emigration Canyon, where she could have gazed across dips and rises into the distant Salt Lake Valley.

Nobody tells James's part of the story, because Murray men are meant to be tough, but I imagine his grief was enormous. I've lived enough to know the weight of *what ifs*. I imagine him holding his hat in his hand, staring east toward Scotland, searching for choices he could have made that wouldn't have ended with his children's mother dead.

Family lore says Jessie took full responsibility for the Murray children when Mary died. She walked up and down a wagon train of more than a hundred souls, talking to every woman she saw until she found a mother willing to breastfeed baby Mary.

They reached Salt Lake City in mid-August, 1863. Jessie White, James Murray, and other Scottish emigrants were sent to settle in Tooele Valley, the place that would eventually be my home. The wide-open valley, like it is now, was sheltered by pine and sage-spotted Oquirrh Mountains to the east and the south, golden Stansbury Mountains in the west, the view north tumbling down to the vast blue-green expanse of the Great Salt Lake. They said it reminded them a bit of Scotland with its moors and lochs and rolling hills.

James and Jessie married two years later, built a homestead near the top of a little ravine nestled into the northern end of the Oquirrhs. It would later be named Murray Canyon. James, an iron miner in Scotland, set about farming in Tooele. He built a comfortable two-story hewn-log cabin surrounded by fruit trees, a large garden, and an animal pen.

I first hiked up Murray Canyon to see the leavings of their homestead when I was ten years old. I gathered rocks and wildflowers and acorns scattered by scrub oak trees, shouted with cousins running back and forth between our aunts and uncles. I was greatly disappointed when we reached the homestead site, not yet familiar with the reckoning of time, the savage arc of change. On a flat bit of ground, we found a crumbling stone foundation grown over and around with weeds, a gnarled and half-dead peach tree, and a bit of fence. How was this our family's history? Why was this worth hiking to?

~

It would be nearly twenty-five years before I'd have the chance again to hike through private property to the old Murray homestead. My mother and uncle Roger had gathered funds for a tall granite headstone to replace the worn and crumbling sandstone marker that stood above the graves of Jessie and James Murray and the seven Murray children who didn't live past childhood. The new stone also included the name of Mary McHattie Murray, offering a space to honor the woman whose resting place is unknown.

My mother made a wreath adorned in specially-ordered ribbon made from the Murray tartan. All of James and Mary and Jessie Murray's living descendants—hundreds of people—were invited to a Memorial Day celebration that would include a dedication of the new stone, a picnic in Pine Canyon, and a hike to the old Murray homestead for those willing and able.

The day before the anticipated celebration, my dad found my brother dead on his bedroom floor from what we'd later learn was a heroin overdose. The year before had been hard on Jared. After marrying the love of his life, he revved into the most destructive manic cycle we'd seen since he'd been diagnosed with bipolar disorder. He became unpredictable and violent. That summer he was diagnosed with schizophrenia, admitted against his will for a couple of days to a mental health facility before he checked himself out. His frightened wife left him, then he moved in with a friend and picked up a heroin addiction. I didn't talk to him much that year. I was going through a divorce, a faith crisis, so locked into my own sorrows that I couldn't bear to carry his. The month before he died, he worked desperately to detox from heroin. He was sick and in pain almost all the time, but he started reaching out to me again, and he seemed to be getting better.

The Memorial Day celebration went on without my parents and my sister and me. Relatives streamed in throughout that day, between activities, to mourn with us in the midst of our intimate wreckage. They brought flowers and plants and picnic leftovers. They told us about the graveside service and the hike. The fence was gone. The peach tree was gone. They were still able to find the old cabin's foundation.

They said things they meant to be comforting like "I hope he's at peace now," and "I'm so glad we know we'll see him again," and "Families are forever."

After what seemed like the hundredth muttered Mormon platitude, I stepped out into my parents' cheery backyard, walked to the back fence and ran my fingers along the silver lace vines that cover the chain-link. I stared southeast, as if I could see through the Oquirrh mountain range to where my children were staying for now with their father, in the home I'd foolishly agreed to let him keep. I tried to find a way to pray, hoping the faith I'd counted on for years might find its way back to me.

I ached as I remembered the dozens of times I'd clucked my tongue after funerals, so sad for those who just didn't understand about God and eternity, certain that if they could just get on board and believe what I *knew* to be true—that we all lived before and beyond this life, that the family bonds created here could be forever and this earth-life was just a blip—the grief would hurt less. This was my first taste of the other side—feeling like the only person saying goodbye in a crowd of people saying see you later.

~

In September 1863, about the same time James and Jessie arrived in Tooele Valley, a group of men began extracting minerals in Bingham Canyon, just a few peaks south of Murray Canyon. They dug webs of tunnels, test pits, found placer gold, lead-silver, and copper-gold.

At the turn of the century, the Utah Copper Company deployed steam shovels and railroads to begin open-pit mining and do the difficult work of extracting the enormous porphyry copper deposit they had been unable to access and smelt.

They dug and they dug, deeper and wider, deeper and wider. They sent their ore to new smelters along the Wasatch Front with names like Highland Boy. The smelters brought jobs and prosperity and massive pollution to the Salt Lake Valley. The pollution swathed nearby farms in what locals called "smelter smut," ruining crops and livelihoods. Four hundred and nineteen farmers organized a lawsuit against five of the local smelters in a case titled *James Godfrey et. al. v. American Smelting and Refining Company et. al.* The judge ruled in favor of the farmers and all but one of the smelters closed.

They sent the smelter smut to Tooele. In 1910 the International Refining and Smelting Company began operations in Pine Canyon, barely south of the Murray homestead that had been abandoned five years earlier when James Murray died suddenly of apoplexy. The smelter up on Anaconda Road handled much of the ore produced by the Bingham Canyon Mine and employed many of Tooele's eclectic mix of immigrants—Scottish and Irish and Greek and Italian and Mexican, and more.

∼

Decades later, my thirteen-year-old mother crouched, hiding with her father and sister in the dark.

"Quick, girls! Hide!" her dad had told them both as he pulled them from the kitchen table and into their bedroom, turning off lights as they moved through the little two-bedroom home.

"Hush! Don't look out the windows!" he warned. "They're looking for me. They're coming to get us."

She says she was terrified at first, but as the night wore on she started to think that things seemed odd. Her father was acting so strangely. Something didn't seem right. She left the bedroom and called one of her brothers, probably Dave, to come check on them.

Just two years earlier, my mother's mother had died from complications of rheumatoid arthritis, leaving my Grandpa Murray to raise the "little girls" on his own. My mother and her sister, Cindy, born barely more than a year apart, were the seven-year-delayed cabooses of their family of seven. In the weeks before their mother, Barbara, died the girls were only allowed to visit her in the hospital once a week. They were dressed and ready for their weekly visit, excited to see their mom, when the call came telling them that she was gone.

In the tradition of tough Murray men, Ellis did his best to hide the grief he felt and worked to provide a happy home for his daughters. He'd retired from Tooele Army Depot around the time his wife died, but he returned to work as a watchman at the smelter so that he could earn enough credits to receive full social security benefits. He would come home after his shift and tell Chris and Cindy about seeing cat tracks in the snow during his nightly rounds. It was years before my mom realized he meant mountain lions and not housecats.

Soon after the night Ellis Murray hushed his daughters in the quiet dark, he was diagnosed with paranoid schizophrenia, precipitated by him being "leaded" during his time at the smelter, which had expanded in 1912 to smelt lead in addition to copper. The poisoning, combined with the stress and grief of the previous years, was enough to break him.

He was always there for them, always loved them, my mother says, but he was never quite the same after that.

~

My childhood home was a sprawling valley of small towns surrounded by open fields. On three sides of my hometown, the mountains rose, rolling, and fell into canyons where I first learned to stand in cold water, to feel the earth beneath my feet and understand that I was part of everything. On summer evenings, if I climbed to the top of my apple tree I could watch the sun setting over the Great Salt Lake. I felt so small. And so vast.

My childhood home was a sprawling valley where, as of 1996 (the year I graduated from high school), 45 percent of the United States' stockpile of chemical weapons were stored.

When relatives came to visit from out of state, we made a point to drive to the top of Middle Canyon, toward Clipper Peak, to look out over the gaping maw of the Bingham Copper Mine, its terraced sides falling down toward the magma and mantle that helped to create its copper ore.

As a child, I stood on the east side of Main Street on the Fourth of July, waving a tiny US flag and watching as tanks and missiles and bombs paraded past, just behind the show horses and the pooper scooper and the marching band. As a teenager, I drove with friends up Anaconda Road to watch fireworks from above the valley, stopped a mile or so away from the site of the old smelter that poisoned my grandfather's body with lead as he kept watch by night, where a giant scar of black slag still seeps lead and arsenic into the groundwater.

My father traveled each day to the south area of Tooele Army Depot for decades, first blowing up old bombs in the desert, then working to help destroy chemical weapons, then taking responsibility for keeping the massive munitions incinerator operating safely and smoothly. Other fathers tested and created and destroyed chemical and other weapons at Dugway Proving Ground, an hour's drive southwest from Tooele. Other fathers drove an hour northwest to Clive, where the euphemistically named Envirocare (later EnergySolutions) facility disposed of Class A radioactive waste.

Mine was an idyllic childhood. I had no idea how dangerous it was, how strange, how the lovely valley that reminded my Scottish great-great-grandparents of home played host to all kinds of poisons.

~

Lead poisoning is not hereditary, but schizophrenia can be, and trauma trickles through generations like arsenic in groundwater.

Most people have only a 1-percent chance of developing schizophrenia. Having a second-degree relative, like a grandparent, who has been diagnosed with schizophrenia tilts that risk toward 5 percent. Often diagnosis is preceded by precipitating events—exposure to chemicals, substance abuse, rapid and overwhelming life changes, loss.

Decades after my grandpa died, my mother spent nights trying to calm her beautiful son's paranoias. Sometimes she'd take long drives in the dark through Tooele Valley with my dad to get away, to feel safe for a few hours.

My mother abides at the center of two generations of mental breakdown. The pain of loss, combined with toxins, toppled my grandfather's sense of safety in the world. Pain and loss and toxins toppled my brother in much the same way. Who knows which of the *what ifs* I've ruminated over might have spared him?

~

Three days before he died, Jared made the drive up a muddy and somewhat snow-choked Middle Canyon. On Facebook, he posted pictures of the canyon, thick with ponderosa pine, the view looking down across Tooele Valley, the view out over Salt Lake Valley—snow-capped Wasatch Mountains rising in the distance, the Bingham Canyon Mine just visible in the bottom left of the frame.

My siblings and I shared a love of the mountains that surrounded us as we grew up. We hiked their winding paths, waded through streams, danced around campfires together and climbed rocks without ropes like idiots. I wonder now, looking at those pictures, if Jared knew he was leaving us, leaving the home he loved, if he was saying goodbye.

Before he left us, I'd resolved to spend more time with him, to talk to him about my total loss of faith in the Mormon Church. Whether he agreed with me or not about the faith part, I thought he'd probably understand better than anyone else in my family the kind of pain and shame that came from standing at the margins of our community. I thought we could probably help each other through our struggles. I told myself I'd reach out to him. Soon.

~

When Jessie White left Scotland it was both slow and sudden—a commitment to a path and a faith that felt so right she could not ignore it. She spent two years learning to live out her faith, deciding whether to stay in Paisley and believe on her own or go by herself to Zion where she could live her faith with others. When she decided to go, she went. There was no turning back.

I have not walked the same path Jessie walked, have not stayed true to the religion she and James and Mary sacrificed so much for. I like to think, though, that I carry their pioneer spirit with me. My emigration from the comfortable faith and easy truths of my childhood was both slow and sudden. Unease about the doctrines regarding gender and sexuality, a theology that created a god who "loved" equally but provided separately, an inkling that any god I was willing to trust would not draw lines to keep anyone out—these were the first stones shifted from their angles of repose, portents of the coming landslide. But oh, how I held on tight for as long as I could. Until, one day, I stood in my parents' backyard after my brother's death and knew that I could never again believe in the way I'd once believed. I could never again let a comforting certainty about forever keep me from loving and trying to save what needed my love and saving *right now*.

I was once so sure that faith in the church that promised us eternity would cure my brother's sorrows. Then, as I began to let go of my own faith in eternity, I told myself I had plenty of time to find my way back to him. Both "eternity" and "plenty of time" were, if not outright lies, lulling excuses to stay passive and complacent.

It's arrogant, I suppose, to believe that I've arrived at a "truer" answer, a "better" ethics. And even if my ethics are better now, I still don't do all I can to live those ethics. But I wonder sometimes if the Mormon insistence on an eternal perspective that I once clung to, that kept me from loving my brother well, is also what has allowed the persistent environmental degradation of my beautiful home, the valley that has gently held so many generations of my family's grief. After all, if this life is really only a blip in the grand scheme of things, if we can count on the earth one day being restored to its paradisiacal glory, why worry about the compromises we make to live here now? Why *not* extract the earth's riches and use its forces to gain power over others?

~

My heart aches for my grandfather, his body toxic with lead, crouching in the dark, desperate to protect himself and his girls from a threat that only existed in his head. I ache for my brother's fear and pain, for my mother who watched two generations of mental anguish. I cannot drive by the sandstone cliffs of Echo Canyon without grieving the death of Mary McHattie Murray, the woman who could have unmade me had she lived. And I hurt for Jane White, Jessie's mother, who rejected the last chance she had to love the beautiful daughter standing before her. Did she live to regret her harsh words?

Nano Taggart

Mojave, Dirge

a companion to Andrew Kent-Marvick / John Foxx

I learned impermanence from
large signs floating down the

Vegas strip with palm tree fronds
and litter: *The Topless Girls of*

Glitter Gulch / $1 draft beer /
prime rib breakfast buffet $3.99.

■

Yucca Mountain almost shaded
a next world's leaking catastrophe.

Inert neon livens an archive that
charges admission: *Take a guided*

tour of the neon boneyard.[1]

■

I found an archive in my mother's
cedar chest, a photo of my whole,

new self in my father's Jack-Mormon hand.

215

∎

Shadows of coming pasts foretell
an empty oasis belonging to no one.

∎

I drank to excess under neon flamingoes
buried at the altar of false place—

false Paris, fake Italy, a stucco castle
pull away the night,[2] shield tourists from

Mt. Charleston and the Great Basin's divide.

∎

Now my archive's inheritor, absolution
turns toward listening and the world's

dark centers are stumbled upon. Knowing
is a map to the blood engine, a map to the

sacred start.

∎

Lake Mead's bathtub rings foreshadow
pleas to pipe Lake Superior for 1,700

miles to the American Southwest.

∎

I'm drinking to my story and the
feigned wonderland that *can't stay*

long.[3] Straight lines escape me.
Calling this *emptiness*, too loaded;

calling it *home*, a lie.

∎

This will be the greatest ghost
town the world has ever seen.

1. "Take a guided tour of the neon boneyard." The Neon Museum (website header). http://www.neonmuseum.org/. Accessed 4/8/17.
2. Foxx, John (Ultravox). *Systems of Romance.* "I Can't Stay Long." Universal Music. http://bit.ly/2qLASzf. Accessed 4/8/17.
3. Ibid.

ANTICIPATE

Laura Stott

Stars

Marbles that burn at the touch
at the game you try to play
in the memory of childhood—
like grasping at the strings of a kite.
Cutting off the tail. Where did it go?
Burning balls of hydrogen helium
warm other planets
where there are blue craters,
eternal sunsets, and swirling mists of gas.
There are ferns growing under other suns
in the shade of rocks and dare
I say, houses. And above—
the blue canvas of twilight,
a quilt of sky sewn with the black
of hearts. Holes pricked
in that shade of night
so the light can come through
fabric, so it could dazzle
and wonder and cause you to gasp
when you stumble out of a tent,
somewhere deep in the woods,
far from where you are now.
Stars are made of memory.
Of glints from the eyes of animals—
light reflected back at you in the night,
of fear, of cat's teeth, of fish bones,
of scales deep in the ocean, of sand,

of the hearts of horses, beating.
And they are up there, right now
keeping the beasts running across the sky.
And when you cut them open
after a death in a field,
after the great shudder, they are full
of light and exhaustion
and the smell of sagebrush after rain.

CRACKED

The Bonneville Salt Flats are a white beach,
the back of a white turtle,
his shell extending over the curvature
of the earth. Underneath, the reptile
is smiling in the sun, his old eyes blinking,
carrying us all slowly
to the edge of everything.

Solstice

Jacob shouts for joy
and for the lions—
the ones we can't see
but we know are there
slinking through canyon maples, the flick
of a tail. On the cliffs, we imagine
the outline of mountain lion
burying its prey. Feral hog
or deer. The mask
of the animals, shallow
in the earth. We are willing
this ceremony of darkness,
the long length of it
coming as fast as breath.
Such a warm December.
The earth smells of continuous decay.
We can feel the trees
even when we don't touch them.
The silver pull
of thin air. Seven years ago
this same week
I saw a snow leopard track
left at a pass in a country
that worships the mountains.
And when I tell the story now,
I say, *once,*
I saw a snow leopard.
But it's not true
even when I believe it.
We are walking towards the spine of God.

Ahead of me now, Jacob
carries his large coat
over his shoulder,
it makes him look so much bigger.
Which is good, because
there, there is the lion!
I hear it crossing the creek.
We eat fistfuls of snow.
We can smell more cats coming,
we are egging on the night
and the roar.

Amelia England

LITTLE COTTONWOOD STOCK

EARLY CHURCH I REMEMBER FROM A LOW VANTAGE POINT.
Mormon Utah Sundays took place in our brown and gold
stake center, the south wall reefed in organ pipes and cabinet
cloisters. There was a bendy microphone on a tilted stand, from
which an assigned speaker was flanked by the bishopric and, for
a fascinating twenty or so minutes, a troop of teenage boys preparing a sacrament of water and white bread. (This meditative
snack session was my favorite part of the meeting.) Behind the
congregation, a large partition opened to a squeaky basketball
court, a dark stage, and a generous backstock of metal folding
chairs—piled, stacked, hung, and loose.

I was preschool-aged, dressed in a lace-bibbed dress flocked
in tiny purple and gray flowers, with only a foggy categorical
of what the speakers were talking about. These weekly recitations were intensely boring for anyone who didn't possess the
steel and sprightliness of a zealot (rare temperament even in a
block of Mormons), which was growing evident in the room's
soft yet pervasive strata of discord—an endless relation of fid-
gets, coughs, exhales, and scratches that, given enough blank
minutes, becomes suddenly, terribly palpable to any nerved-out
child in stockings.

After the usual lineup of strangers and church officials spoke, it was my mother who took the podium. This was unusual and bothersome: my parents and brother and I normally sat quietly in little brown pews near the back, and no one had alerted me to a public family announcement. But discussions had been had, agitations obliged, and queries settled among adults. My mom had resolved to leave the LDS faith she was raised in, and wanted to state it publicly. As tiny as I was, I think now she would be happy that I'd remember it.

After the resignation, it was natural that my siblings and I would grow up knowing our mom was different from those of classmates and neighbors. Sometimes we misinterpreted her exit as inconsequential, and other times it spurred us into long philosophical entanglements with whatever commotion was at hand—theological or secular.

My dad kept his active membership as my mom worked beyond it, and what would remain of their split-faith marriage set us a unique course of half-stepping with the church for the rest of our child lives—an every-other-Sunday approach to doctrine and community. The rest, as we would mold and rework on our own time, was the great beyond.

~

In the year leading up to my eighth birthday, my ex-Mormon mom and still-Mormon dad began to prepare me for my upcoming baptism. This was a typical rite in most LDS families but less clear-cut for me. Growing up with my alt-ish clan in Alpine-Utah suburbia, I liked having one parent who had formally defected from the monoculture. In the long run and for better, it acclimated me to big cosmic paradoxes, establishing for once and always the multiplicities of story and code and logic. As my parents discussed my baptism and explained their intentions, I knew very well I had the option of keen and livable detours, even if all the Mormon eight-year-olds of history had already forged a path.

My mom's breach had steeled me against a cultural majority I would never quite belong to—its premises that dominated our public schools, community celebrations, neighborhood gossip, and social politics. Not a year went by without some non-secularity from my elementary teachers, be it "Heavenly Father created us to be whole and complete. If I see anyone drawing rude parts on their body diagram, we're talking to your parents," or "Oh yes, I've heard about your family. You're in the same ward as my nieces," to "Who here wants to go to BYU when they grow up?"

Only in history and all its embarrassing overlaps did these authorities sidestep Mormonism's spiritual and cultural exceptionalism. This happens in microcosms: it can be difficult to concede that what feels like everything to one's home and birthright can feel like confinement to another's. (It would take me a few more years to realize Joseph Smith was a contemporary of Karl Marx, and that the Mormon Pioneer Trail was just one of many serious westward colonizations.)

Inside my church education, my teachers promised that baptism was a righteous and essential tradition. As recounted to me in Sunday school, John the Baptist was an important friend to Mormon Jesus. He hustled solemn rites in the Holy Land and, according to the visual aids, he was burly and good-looking. It's when John baptizes Jesus that Heavenly Father reveals himself in the sky and Jesus as the pleasing Son of God, and the Holy Spirit descends as a white dove. And as clarified in the Book of Mormon, John was key to prepping Saints for the coming of Jesus. (Vaguely I recall how verily Heavenly Father appeared to John to signal the holiness at hand.)

Just as my schoolteachers confined history, these Sunday school lessons offered little context for baptism beyond the Mormon doctrine. I knew it involved personal repentance and faith in an enigmatic authority, but metaphysical details were lost on me. "Getting baptized" was reduced to wading into a large tub or tiny pool—depending on how you squinted at it—shrouded behind a vinyl accordion divider in the LDS ward stake house. It was a conventional operation, devoid of honeycomb and doves and bearded hermits, and all the trappings of deep and old-timey religion.

I was a bit sniffy and precocious about the whole business. The tiled tub was dingy and disappointing. I couldn't reconcile Jesus and sexy John in a chlorinated tank. And I certainly couldn't justify "choosing the right" and "seeking repentance"— those commands only served for neighbors to patronize my family between school and church, administered with their special blend of evasion and confusion.

My parents made a cool and exciting proposal: Would I like to be baptized in our local Bee Pond, the especially cold one we frequented for picnics and swimming? This could be an excellent compromise. For my mom, it was a celebration of her hometown, where mountain water flowed from the Lone Peak Wilderness and filled up the Mormon grid of dairy farms and fruit orchards. For my dad, it further strengthened his odd patriarchal standing, the man with the apostate wife and overly intellectual testimony. And for me, it felt special. It was reassuring to appropriate this ritual of purification—another curious but well-meaning way my parents worked to make our religious apartness less of a hassle.

~

With my parents in accord and my pond date set, I became a great believer in my baptism. The Chapel of Nature offered much clearer doctrines than the Alpine 12th Ward, most importantly those of individual worthiness and philosophical virtue. Our family scrapbooks and photo albums show how seven years was my perfect age in which to wax romantic. There's me nuzzling a bouquet of wildflowers. Here my brother and I are perched on a red sandstone cliff, smiling down at my dad's camera. Here we have an original poem about my love of waterfalls.

I made all my best memories outside. There was the cloy of woody orchard smells in my cousins' tree house, the tire-swing meadow in some parents' friends' children's sprawling farmstead, the trilobite fossils spilling into the road by my grandma's cabin. A single horned toad, white bellied-up, stretching toward an apocalyptic horizon of west basin flats. Powdery Christmases, glorious springs folding into dry summers and billowy falls—happy intersections for the cure of Nature.

The Lone Peak Range was always there. It filled my north bedroom window, washed and crested in snow, then runoff, then wild green, then back to snow. On a strange day before a tornado hit downtown Salt Lake City (a rare thrill this far west of Kansas) my parents and brother and I hiked to the highest peak, and I remember the hot chill of ozone harrying down my pink shirt and sweaty hat band, like the mountain would bolt beneath us.

And I had memories of the desert. The same year I would be baptized my parents bought a rural southern Utah parcel, in which my brother and I devoted dozens of weekends to pocketing southwest Native artifacts. It was an area previously occupied by homesteaders, and before that Ute and Paiute people, and before that Ancestral Puebloans, and before that mammoths and archaic tribes. Relics from each society would lie quietly for several centuries until we wandered through their provenance.

Christian and I understood the basics of pre- and post-colonial exchanges in our home state, most of the somber ethics of massacres and siege, and incidentally how we our very selves were part of the latest wave of land seekers, well-intentioned or not. Still, amateur archaeology and wilderness exploration felt like the most natural hobbies in the world to us, and we weren't yet savvy enough to resist treasure-hunting. The joy of wandering terrain to have a flint chip or potshard present itself unmistakably from the sagebrush—I thought it was the closest I would feel to pure, manifest generosity from my home landscape, as though the sand itself was pleased to have me there.

Over what seemed like a happy phase for our family we went on these excursions often, during a time when I understood that southwest public lands were under attack but it did not affect my productive sense of solitude with my siblings. Our parents asked us fair questions, reminded us which sites were open for rock-collecting or leaf-pressing, which formations held up to scrambling and which soils could not bear footprints. They divided opens, and opened the sacred. "Nope, take only pictures," my dad would say, or "Those people are wearing the wrong clothes for hiking." One Saturday in a blazing riverbed he yelled at two Germans scratching their names into a sandstone wall, which I happily relayed to park rangers for the remainder of the weekend.

~

On one of these customary family trips, my mom took my brother and me to an old ranch trail built around Native dwellings and pathways in southeast Utah. I have never returned to it or found its name, but it seemed it had recently been appropriated as an unofficial visitor entrance—a gateway to an ever-descending series of ancestral sites and red rock paintings sprung somewhere between tepid BLM status and rural folklore. The landscape was dry and laid bare and the season hot, a kind of dusty and brilliant whiteout, with only a few uneven flycatcher calls among the short juniper and, farther along, tall and golden ponderosas along a fragrant spring.

My mom carried lunch in a bright blue backpack and agreed to hold the water so my brother and I could explore the ranch. We normally made ourselves at home in these sites but this one felt like a mystery, absent of all the familiar brown-and-yellow signage, the bear-proofed trash cans, and the chained-off viewing platforms of a state or national park. It felt like true multiple-use territory—operated over several generations of Pueblo to Mission to sheep camp, and then reconceived again for some privatized acreage grab. There was an outhouse and a motor home further down the road, with several structures built of gray and warped timber, others in plotted clay and celled off like an ancient petting zoo. We wandered quietly among the corrals and foundations toward a red stone tower, intact but crumbling into a dry wash swathed with what appeared to be chipped river rock.

As we approached the tower's base I stopped quick, suddenly realizing what sang before us in the sunlight. Unattended, unmarked, and lounging like nothing we had seen before, were hundreds of broken arrowheads in the sloping sand. Christian noticed it almost as quickly as I did, brushing past to marvel over the hard and precious glints of muddy red, sharp black, and blue gray, scattered and bare for the taking. Giddy by our good fortune, we dropped fast to our knees to scoop them into our shirt cradles. It felt wildly impossible, like someone had left everything out to trick us.

"Hey kiddos—" Our mom had noticed our maneuver from behind, and with an awful lurch I realized she was about to impose a sanction we would not be able to circumvent. I turned to her with my hands full of warm serrations, and she tilted her head, sympathetic but firm. "These aren't ours to take."

Christian let his shoulders sag and mouth gape in exaggerated dismay. I did the same. We respected our mother, but knew she would humor a good show of negotiation. "Are there rules here?" I asked. "Why are they on the ground like this?"

"See what that says." She pointed at an old sign posted down the slope of the tower, maybe forty feet from our main path. We stepped away from our cache and slumped around to read:

PLEASE DO NOT DISTURB THE ARTIFACTS

It made no sense to my heady surge of looting logic, especially when placed at such an awkward vantage point, and in this strange tract that took well over an hour to access. My mom held back, quietly validated, as Christian and I stood horrified and tried to refigure the sign. As I was about to point out to everyone that we seemed to be the only hikers around that day, a girl's voice called out from the motor home down the road.

"Hi, folks!" We turned to the trailer to watch this new person step out, jean- and flannel-clad, with dark hair and a teenage face. She appeared to be Native—I assumed Navajo from what I knew of the area, or Diné as my mom would later distinguish. I had barely noticed the trailer before and had assumed it empty, as it did not look out of place in the motley of old ranch buildings.

"Hello," my mom smiled. She spoke to most young people easily. "Are you keeping cool out here?"

The girl laughed politely. "It helps to insulate," she said, gesturing back at her shelter. The windows gleamed with brash chrome sun protectors—the kind I knew were used to shade a car windshield in a hot parking lot. "Did you find your way easily?"

"We got turned around a couple of times when the dirt roads started," my mom said as the girl approached us. "This is our first time here. It's incredible what you've kept preserved. I'd love to know the history."

The girl nodded to agree. "Thank you. It's my family's property so I stay to keep an eye on things," she said, and then, "Everything we try to keep unchanged. As you walk around it's important not to displace or damage the objects."

My brother and I stood petrified, hoping terribly the girl would not look and discover the scene of our sifting. Thankfully my mom continued to chat and ask questions, leading our host away from the tower and leaving us to ponder and puzzle and choose the right, as she knew we would.

The two of us alone in the shade, Christian turned to me indignantly. "I've found more than all the cabin arrowheads put together," he said. "They're just out here. Shouldn't they be in a museum?"

I nodded, knowing he meant the glass hutch at home in our dining room. But I also knew we were both more than just disappointed, growing a little embarrassed in the presence of this girl and her history we knew very little about. She had authority greater than I had ever encountered, and even in my greedy survey of the site, I couldn't bear for her to think I was the kind of revolting child to disturb her home and artifacts. And she and whoever she worked for, whoever she was related or beholden to, knew the arrows were there and had decided to leave them, which meant they had, at minimum, a small measure of trust in their visitors' integrity, even in a site that had been rearranged for centuries.

And I couldn't admit I had come there to steal—that would be bad. I was there to appreciate and treasure a newfound object, to bring company that would add beauty and goodness to my world. Or relocate another's relic to my passionately imagined stories. The temptation was awful.

"Did you hear that, kids?" my mom called out to us to relay something the girl had just explained, pointing at our tall and shady monolith. We craned our heads at the old stones above us, noting a few peepholes and wooden crossbeams sticking out of the clay, what at one point must have been a second story. It was backlit from the west-descending sun, a bright halo against the hot blue sky. My mom's voice lowered a bit. "There are bodies in there."

Bodies! Christian and I looked back at each other with a gleeful prickle of fear. "Like Indians?" he said. I strained to file everything in my limited chronology. They were likely mummified and ancient, or maybe boxed up in little cowboy coffins, or perhaps they were freshly dead. It spooked me, but I wanted very badly to find a way under the stones to see for myself, or at least climb up the side to snoop in from above.

The girl smiled but didn't answer. "We shouldn't look directly into the buildings here," she said, and stepped back toward the main trail, heading to walk around us and return to her trailer. I glanced along the dark little livestock huts, and further along the camp shacks and open sties. Each was built with that gray weather-cured wood—slatted, gapped, very tempting to peer through. The girl made a salute goodbye, holding her palm open and still. "If you're okay for the hike, I'll leave you to it—"

My mom smiled, thanked the girl, and gestured to my brother and me to walk back to her. Christian obeyed, leaving me alone and thinking over the newly piled troves. With our time up, I looked down and made a quick decision, because I knew if I could not take the arrows, I preferred no other visitors to see. I dug into the sand at the tower's foundation, arranged two dark rocks, and secreted the points into their shady new recess. They were out of sight and sunlight, snug and hoarded at the base of the tower.

If there were bodies behind the bricks, I felt they were the only witnesses to my shame, which was rising fast but not fast enough to have me undo anything, small as it was. The girl had not seemed to notice, or she was at least gracious enough to let us leave before resetting everything as it was. She must have had to do this often—pause her reading or cleaning, stand out in the dry air, and answer topically, choosing when and how to transmute her surroundings or speak her history. Eventually I'd grow to hope she understood my mistake, or that she was forever annoyed with it—but in either case knowing she had chipped a small window onto deeper doubt and mystery than I could handle at the time.

~

If I were asked to audit my moral development, I can muster up a reel of murky checkpoints and frustrations to substantiate my conclusions. Some riddles were solved over ritual and acquisition, and most have hung around like excess while I wait for more clues. Peaks and deserts in my home landscape act as restoratives, but never in the ways I expect. Whether I'm living in wide-open solitude or just sharing for a weekend, the Southwest makes a jagged pattern.

By eight I had been told baptism opens up multiple lines to Heavenly Father and the Holy Ghost, which sounded very special and a little scary. My Sunday school teachers offered many anecdotes proving the existence of celestial guidance. The Holy Ghost nudged them to save babies from tumbling down flights of stairs, protect missionaries, predict flight crashes, hunt elk, choose wedding dates, and cull gentiles destined for special conversion. It helped them grapple with science and history and political unease, make contact with dead family members, and tilt their lives toward lofty promotions and stronger testimonies. I felt out of step with these miraculous claims, but the reports were curious nonetheless.

"I'm getting baptized on the Fourth of July," I'd remind my primary teachers, the kids at school, my cousins and aunts and uncles. I had turned eight the May before—the age of accountability sung about in LDS primary baptism songs—and collected two new facts about the ritual: I had to be totally submerged or it didn't count, and the gesture of plunging and resurfacing in the water symbolized death and resurrection at the hand of a priesthood authority.

"I'm not getting baptized in the church, it's a pond," I'd continue. "It's Bee Pond and it's so cold you can barely feel your body. I've already swam in it and gone completely under the water. I think I'm the only kid here who's getting baptized outside."

"I got a white dress with three roses on the belt for getting confirmed," I told any woman who asked of my shopping. It was rare to be outfitted for a special occasion, and I was particularly pleased to match this style with the white flowers on my white Sunday shoes. My mom also took me to the supermarket beauty aisle to choose a pair of white tights, which were so opaque when worn it felt like the lower half of my body was made of milk—smooth and ethereal for my new life of repentance. (But unsuitable for pond water. For the actual immersion, I'd wear a white dad-size T-shirt.)

I held these pitches like jewels. *Here is my long journey with a moral arc*, it meant, but even as I willed and rehearsed for it, I was confused. I sensed bigger stories ahead—an unexpected question or visitor, signs and pamphlets telling me to leave no trace and deface no treasure, a longer and unsatisfying rehash of the doctrine. My brother would look at me, apprehensive that his next year's rites might not prove as monumental as I made them to be. He listened to my reports from Sunday school ("After I get baptized I receive the Holy Ghost from Dad and Grandpa C. T. and Grandpa Gene") and my observations on being the oldest ("We have Dad as our world father and we have Heavenly Father for heaven"), but the synchronicity of our relationship meant that if I were on track for major maturation that year, Christian would get it too. He was yet convinced.

I had only a small inkling at the time—that my deepest rites and confirmations would not arrive at once but instead accumulate on the periphery. I had only a few more doctrinal rituals like this left in me, as the religion would ultimately fail to take. I'd push and bury and ignore, but by college I would send my letter of resignation from the LDS church, and by then affix my gospels to a much less stable cosmos.

My grandpas would attend as promised, cited as worthy priesthood holders—respectable patriarchs with well-developed careers and swaths of descendants. Both would die from cancers well before their wives, and before I could ask more than a handful of questions.

And my dad was there. Over breakfast he had asked if I had hesitations or wanted to understand more of what would be happening that day. He couldn't lack for perplexity—all into my adult years he'd write me letters, ask to verify and seal his own observations on religion, relationships, movies, and all his great insights and terrible misunderstandings. Perhaps unintentionally, he'd be the one to hold me under the water and mystify me of its purpose.

And my mom stood on the shore, as her gender and apostasy excluded her from walking into the font with me. She wore a long summer dress, black and gold and splashed with big pink and periwinkle flowers. All morning she ran the ice-cream maker and its boarish sound on the back patio, and cleaned the house and answered the phone, and laid out chicken kebabs and white bean salad on platters shaped like goldfish. I knew even then she was conflicted about my initiation, but these little acts of accordance between her and my dad would foster better insight than I'd ever report from the baptism: that goodness requires bigger time and more ample company than my own.

But here's where we were that day: north like all the other towers, more ancient than anything I had been blessed upon, stood the Mount Jordan Wasatch Range and Lone Peak and the tiny fraction of the data I would collect from it—that Question Mark wall, quartzite and cottonwood, thirty million years steady. Jacob's Ladder and wreckage and artifacts of long dead, and a sloping field of granite bombs ascending to the highest summit and its full-circle survey of the Great Basin. And wellsprings jumping at the fastest way down, sailing a century's worth of suburban developments and old apple orchards to pool in shady coves—ciphers I could only beg one summer at a time.

In that water there was sweet and extraordinary cold, and the pleasure of sunlight floating at the surface. The small roar of the spillway drowned out my dad's prayer to everyone but me, but I would not remember the invocations. And when I closed my eyes and held my nose, I felt the enormous quiet of submersion—a child asked to defer or calibrate her language or choose the right, and instead tipping backwards over a catechism of wilderness.

Dayna Patterson

BREATHE IN

Breathe in. Hold. The Ama in Japan pump their lungs oxygen-full, their blood abuzz. They dive from dinghies into freezing ocean, immerse like mermaids to sea-harvest pearls and food. 30 seconds. Grasping what was seeded from sand under menace of shark-lurk and blue-noose. 60 seconds. Sea cucumber. Abalone. Urchin. Octopus. 90 seconds. Pushing up with robbed mouths.

Breathe in. Hold your face under bubbles, nose and mouth, while big sister counts the seconds to a hundred. *You almost made it*, she says. *Do it again.*

Breathe. Like the tide, what washes in and erupts on shore, molecules that have been here before, each intake a partial resurgence of the old. In a shared room, swapping molecules with other breathers. Susan's exhale your next inhalation. What was inside her now inside you. This strange intimacy of secondhand breath. Thirdhand. Fourth. The whole earth a shared room.

Breathe. Bend at the waist, arms crossed over chest, till black lights disco and sleep-heaviness overtakes you and gravity's big hand pushes you down onto the gym's blue wrestling mat or into the arms of laughing friends who wait for your resurgence.

Don't breathe. You don't need air more than this stroke between the legs, between the sheets, between evening and nightfall, insistent rub, fingers' merciful friction. Hold. Keep holding. Starve your blood abuzz.

The whole earth's atmosphere frailer than we'd imagined, thin envelope of the apple's skin, easy to chew through. Easy to break the triple bonds of nitrogen with chemicals compounded in all-white rooms. Just now we are grasping what we've seeded.

COLLECT

Lance Larsen

SACRAMENTAL

My friend, a believer, fears both gluten and God,
so each Sunday when the tray wends its way

he takes a crust of bread and touches it to his lip
like a priest kissing prayer beads and calls life

good and calls God bright. And thus lets a shred
of Wonder into his world, emblem turned flesh.

What faith, to take in hope by chewing on nothing,
then stow what's left and later empty his pocket

of its holy scraps over an anthill. As for the rest
of us, dogged pilgrims, don't we still need

crumbs to bolster our belief? Aren't we all ants,
mandibles and churning legs, curry and carry,

give and mostly take, bearing the manna down
into the bunker, into the dark kingdom of praise?

Nest

The things I saved up there—mantis legs, cat fur,
porcupine quills tied with twine. I thought
this was religion. To climb through leaves

and pocked apples to the highest bough, to finger
what no one else wanted. Cicada husk,
dried fish tail. Not death, but what death left

behind. I touched tongue to rabbit skull, tasted
the eye holes. So many creeds, and only a crooked
wind and the sulfur glow of the railroad yards

to help do the sorting. Snake skin wrapping
my knuckles, the clink of wisdom teeth, my aunt's.
Worn down enough to make me think of food.

What it might mean to chew. And be chewed.
That divination. Then putting everything
back. Bone puzzle, flesh pieced against fur.

And swallowing as I climbed down—the creature
above and inside me now. Anything left over
circling like a hawk or unanswered prayer.

Twila Newey

ODE & ELEGY

Expanse claimed me early
years before father pushed me
under chlorinated water &
pronounced my small body clean,
proclaimed my membership
in a walled church drawn
by lists of prescriptive rules
& stored food for safekeeping.
Even so small I knew I belonged
more to the temporary
congregations of passing clouds,
communities of trees & other
occasional passersby—a deer,
a hawk circling, blue relief—
a nod of my head prayer enough
for our mutual moment
in the long world. We tiny notes
—hair, feather, leaf—float
through air in our time, each
as precious as a single drop
of this glacial pool where my children
baptize their toes—water
skin, sky—all walls eventually
crumble. All bodies become the dust
we tread this trail where chosenness
lists on wind, breaks open
in repeating peaks of earth, solid

waves made of time so vast,
we sing back only
our stunned silence.

Kathryn Cowles

HYMN

with 8 birds on a wire
or rather on 3 wires . . .
4 birds on 3 wires, one bird on one . . .
5 of 'em now on 2;
on 3; 7 on 4
Ezra Pound, *The Pisan Cantos*

1
all is well, I sang, little
learning how to do the harmony parts,
Saturday church choir, *all is well*

the blue sparrow babies have hatched
and we have kept the cats
away thus far

and one day everyone decides
to bale their hay
every single field down
all at once everyone

all at once
my friend is sick
sick and far away and I hear
will die and I
can't get my head
to think it through
all is well, I sang, *all is well*
tho hard to you

2
so I wrote another friend
a goat on a spit for you, Brenda
we took a photo, I said, transcribed,
put it down, list, list,
sent a postcard
is it getting hot in here

3
I am cycling in the mountains
here is what I see
my arms stretched out in my shadow
three horses facing away

the cows have got out, one white
excuse me while I take this hill

4
don't you call coward on me
I put the knife through the fish's skull
once caught, all alone,
into its hot, hot brain, again, again
to be sure it's just

here lies / the Idaho kid
the only time / he ever did
he transcribed bird bird bird bird in Pisa
counted them for comfort
because everyone needs a latch
comfort, comfort
knife caught hold
in a cliff
and if I die, I sang, *and if I die*

5

the spit is picking up, Brenda
I have a bug in my eye
I can ride a hill down w/ no breaks now
my one eye is streaming from the bug
the spit is turning fast, Brenda
a knife to the brain is quicker
than a whack, whack, more humane
I cannot get it in my head
I see a blue bird, a bale,
a white cow
every single field down
happy day, I sang, *all is well*
every single thing down, picking up

Go

Clouds like a sheet overhead
like a parachute opening
cause me accidentally to look
directly at the sun so now
I've got sun spots in my eyes
that move from thing to thing as I shift my gaze—
superimposed if temporary /
I feel a sudden affinity with trees
we are all sitting still in the breeze
while the water and the air
and the birds and the sun spots
and the loud-winded flag behind me
and the cars and trucks and the clouds
go by and the two fishermen on the lake
and the fish under the water too
the spider on the bench and all
the insects besides and a group of four
in a golf cart fast on the sidewalk go /
the swallows cut the air in planes
even the babies
do it for its own sake
looks like, though I'm sure they're
catching bugs, but oh,
black sleeves like scissors
snippeting the air they're
the fastest thing around.

Tamara Johnson

The End of the World

Only in the opening and closing of this confession, do I dare cross that boundary of modesty and cleave you to myself, for surely, as a passionate reader, you know that we take the best works into the intimacy of our souls and make them our own.
    —Julia Alvarez, "Response to Sor Juana Inés de la Cruz After Reading Her Poems"

I GO TO THE END OF THE WORLD TO THINK ABOUT EVERY-thing that's happened. Most people call this place The Point—although there's nothing pointed about it, just an unpaved lip of canyon jutting out between two trees until the dirt pushes up into a pout of pineapple weeds, agave blossoms, sage, wild onions, and hundreds of rhyolite cobbles the size and shape of baby heads. A coyote trail will take you all the way to the river if you follow it, but most people won't. It isn't weird to just stand here, maybe watch the sun drop into the ocean as a semicircle of mountains disappears behind you like a grin. In the morning I squat on my haunches, inspect the previous night's detritus. Some things I've found here: an empty wheel chair, Bart Simpson mask, ketchup packets, empty Swisher Sweets bags, fur and bones, laundry line with a Betsy Ross–style flag tied to it, graffiti, scattered bike parts, framed photo of a guy in military dress, wads of bright blue bubblegum with all the teeth marks, feather boa. Usually, though, I just find little tobacco piles and different kinds of candy wrappers. When the tops of trees almost touch like this, some people call it a kissing canopy. The twin invasives—Indian laurel, Chinese banyan or curtain figs, depending on your vernacular, create a mood of conspiracy. People often whisper. Once I almost stepped on a kid in a sleeping bag. His eyes got wide when he saw me. He said it was his first time. *Dropping acid? Sleeping rough?* I didn't ask. He raised the mouth of his sack with his left hand, and when the right emerged it was gripping the neck of a beautifully polished guitar. His pillow was clean, the air between us peppery with nasturtiums.

In order to better understand the possibilities of space-time convergence, early astronauts began to use (as I imagine they still do) certain knowable, precise, but speculative language choices to express the experience of movement in an absence of days, nights, years, and earthly seasons. Early in the 1970s other people, too, lawyers mostly, began appropriating the language of space travel to speculate on a past that had become unfixed from the usual rotations. When former White House attorney John Dean famously used the phrase *point in time* three times in forty-five seconds during the Watergate hearings, court watchers found the obfuscation outrageous, rightly pointing out that there was no way to accurately determine whether the span referred to seconds, days, or years. But the phrase caught on. Now many of us use it as a matter of habit. *At this point* in the narrative. *At that point* in the game. A not unreasonable way to describe vagaries unimportant to the overall conversation or turning—turning being an earlier way to describe what conversation is.

Turnover is a common usage for properties, or perhaps employees. The thing is vacant. The person is elsewhere. Dislocation. Demolition. Renovation.

Once in a while a fog flows into the canyon from the west,

then, I squint so that individual water droplets appear more like a body that is able to lick up at my toes and drown the monkey flower we planted together last winter. Actually, Ranger Bautista has started the project by the time you and I happen to walk by...There is a gigantic pile of wood chips, three or four unmanned shovels. We are already sad, but trying. You are doing your best to get sober. All around us, all I can see is good eating: epazote, prickly pear, manzanita and lemonade berries, squab, acorn, squirrel, mallow, black sage, amaranth, nettles, sour grass, purslane, curly dock, rabbit mugwort, sweet clover. But a park is not a commons. We leave the bounty and the hawks surfing the thermals.

How old? Fifteen? The Church Patriarch arrives by appointment to give me my blessing for the future. A thing I am not prepared for is his tape recorder. I don't know why this detail surprises me more than the cold oil on my head or the declaration that I am of the tribe of Ephraim. A thing I am not surprised at all by is the topic of marriage. I am told that if I remain worthy I will have the privilege of going to the temple and bearing children. Because I want nothing more than to stay single forever, I consider this ordination my first koan.

In 1916 crowds of well-dressed spectators gathered on the cliffs to watch the river dislodge Isolation Hospital from its banks. In a photo of the aftermath, the rectangular wooden building looks more like a tool shed than an infirmary. In a large, open window a woman's long braid catches the light against her white shift. Or maybe it's a young man in suspenders and tie smiling for the camera. Probably neither. Suppose, for the sake of argument, that I can return a hundred years from now as I thoroughfare. It's a ridiculous supposition, I know. But no more ridiculous than the state I am in, standing here with my self-importance, a public works project. Public school hand-me-downs. Tax subsidies.

A Mormon girl who squinted over so much fine print she ruined her eyes. One of the very few times I remember my mother getting upset was over a question I had about nuns and why our church didn't have any since we already called everybody sister. When I was prescribed my first pair of glasses, around the age of twelve, the laser precision with which I could see every leaf was painful. I didn't know the word yet, so I used the Spanish word *prueba*, or puzzle. Proof. Thesis. The school bus window is dirty and my reflection not so flattering. I had much preferred my earlier, impressionistic, vision. Still, I wanted to see clearly.

Someone begins leaving record albums in the driveway of my parents' home. I bring them inside, admiring covers and holding the vinyl by its edges as I had seen my father do so many times. England's Newest Hit-Makers says one cover, but inside Their Satanic Majesties Request. The hum of the freeway is such a constant that when we went as a family to Glacier National Park the quiet kept me awake all night.

Once the pandemic hits, the trails and beaches become so flooded with people the governor orders all parks closed and advises everybody to go back inside. I'm trying to imagine what it would be like to close a circle, to return to an earlier version of myself as you have. When the early student app, *Rate My Professor*, first came online I was pleased whenever someone awarded me the "hotness" icon, a red pepper. Perhaps I was remembering my first real literature class—lone girl among frat boys, gawking at our professor. She would fiddle with a long pearl necklace explaining that Samsa, as in Gregor, could be translated from the German as "I am alone." Sylvester Hulet walked from Council Bluffs, Iowa, with the Mormon Battalion. No, he rode a horse. We know this because he lent the horse to Amos Cox, brother of his beloved Orville, after Amos was gored by a bull. I want to be accurate. Everything about my great-grand-uncle codes as queer, but the word he chose was bliss. I asked you once what you would do when you were forty-six and I was fifty-eight. "Love you," you said as you kissed my eyelids. "I'll just love you."

~

Back in my mandated isolation I find the Yelp page for University Heights Park: "Nice view, but not really a park." "More of a nook." "A look-out point." The average rating is 3.5 stars. I read more about Sylvester, admonished not for speaking in tongues but for doing so without authority. Deceived by trickery for the Devil's own ends, he is forced to sign a confession and promises not to engage in charismatic practices.

Steve Langdon pushes me against a stack of Kumeyaay translations that his mother has piled in her garage. I'm here willingly, but the force of his body and the feel of his top teeth pushing into my lip are so noteworthy that I record the occasion in my diary. My father reads it. Certainly this is the moment I switch from journalism to poetry.

But some things need to be said prosaically. We finally get you into rehab, you leave with another woman, a high school sweetheart. The landlords start tearing down your apartment immediately. The virus is already upon us. It is Mardi Gras. I go to Las Vegas with Gina, just a twenty-four-hour trip, and in the morning we visit the Neon Museum, a dirt lot, really, with all the old signs. The monk hours I'm keeping now aren't very difficult but the blue of the artificial light hurts my eyes. My grief is enormous, not at your leaving but because of the cruel and unnecessary epitaph, oddly familiar, even compelling in its arc of teen vampire plot points. Men I don't know well, and a few I do, all say the same thing to me: *You're both better off.* As if they could possibly know. Or, if they somehow know, that it would ever be their place to tell me. Women who hope to provide comfort say things like, "You'll get another one," or, worse, "You still have life left in you." I put on my politest face and say thank you to the landlords who have reluctantly paused the parade of (de)construction workers: the stomping and spitting and the use of the common area by random men, the touching and turning of shared locks and doorknobs, the up and down looks. It's terrifying, this new realization that my single-minded point of view is no longer taken as seriously as before you left. *Please,* I ask. *If I can't finish this essay how can I possibly manage to pay rent?*

It takes four days of arguing and threatening, but they relent.

~

Sylvan/Sylvestus/Sylvester

The End of the World could hardly be more delightsome: drab, fat, towhees; the aptly named poppies bright against thunderclouds. An absence of cars on the interstate makes it easy to see the freeway's undoing: motorway becoming bikeway. Wagon trail returning to walkway, to bunny run. Steve, son of Margaret, teaches Jeff, son of Sylvia, how to play guitar. When our mother is dying Jeff picks me up early. We take the 15 listening to Motorhead, then Schubert, speed past red rock. It is mid-July and other families are also preparing for homecoming. At American Fork the sun is sinking. We stop in for her roommate, who is like an aunt to us. She drives to the hospital, well familiar with the way to the ICU already. I take the night shift, Jeff the day—hauling his guitar and amp up near her bed so she can hear him practice, which she enjoys. "Look! They gave you the VIP room," says her neighbor and friend Mary Ellen, who is masked up for her own health reasons. And it's true. The window looks out onto a hillscape. Two horses munch grass, switching their tails. I think of the Auden poem "Musée des Beaux Arts," which is so much a part of my body that it rises spontaneously as a hymn: *About suffering they were never wrong, / The old Masters . . .*

Seventeenth-century nun Sor Juana Inés de la Cruz had the largest library in New Spain. She reluctantly relinquished it, leading one of her translators to ask this impertinent question: "[I]n spite of all her acumen, learning, and astute intelligence, she somehow failed to take into account the depth of sexist bigotry that prevailed in every sector of society. Why did she allow herself to be caught in the snares set by a misogynistic hierarchy, embodied in the person of Manuel Fernandez de Santa Cruz, who had once been her friend and associate but who attacked her in a portentous letter, purportedly by another nun, the fictional Sor Filotea ..."

A woman can be a perfect genius and still: How, in her perfection, *did she allow* this *misfortune* to happen?

In Buddhism, as in Catholicism, female monastics are called nuns; or, *bhikkuni* (female *bhikku*). Though they are not required to symbolically marry, as Catholic nuns are, their social status as women has been presumed to be deferential to that of even the lowest monk. And, although the story is probably a later invention, the first rule of a woman's order (or eighth, depending on your source) is that "almswomen, even if a hundred years standing, shall make salutation to, shall rise up in the presence of, shall bow down before, and shall perform all proper duties toward an almsman, if only just initiated." Even without creating a gender-specific title (nun, daughter, wife), the feminization of the existing word (female priest, female son, female husband) is enough to change an entire set of expectations in what would otherwise seem an identical position. For this reason I was delighted to serve as *best man* in my friend Daniel's wedding ceremony. I should state for the record that I identify mostly as a cis-femme. In other words, I may be an old maid but I am no maid of honor. I identified with Sor Juana, the nun, because I couldn't yet imagine a differently gendered title beyond the ridiculous bachelorette of *The Dating Game*. I was well into adulthood before I realized that women, like men, had ego that deserved protection and that my own mother was smart and capable.

My mother and father were both Idaho farm kids. His family raised sheep, hers cattle. Sometimes I joke that the best thing they did for us was to move as far south and as far west as possible. In truth, they were both more nomadic than anything. Of the four children Jeff and I are the only two still here. A biography that my mother wrote for her fiftieth high school reunion lists paragraphs of travel locations. We children merit barely a mention at the end. Mostly this makes me happy although certainly my father helped her write it—not because she was incapable, but because his words carried more weight, were more official. My mother poured her talents into culinary delights and into caring for all of us: her patients, her friends, her neighbors. A middle child, she would often say, "No one took care of me much," but she would smile at the memory of solitude. Before she was the farmer's daughter of fantasy. The place I go is similarly woodsy but not unmanicured. This is not the butch place of survivalists but of my mother's brothers singing arias while driving a tractor or practicing *Swan Lake* under the moonlight dressed in long johns. Sister Sylvester at his weaving. Brother Orville, kin but not kin.

The place I like to stand is beautiful in its unbecoming. The ragged edges of the point break off into a tangle of black-eyed Susans and escaped mallow as high as my lungs. It's hard not to believe that the world is trying to shake us loose, but this is wrong thinking. Long ago you and I sat in the presence of the great trees and made each other pinky promises, proclaiming one another *nothing special* and granting ourselves the privilege to escape whenever necessary. I had shaved my head almost to the scalp. We resembled brother monks more than husband and wife and this, more than anything, made me happy. Before Sor Juana devoted herself to higher learning she asked her mother if she might pass as a boy. When Bishop Fernandez de Santa Cruz betrayed her he hid behind the false identity of a woman. There is something in this. I am straining to see the concrete strictures of river below. I know where the water is because of the trees around it and how the ducks fly to and from in the crepuscular hours. I have lived in places without even a decent window. I have rented rooms that aren't even rooms. I have been illuminated to the outside, reaching for a book. A record. A sliver of moon slipping in through the blind. A whiff of jasmine. Standing in front of my library whispering, "Teach me how to be old like a tree." *You were always free to go.*

Edith Grossman. Translator's Notes xviii, *Sor Juana Inés de la Cruz: Selected Works.* New York: Norton. 2014.

Lenore Friedman. *Meetings With Remarkable Women: Buddhist Teachers in America.* p. 7. Shambhala Publications. Boston: 1987, 2000.

(UN)CLAIM

Reb Cuevas

Jicama

it was jicama
soused in lime and chili
that my cousin threw
into my father's face
when he thought
he'd have her try
something that he actually
liked

the flavor nipped
her tongue
like the expectation of sweet
swapped with bitter
and she'd had
enough

trust warped by
too many try-this-it's-goods
ending in curdled milk
a garden flower
her spitting in the sink

and my father's laugh

a huff that purples his face
when he means it

and he always does

My father: a cook.
My father: a carpenter.
My father: an immigrant.
My father: a man who laughs.

My father: an engineer
in utah,
joking to his neighbors
that "this land
belonged to mexico once,
didn't it?"

and laughing alone
because *his* was the face
they questioned
when we moved in-
to that rambler
by the church
belonging to my mother's
parents

My mother: the link
to that place,
and the cul-de-sac
with the basketball
hoop in the curve

and the net
from her
childhood

The neighborhood: a redbrick block

of backyards
hedged-in orchards

apple, peach,
and cherry

where my mother
played, and now her
children

each of us liminal
in our belonging
depending on where we fell
genetically
on my father's
earth-toned
gradient

My father: a fleck
of pepper
in a pot of cream

a south-of-the-border
sojourned
spice

his tastes are an escapade
for utahed tongues
their curiosity
his playing ground
sometimes

and jicama is clever
by nature

an apple without seeds
trying to belong with salt
it wants to be all things

with lime and chili
it wants to take my father back
to the places that are his
by nurture:

to a coiling river
the volcanic air
the bee farm
and the sprawling orchards

mango and papaya

my cousin didn't like it
it's an acquired taste

Sarah Newcomb

WHERE GRANDMOTHER WALKED

Grandmother's Gift

WARMTH POURED OFF THE WOOD-BURNING STOVE IN THE corner of the living room, which crackled with the sounds of wood shifting from within. The fragrant scents of coffee and fire mixed and filled the air. Just off the living room was a large picture window looking out onto the small island community of Metlakatla, Alaska. In the window hung suncatchers and crystal prisms, which caught the late-afternoon sun and sent rainbows of light dancing across the room. In front of the window was an oval dining table with two people sitting at it.

A seven-year-old girl with waist-length black hair was spooning kippered fish onto a large round cracker. After taking a bite she let her dark brown eyes wander to the pictures of children and family that covered the walls and trailed down a narrow hallway. When she looked at them she liked to recall the names of her cousins, aunts, uncles, and anyone else she recognized. She found a few pictures of herself and felt the familiar happiness spread over her that came in knowing she belonged there. Her eyes wandered to the older woman sitting next to her. Short white hair curled against her grandmother's head, and gentle eyes so dark they were almost black looked far away and lost in thought. The woman pursed her lower lip for a moment and then lifted her coffee mug to take a sip. She placed the mug back down on the table and wrapped her fingers around it, moving them slowly as if to soak in the heat.

The two stayed this way for some time, eating and enjoying the quiet. The girl was watching her grandmother when the older woman's head turned, and their eyes met. Grandmother smiled and deep wrinkles rippled across her face. Reaching out she took one of the girl's hands in her own and gently squeezed. The girl smiled in return, then lowered her eyes to where they held each other and wondered at how incredibly soft her grandma's hands were. Grandma squeezed a second time before letting go, then returned her hands once more to her coffee mug.

The memory is so thick it feels like I can reach out and touch it, like a heavy mist which has fallen around me. It feels like home. Grandma had seemed eternal when I was a child, like she would live forever. Even now, years since she passed on, it is hard to believe she is gone. I remain perfectly still while holding on tight to the connection. I want to relive the memory just one more time, but I can already feel it slipping. I do not resist, but instead release my hold. I know it will come back to me; it always does. I feel it float away, but the gift Grandma left me remains. Some gifts are priceless, and the one that my grandmother gave to me was the experience of being unconditionally loved and accepted. I am left in awe of the impact of that love and how it has stayed with me throughout my life. It took a long time for me to even comprehend what I had been given.

Raised by Strangers
If I had understood my circumstances, I would have done things differently. Once I did understand what had happened to me the pain and regret were palpable. I began to mourn for my grandma, and the choices I would never be able to make. I wanted to tell her I was sorry for not visiting more and tell her what she meant to me. A child has no way of comprehending their very heritage being taken, let alone knowing to ask for help.

Not even Grandma knew that I had been raised to reject a part of myself—the part of me that was her.

From the time I was born I was almost completely raised far away from my Tsimshian tribe. My mother had left the reservation early in her life and joined the Mormon Church, also known as the Church of Jesus Christ of Latter-day Saints. My mother was the only one from our Tsimshian family to join the church. It was an interesting childhood, and I became accustomed to constant change. My father's jobs moved us often and as a result we uprooted every few years to a new state. As a Native American I never quite fit in at school or church. I was treated kindly, but I was also treated as different. I would forever be an outsider. Eventually I learned to focus on the positive and began to enjoy the adventure of it all. Seeing new places, meeting new people, and experiencing various cultures became some of the best experiences while growing up.

In many ways the church helped me with all the changes. It was consistent and familiar everywhere we lived and became one of my favorite places to be. I loved the church basketball games, potlucks, and activities with other kids. I loved singing and looked forward to every Sunday, hoping my favorite songs would be chosen. Each time we moved and started over I knew that the church would be at our new home waiting for us. The church leaders taught me about God, the Bible, and the Book of Mormon. The church also taught me about my identity as a Native American.

"Sarah is a Lamanite," the primary teacher paused to tell the class. I felt my protective smile slide into place, and I froze. Unsure of what to do I kept completely still while the other children's eyes were studying me. I felt the weight of who I was as it pushed down on me not for the first time, Native American— Tsimshian of the First Nations, and I was a Lamanite.

During children's music time we all sang about my Lamanite ancestors in a song called "Book of Mormon Stories." I was surrounded by Anglo children as we would sing about how my people had been given the land in the Americas if they lived righteously. Our voices echoed around the room while children and teachers in unison raised one hand behind our heads in a fist with two fingers extended. This movement was meant to represent the feathers that Native Americans wore in their hair. I was connected to the Book of Mormon in a way none of my classmates were. In some ways I felt special because of that.

When I did visit my tribe, I did not need to ask my grandma or Tsimshian elders about our culture or where we came from. At church I had been taught that my tribe did not have the full knowledge of our history, and they did not know that the Book of Mormon was a sacred lost record about our ancestors. I trusted the teachers, leaders, missionaries, and apostles when they spoke of who the Book of Mormon was about. Strangers knew more about my ancestry than my own people did. I was lucky, chosen even, for I would help bring redemption to my people.

The more I found out about my ancestors in the sacred scriptures the more disappointed I became in them. As a child I sang that my people were given the land if they lived righteously. As a teenager I finally understood that they had chosen to turn away from God and live unrighteously. As a result, God cursed them by completely abandoning them. I struggled with sadness as I imagined how unrighteous an entire cultural group must be for God to completely forsake them.

I was also taught that God then marked my ancestors with dark skin, as a sign of being a cursed people. The purpose of the dark skin was so the righteous people would know that they should not mix or marry with my people. I was taught that my ancestors became idle and mischievous, and that they were a scourge to the righteous people. I read that due to their bad choices they were unable to keep the land of promise, because God only promised it to them if they lived righteously. As a result of their unrighteousness God guided Christopher Columbus to the land and gave away the land of promise to those who deserved it more.

I was a Native American child being taught manifest destiny at church. I was taught the reason for Native American trauma, genocide, and loss of land was our ancestors' own fault. If only my ancestors had been righteous, God would have protected our people and our lands. I desperately wished that they had been good people, because perhaps then Native American families and children would not have been harmed so terribly in our country.

Identity

The older I became the more challenging visits home to the reservation were. One year, when planning a trip to see Grandma, I became excited about being old enough to learn the traditional dancing. I was perhaps ten or eleven. I had been looking forward to learning for a long time, but my mother quickly discouraged me from this idea and told me that I should not join in the dancing. I accepted what I was told and put it out of my mind. These were incorrect traditions and a remnant of our people turning away from God. My life needed to stay grounded in the gospel as taught at our church.

During that summer visit I entered the longhouse. As I walked into the building the smell of cedar permeated the air. Wood carvings and masks were displayed in the entry room, and it felt as if the masks were greeting me as I passed them. A small group of children sat at a table with their heads bent together as they practiced their beading. I paused a moment to watch, and wondered if I could teach myself to do what they had been taught. The beat of the drums increased, and I heard a woman's singing join the rhythm. I followed the music and moved further into the building, entering the second and much larger room of the longhouse.

A wall to one side was lined with wood benches to sit on, and at the far end of the room stood a low stage. A man was on the stage playing a large box drum, and a woman was standing on the floor just in front of the stage singing in Sm'algyax—our first language. The people were dressed in exquisite traditional regalia. They wore dresses with button blankets wrapped around their shoulders. Mother-of-pearl buttons outlined the black and red fabric in the shapes of the clans—Eagle, Killer Whale, Raven, and Wolf. The dancers were moving in a large circle around the room. I felt my entire being stirring, as if the dancing and drums were calling to me. I ached to join them, but instead moved to a bench to observe. I knew I was not allowed to participate, but as I watched I wondered how something so obviously beautiful could be bad. Why did God think our traditional ways were so evil that He had to abandon us?

By this point in my life, I had become so accustomed to pushing down the distress within my torn identity that I was not conscious of it. Yet as the drums beat, and as the people danced and sang, I became mindful of the split within myself. I was in the only place I had ever truly belonged, but in that moment began to feel like an outsider among my own people for the very first time. No one was actively telling me I had to choose between being Tsimshian or Lamanite, but I knew in that moment I could not fully embrace both. In the coming years I would do what my parents and church leaders had taught me to do, and I choose to be a faithful follower to God and the Mormon Church. My mother often spoke of the importance of redemption for our people. I was a Lamanite, and with that came unique responsibilities.

For many years I was able to overlook the unease of that choice. However, once I became a mother everything changed. I was suddenly very aware of the subtle racism all around me at church, that before motherhood I had always ignored in order to cope. I withdrew, hurt by the rejections that had once rolled off me, and I worried for my children's futures. I did not turn to my grandmother or my Tsimshian family for help because they were not Mormon. Instead, I turned even more towards the very thing that had fractured my identity—the church.

Over the years I withdrew more and more socially, which was not like me at all. Yet at the same time I was unaware of the real changes happening inside myself. Motherhood had awakened me in a way nothing else could have. I expected more for my children—from myself, from family, and from those who were considered leaders. During the early years of raising my children I decided that to protect them from the social discomforts I had experienced, all I needed to do was have more faith and actively seek God. If I could gain all the knowledge God would impart to me, I could pass it on to my children and strengthen them for their years ahead. My quest for knowledge was insatiable and I spent years reading all the official church materials I could get my hands on. I went into it thinking I already held the truth, and just wanted to be the best and most faithful Mormon mom I could be. Much of what I read surprised me, and I began measuring the wisdom of the things I was being taught at church against the wisdom of what my grandmother, aunts, and uncles had taught me.

At the end of this pursuit, I instead found myself leaving the church with my husband and four children in tow. Months of tears followed in which I attempted to cope with the changes to relationships with Mormon family and friends, and with the loss of the church culture I had loved and been raised in. Each day felt as if I was on autopilot. I understood my decision, but I could not fully wrap my mind around how much it all hurt.

Direction
One day during that first summer after we had left the church, I lay down to rest. I could hear my children playing in the next room, and their sweet screams and giggles echoed through the

house. While resting I was listening to a podcast when it suddenly hit me: I was not Lamanite. I was shocked by the implications of that one small fact. Unable to contain my surprise I jumped to my feet and started pacing. I cannot say why it took so long for me to realize this obvious detail, but once I did my entire world was rocked.

Questions raced through me with no answers. Why was I lied to about my ancestry? How could anyone do that to Native Americans? My ancestors did not cause their own genocide or lose the land of promise through evil choices. My ancestors did not turn away from God. My darker skin was not the result of a curse. With my heart pounding I walked out of my room, through the front door of the house, and stood in the sun. I was no longer afraid of my skin darkening, and I embraced the heat of its rays as tears streamed down my face. It was not my people who needed redemption, but those who had lied about Native American identity who did.

In the weeks that followed I struggled to process the weight of it all. I kept pacing through the house and yard day after day. My inability to sit still was laughably annoying to everyone, myself included. One day I walked past my old running shoes and decided I might as well embrace it. I slipped them on and fell out the door. The sounds of my feet hitting the pavement set a rhythm and I kept my breathing measured against it. The ability to think things through seemed to loosen inside of me.

While I ran, I felt the vibrations of life as they rose up around me; the wind and sun warmed my skin, and the trees rustled in the breeze. Everything felt vibrant. Coming up to a park I moved off the pavement and ran with the soft grass and earth beneath my feet and relished feeling alive. It was during these moments of being completely alone while surrounded with life that I began to reflect and work through what had happened to me and the choices I had made. I also began to make plans and find direction. I had not spent time with my Tsimshian family as I should have. A few of them had already passed away, taking with them the opportunity for me to make amends for my mistakes. I could not let any more time pass and risk losing others that I loved.

Shy and unsure of myself, I reached out and called my uncle Bert who had always taken the time to stay in contact with me. His voice echoed support over the phone as I attempted to explain what had happened. As he spoke, I could hear Grandma's wisdom being passed on and realized that he had made efforts to stay connected with me in some part because of her teachings. My bond with him had grown in the years since Grandma's passing and I cherished him for all his efforts. Again, I was struck by another gift that I had not seen, and I was incredibly grateful he was not gone. I had time and would not waste it.

My heart sped up with each attempt I made to reconnect with aunts, uncles, and cousins. Uncle Bert's encouraging words were always cheering me on in the back of my mind. Expressions of love from me were awkward, but I was determined to be genuine with my thoughts and feelings. Too much was at risk; I could not miss another opportunity. If anything happened to anyone, and I had not tried to let them know how much they meant to me, I would never forgive myself.

In the summer of 2019, my husband and I flew to Alaska with all four of our children to see the family. At ages thirteen, eleven, nine, and five, my children had already missed opportunities to grow up with their Tsimshian family, as I had never brought them home to the reservation. It was the most beautiful experience of my life. I watched the same people who were so kind to me as a child embrace my own children in a way that they had never experienced. Laughter and hugs replaced all the tears I had cried. Meals and family get-togethers filled homes night after night. Love had always been there waiting. It only took me finding the right direction to walk in.

~

Running

This was the first visit I had made in which my grandma was not alive, and I felt the impact of her absence. I had known it would be hard to not have Grandma there, so it did not surprise me when I struggled with that reality. For Grandma I had planned ahead and had packed my running shoes; the same shoes I had run hundreds of miles in to find my way back to her. I wanted to feel beneath my feet the land where my grandmother had once walked.

The morning of July 4 was cool, clear, and beautiful. My uncle Archie dropped me off at the meeting place for the women's distance race. He wished me luck and smiled his big smile as he drove away. I shifted back and forth on my feet, fidgety as I stretched. To calm myself I closed my eyes and listened to the sounds around me. The other runners were chatting; they all seemed to know each other. Someone made a joke and the group burst into laughter for a moment. I heard a few cars drive past and in the following quiet could hear ravens cawing in the distance. Everyone started moving and I opened my eyes to see that a large van had pulled up and the runners were climbing in. I followed and found a seat, then we rode a few miles out of town.

The van stopped in a parking lot by a small lake to let out the women runners. The driver got out with a stopwatch and started us off quickly. I started running, only glancing back to see the van pull away as it left to drop the men further out of town for their longer race. I felt my nerves ease some as I set my warm-up pace. I wanted to just enjoy the run and be in the moment as much as possible.

The most beautiful smell in the world is that of the Alaskan rainforest—clean, damp, and blending with the sea air. I welcomed it in and felt the cool crispness fill my lungs. On the left side of the road was Yellow Hill, a massive hill with stunning large yellow rocks that climb to 540 feet. One of my favorite memories is hiking it with family during childhood visits. I looked and saw that the narrow wood boardwalks which lined the trails had been kept up and miles more had been added around the base disappearing into the trees. I was running just behind the woman in the lead when she picked up her pace and pulled my attention away from the scenery. I sped up and stayed just a few feet behind her. It was a little faster than I was used to, but I hoped I could keep up.

It was not long before my body protested at the pace she had set, and I considered slowing down. I was unsure if I could keep up for the full two miles, but quickly decided to ignore the protest and pushed it out of my mind, my competitive side getting the better of me. I wanted to do my best, especially for my kids, so I challenged myself to at the very least keep up with her.

To motivate myself I focused my mind on the reason I was running. My thoughts turned to my grandmother and I began whispering to her. I was surprised at how talking to Grandma while I ran felt like the most natural thing in the world. I told her I was sorry it had taken me so long, but that I was finally home. I told her I missed her.

About a mile in I evaluated my pace as I gained on the other runner. At one point, when I was side by side with her, she looked over at me and told me I was fast. I smiled as big as I could and said thanks while measuring my breath to appear unwinded. It always amused me how much running is a mental game. I continued pretending that I was not dying inside to psych out the other runner. I had planned on doing my best, not thinking I could win, but suddenly wondered if perhaps I could. Maybe I could win it for Grandma. I almost regretted that thought because once that idea got in my head I had no other choice than to try. I kept my breathing as even as possible and focused on the form of my gait. Soon after, the other runner started to slow down a bit and I took that opportunity to speed up. With a huge grin on my face, I ran as fast as I could go.

More than once I felt my body screaming to stop. It had been years since I had felt that kind of burn, and I wondered how long I could keep up such a pace. But every single time I faltered I chose to talk to Grandma instead and ignore the discomfort. Over halfway through the race I saw some children playing and riding bikes, and they stopped to watch me as I ran by. I reached the town and passed a small convenience store and houses which lined the street. My eyes caught some movement and I looked up at eagles flying high and circling over the trees. The beautiful life within the community had not changed in all the years I had been gone.

I could feel my legs beginning to slow down, yet I had no idea how close the other runner was. I never looked back. Instead, I tried to recall all the memories I had with Grandma and family growing up. Picking berries, going on walks, having a crab bake on the beach, and all the joy of being with everyone floated through my mind. I continued to whisper to Grandma about so many things I cannot remember them all. I felt warmth and energy spreading over me each time I spoke to her—it felt like unconditional love had surrounded me just as it had when I was a child. I sped up to a sprint when I turned onto the last stretch, sensing her joy, and crossed the finish line first.

Thomas W Murphy

GRAVE CONSEQUENCES:
ON REVELATION AND REPATRIATION

"HOLD STILL," THE SCOUT LEADER SAID, AS HE APPLIED black face paint outlined in white on one half, and then white bordered in black on the other side of my face. Participation in the Order of the Arrow was a distinguishing honor for young Boy Scouts in the Tendoy District of the Grand Teton Council from Pocatello, Idaho. To play the role of a medicine man, wearing a bison headdress and feathers, in the induction ceremony was an extraordinary responsibility. Adorned in Indian regalia at Camp Little Lemhi in the Targhee National Forest in traditional Shoshone territory, I represented the passing of an environmental ethic from the original stewards of the land to settler colonists who had taken their place, or so it seemed.

"You need to take those off," an adult leader insisted. Without my spectacles I could not read the secret script he handed me in a booklet. The ceremony started in less than an hour and I couldn't possibly memorize my lines in that short amount of time. Frustrated, the leader consulted his peers and finally consented to allow me to don my eyeglasses underneath the bison's horns and over the top of my makeup—but only when it was my turn to read lines from the pamphlet. "It's just not going to look real," he sputtered in disappointment. Eyeglasses in hand, I stumbled through the rest of the ceremony, myopic in action as well as vision.

Nestled below the Palisades Dam on the Snake River, in the Yeaman Creek Canyon at the upper end of Swan Valley in eastern Idaho, Camp Little Lemhi mimicked indigeneity. Scouts practiced archery and canoeing and learned "primitive" crafts like starting fires, wildlife tracking, and basket weaving. We slept in campsites named after Shoshone, Snohomish, Seneca, Chippewa, Apache, Paiute, and other nations. Boys selected for Order of the Arrow took responsibility for cleaning up camp at the beginning of the next summer season. An overnight vision quest, accompanied by fasting, offered the promise of a deeper meaning to this foray of service. The pretense was marked by the general absence of Indigenous peoples. While Pocatello, the city from which most of the boys came, adjoined the Shoshone-Bannock Tribes at the Fort Hall Indian Reservation, I do not recall any scout troops from the reservation. Most scouts from the Mormon Indian Student Placement Program, an official church-run foster service placing reservation youth in the homes of white Mormons during the school year, went home for the summer and did not join us at scout camp, except when brought in as a visiting group to perform a powwow song in ceremony.

I wondered why the men had chosen me for the role of a medicine man. Had they heard stories about my Lamanite ancestors? "Lamanite" was the label, drawn from the Book of Mormon, my parents had applied to our distant Iroquois heritage. It surely wasn't my archery skills, abysmal at best. Perhaps it was because I was a senior patrol leader, or maybe it was winning a "Big Foot" award for my ability to remember names of trees and to identify animals by their tracks and signs. Should I have told them that I kept notes on our nature walks?

Scouts swore an oath to be "honest" and "trustworthy." Yet, a faux ceremony in which white boys played Indians under the guidance of settler colonial men seemed to obscure more than it revealed. This ritualized way of remembering was not an "honest" and "trustworthy" portrayal of the past. The image of a dying Indian willingly bequeathing responsible stewardship of the land to a new generation of settlers owed more to wishful thinking than historical facts. "Playing Indian," I would later learn, helped ease the nagging conscience of settlers benefitting from a violent and fraudulent displacement of Indigenous peoples while depriving their living descendants a voice in that act of remembrance.

Getting to and from the scout camp in the early 1980s was a frightening experience. Rumors told us that the Palisades Dam was another earthen structure, just like the Teton Dam that had collapsed in 1976. My dad and stepmother purchased the inundated Arctic Circle in Rexburg for a bargain price after the flood. They told stories of shoveling layers of mud out of the restaurant and of water covering the pasture at their house on the outskirts of St. Anthony. I helped them build a new home in Sugar City where scarcely a building had survived. The road to Camp Little Lemhi crossed the river at the base of the Palisades Dam. Looking up at that massive structure made me uneasy. Images of the Teton Dam flooded my imagination. Even up the canyon, older boys warned that portions of the scout camp itself might be swamped if this dam broke too.

The fishermen in my family had qualms about dams on the Snake River. They told stories passed on from old-timers of walking across the river on the backs of salmon. Yet, irrigation from the Minidoka and Palisades Dams had opened up agricultural opportunities for the Murphy homestead near Hazelton and at the dairy farm on Kasota Road near Burley where I had spent most of my childhood before my parents' divorce in 1974. Those farms each hosted their own memories. My aunt told me about my paternal grandfather lamenting that one of the Japanese day laborers working in the field on the Hazelton homestead in the 1940s was a medical doctor, incarcerated at the Minidoka concentration camp in nearby Hunt. I-84 bisected the Murphy homestead in the mid-1960s, stranding the bulk of the fields from irrigation. After the freeway dammed the ditches the family had no choice but to lease most of the farm to neighbors with water rights. We knew all too well the value of the Minidoka Irrigation District to settler livelihoods. My maternal grandfather made his living "riding ditches" but fishing was his first love. Oh, the stories he told about the fish of bygone times! The land, too, held stories. Projectile points, or "arrowheads" as we then called them, eroded from the banks of the river on our Kasota farm and served as a reminder of a once-flourishing fishery. "Damn those dams," we said. "Couldn't live with them, couldn't live without them."

As an eager reader, even of the Book of Mormon, I was delighted by a gift of a new book from my mother: *The Lemhi: Sacajawea's People* by Brigham D. Madsen (Caldwell, ID: Caxton, 1980). I remembered Limhi, the Nephite king in the latter-day scriptural revelation who led his people out of bondage and into freedom in Zarahemla. The Nephites and Lamanites were purported to be named after two sons from an Israelite family that had migrated from Jerusalem to the Americas twenty-six hundred years ago. I devoured the book but I distinctly recall my bewilderment. If the Lemhi were descendants of people from the Book of Mormon, why didn't this eminent Mormon historian mention Lamanites or Nephites? What about Zarahemla and King Limhi? Why did he call Tendoy a chief rather than a king? Where were the chariots and the steel swords? What about the Hebrew record keepers who engraved their stories in reformed Egyptian hieroglyphics? Had their skin color changed over time? Reading nonfiction as a teenager was my first inkling that the stories from scripture did not match the ones coming from history.

From scripture I had come to expect people's skin color to change, chameleon-like, in response to their righteousness and wickedness. According to the revelation Joseph Smith claimed to translate from a set of gold plates he said he found in Seneca territory, Lamanites were cursed by God with a dark skin for their wickedness. If they changed their behavior and joined the church they could become white again, or so the scripture said. LDS general authorities testified of such changes in children from the Indian Student Placement Program. The word of God revealed a future in which the descendants of the Lamanites would "blossom as the rose" and become a "white and delightsome" people, although that prediction changed to "pure and delightsome" in 1981.

I remember as an eight-year-old swimmer on the Burley Barracudas swim team noticing the changing skin tone of my teammates. A girl I had my eye on progressively darkened as the summer season wore on. In the twisted mind of a child, I started sinning deliberately in hopes that I could match her suntan. It did not work! That was six years before the Church of Jesus Christ of Latter-day Saints (LDS) changed the word of God. Naively informed by racism I had yet to recognize, I believed that it was the conversion of my ancestors to Mormonism that had given me a light complexion. The more obvious roles of the sun, climate, and intermarriage with European settlers had yet to occur to a kid who had confused scripture with reality.

That misunderstanding would change when I entered college, first at Utah State University and later at the University of Iowa where I discovered the academic discipline of anthropology. Anthropology gave me a chance to explore my interest in Indigenous cultures without abandoning my eclectic passion for both the sciences and the humanities. There were no "Nephites" or "Lamanites" in my archaeology classes. In fact, I learned that the Book of Mormon contained the wrong plants, animals, and technology for ancient America. Indigenous people walked this landscape millennia before the events described in the scripture. In biological anthropology classes I learned that differences in skin color came primarily from variable exposure to ultraviolet radiation. While skin colors have changed over time due to climate, migrations, mutations, and gene flow, those adaptations have nothing to do with religious beliefs and practices. In linguistic anthropology courses I learned that the languages of ancient America had no connections to those of Hebrew and Egyptian peoples or anyone else in the ancient Near East. In cultural anthropology courses I learned that American Indians had histories and cultures of their own, much more like the ones of the Shoshone people that our Mormon ancestors had called "Lemhi" than those of Nephites or Lamanites.

An archaeological field experience in eastern Iowa, land of the Meskwaki Nation, opened my eyes to repatriation issues in 1992. "What did you find?" my classmate asked. "I think it is a bone. Maybe a clavicle," I replied. We were excavating an alluvial fan in the flood plain of the Mississippi River. The site, located on a farm, included postholes from the oldest known house in Iowa from an era archaeologists called Paleoindian. Our professor, Dr. Mary Whelan, was not about to let undergraduates excavate that important location. She had us in another field, a "plow zone," closer to the farmhouse. The materials in this section of the site came from a much later period archaeologists called Hopewell. When I turned that bone over in my hand I did not know that a clavicle was a distinctive feature of primates. I had yet to take a biological anthropology course. The only primate in this section of North America, from the time period we were excavating, was—well—us. Unaware, I bagged it, marked the bag, made a notation in my field notes and then continued slowly troweling the deepening surface of our quadrat. At the end of the day, I turned in the materials I had collected without saying a word about the find to the crew chiefs or professor.

Two days later Dr. Whelan started the day with a lecture about process, procedure, and ethics. One of the students, she said, had not only found a human bone but had failed to report it to the field instructors. They did not find this clavicle until the laboratory technician sorted through artifacts the following day. Finding a human bone changed everything. She shut down not just our quadrat but the entire section of the excavation near it. A third of the class had to move, open up new quadrats far away from the area that might contain a burial. A lively conversation about human remains and the ethics of archaeology occupied the long van ride from campus to the field site that morning following the lecture. In 1990 the Native American Graves Protection and Repatriation Act (NAGPRA) required institutions receiving federal funds, such as the University of Iowa, to notify and consult with Native American leaders regarding inadvertent discovery of human remains and sacred objects. Tribal governments could request repatriation of affiliated remains.

Our discussion shifted to Dickson Mounds, a site not far away on the opposite side of the river. For decades the state of Illinois had displayed more than two hundred Indian skeletons over the objections of a group called the United Indian Nations. In April of 1992, only two months before our field school had started, the state had closed down the display after consultations with local tribes. Raised with settler ethics, I had taken for granted that it was okay to dig up and display human skeletons. I had grown up listening to stories of Zion's Camp, under the direction of Joseph Smith, excavating the skeleton of Zelph from a mound not too far to the south of our field school and Dickson Mounds. My understanding of that favored story from my childhood shifted as I began to consider, for the first time, how I might have felt if Zelph had been my great-grandparent.

Graduate school at the University of Washington beckoned me west again to Coast Salish country. In the Salish Sea basin I developed my first close relationships with Native people beyond that of my wife, Kerrie. Kerrie is a direct descendent of the Cherokee woman Peninah Shropshire Cotton, a nineteenth-century servant who became a plural wife in the home of Daniel Wood in Nauvoo, Illinois. Peninah, acclaimed by the Daughters of Utah Pioneers as the first Lamanite to join the LDS church, came west to Shoshone and Ute territory with the Mormons, where she raised their children orphaned in war. Kerrie taught me that Native ancestors should have names and stories of their own. "Who were they? Where did they come from?" she asked. With Kerrie's encouragement I followed the genealogical trails forged by my grandmother and mother back to the Mohawk Valley in what is now called New York State. There my mother had found Susannah Ferguson Youngs on an inscription on her daughter's death certificate, and on census records from 1810 to 1850, in the household of her settler husband, John Youngs. Susannah, we learned, was born around 1786 in the Mohawk town of Tion-onderoge within the township now called Florida and moved, after her marriage, to the former village of Wautego, called Otego by the settlers in the Susquehanna Valley. The Mohawk Nation is one of the Six Nations of the Haudenosaunee (Iroquois) that also include Oneida, Onondaga, Cayuga, Seneca, and Tuscarora.

In reminiscences from the community of "old Otego," stashed in a binder at the Heritage and Genealogical Society of Montgomery County, we found stories of "swarthy" women living near old Indian trails, harassed by drunk white men. One of those was a "widow Youngs," smoked out of her own home by a would-be mason who sealed her chimney as a prank. The detailed geography in the story matched Susannah's home as indicated in a census report and an old map. Susannah's granddaughter had later relocated with her husband to Sterling, Kansas, in Wichita territory. There they met Mormon missionaries, converted, and followed them west in 1901 to Albion, Idaho: Shoshone land. In our tour of western New York, Kerrie and I never did find Susannah's grave but we found that of her settler husband and one of her daughters nestled in between two farmer's fields near Otego. Is Susannah, I wondered, in a museum somewhere? Was she put on display? Is she someone's science experiment? Just the thought of it hurt. This missing Indigenous woman is my fourth great-grandmother!

I had once camped as a Boy Scout at Little Lemhi in a campsite named Snohomish. Kerrie, our daughter Jessyca, and I located north of Seattle in 1994 in the traditional lands of this Coast Salish nation, whose citizens were to become close friends and adopted family. While still working on my doctorate I found part- and then full-time employment at Edmonds College in Lynnwood, Washington. There, members of the Native American Student Association asked me to be their advisor and help plan an annual powwow. Budding relationships with Indigenous students, their families, and communities blossomed after I published a controversial article titled "Lamanite Genesis, Genealogy, and Genetics" in the anthology *American Apocrypha* (Salt Lake City: Signature, 2002). This article drew from new DNA evidence to show that ancestors of American Indians had been in the Americas since time immemorial and that their closest relations could be found in northeast Asia, not the Middle East. My conclusion that while the Book of Mormon might be scripture, the people and events it describes are fictive drew the public ire of my church and the appreciation of the urban Native communities of the Seattle area. Without compromising my conclusion, I successfully defended my membership in the church, insisting that scripture and science need not be confused with each other.

Angelo Baca, a Diné and Hopi student at the University of Washington with Mormon heritage, reached out to me after reading newspaper reports. He asked for my help with a film, *In Laman's Terms: Looking at Lamanite Identity* (Seattle: Native Voices, 2008). The goal of the film was to provide a place for Indigenous people entangled with Mormonism to tell their own stories. We traveled together back to the land of the Haudenosaunee and the Hill Cumorah, from which the Book of Mormon stories emerged. We stood on the same hill where Joseph Smith called upon an angelic familiar spirit before taking a set of gold plates that I had begun to realize would never have rightfully belonged to him. Using a seer stone, buried in a hat, the Mormon seer produced a tragic narrative that ends with the Lamanites, purported ancestors of the American Indians, destroying an ancient white civilization of Nephites in epic battles at the base of Cumorah. The archaeological record of this glacial drumlin, though, told a different story. We wondered what stories the Seneca had to tell and what they might think of Mormon scriptural accounts.

We spoke with G. Peter Jemison, a site manager and the Seneca representative under NAGPRA, at the historic site of Ganondagan just a dozen miles away from Hill Cumorah. Jemison corrected the stories we had been taught. There was no clash on Haudenosaunee land with an ancient white civilization pulled in chariots by horses, wielding steel swords, raising cattle, sheep, and goats, or eating wheat, barley, and oats. Rather the Haudenosaunee had a Great Law of Peace that helped reduce warfare and minimize casualties. The loss of just a few lives in battle was devastating to Seneca leaders who had a social responsibility to care for the families of those who died. "We were never the kind that thought you had to really wipe out every last person," Jemison reflected. He found the Book of Mormon stories incredulous, the racism "harsh," and the accusations about our shared Haudenosaunee ancestors unfounded.

As an adult I had come to realize that Latter-day Saint revelations told us much more about ourselves than they did about Indigenous peoples. I found a path closer to the truth was to be forged in relationships with living people rather than spirits of the dead. Although my faith evolved, I did not reject the environmental ethic I had learned as a Boy Scout, neither did I turn away from a commitment to service. At Edmonds College I worked collaboratively with Coast Salish nations to build an environmental anthropology field school where students, under the guidance of staff from tribal governments, could weave together science and traditional knowledge to restore habitat and revitalize community. In Coast Salish country, I learned, plants and animals are people too! "You need to learn their names," I teach my students. "How else can you build a relationship?"

Through partnerships extending over two decades we have restored habitat for fish and wildlife, surveyed Dungeness crab and spot prawn populations, helped estimate Coho escapement and brood stock Chinook in the Stillaguamish River, sampled plastic concentrations at Edmonds' Marina Beach and on Everett's Jetty Island, hosted salmon festivals and powwows, built ethnobotanical gardens and an outdoor cultural kitchen, documented the return of wolves and fishers to the Cascades and Olympics, monitored wildlife passage structures and green belts with cameras and traditional tracking skills, and traveled on Tribal Canoe Journey as far north as Bella Bella, British Columbia, and as far south as the Columbia River. For several years I took urban students from western Washington to the rural community of Kettle Falls in the northeast portion of the state.

We partnered with Colville Confederated Tribes, the US Forest Service, and livestock operators on school-based wildlife tracking and monitoring programs. We had dinner with cattle ranchers and listened to their concerns about wolves. We toured the Grand Coulee Dam with a retired engineer from Colville, and then sat with tribal elders above the once-flourishing Kettle Falls to hear their stories of inundated cemeteries and the loss of one of the world's largest salmon runs. I asked my students a question one evening as we sat in a circle on wrestling mats at Kettle Falls Middle School, where the school district provided us a place to sleep. "How many of you have ever spent the night in a small town?" Not one raised their hand. I built a career putting into action the legacy of service-learning and environmental stewardship I had learned as a young Latter-day Saint growing up in southern Idaho. I became a diplomat employing empathetic listening to negotiate between an urban and rural divide as we all navigated difficult balances to protect the places that we loved.

In September of 2011 Kerrie and I stood in Port Angeles, Washington, with Klallam friends and colleagues to watch the launch of the demolition of the Elwha and Glines Canyon Dams. Here, too, elders shared stories, documented on the Lower Elwha website, of fish coming "in so thick that you could walk across the river on their backs." They spoke of their ancestors and creation site submerged deep under the water and inaccessible for nearly a century. As the dams were about to come down, Klallam elder Maudie Sampson exclaimed, "It's about dam time! Aye! My dad use to work at the dams, at least he would have gave us a warning if the dam broke, so I'm glad they are coming down, not only for the danger, but to help bring the fish back also." These dam removals, among the largest in the West, freed the Elwha to visit their ancestors and are bringing flourishing salmon runs back to the Lower Elwha Reservation downriver and the wilds of Olympic National Park upriver. These exemplary dam removals beckon for deeper conversations with Shoshone people about the fisheries and cemeteries that they have lost on the Snake River.

Closer to home we worked with Snohomish County, City of Mukilteo, the Washington Department of Fish and Wildlife, and Tulalip Tribes to remove barriers that had prevented salmon migration into Japanese Gulch for about fifty years. This Puget Sound tributary begins at Paine Field Airport and drains north into the Salish Sea next to the site of the Point Elliott Treaty, signed in 1855 by leaders from Snohomish, Duwamish, Snoqualmie, Samish, and other Coast Salish nations. This treaty promised the original peoples of this land that they could hunt and fish in usual and accustomed places in perpetuity. Yet, a century later, transportation infrastructure blocked salmon from returning to the stream in the very shadows of this historic promise.

Japanese Gulch is not only culturally significant for Indigenous peoples but also to immigrants from Japan who called it home from 1903-1930. My archaeology students conducted surveys and an excavation as mitigation for the damage to Japanese cultural resources caused by the restoration of the stream to its historic channel and the construction of fish ladders requested by Tulalip Tribes. In November 2012, two weeks after construction ended, we documented Coho spawning again in the stream after a decades-long absence. They have returned every year since.

Oral traditions connected the Japanese families from Mukilteo with those incarcerated at Minidoka during World War II. The school pictures, the leather soles of their shoes, household ceramics and broken glass told stories of families that recalled, for me, memories of Japanese laborers on the Murphy homestead in Hazelton, Idaho. Masura Odoi, a Japanese elder, remembered an idyllic childhood in Japan Town Mukilteo he called "a Garden of Eden" in contrast to his experiences at Minidoka. I returned to the stream with human ecology and bioanthropology students for the next seven years, monitoring water quality and counting the salmon that had finally come home. When we found that pollutants coming off of roads in the watershed were killing Coho before they could spawn, my cultural anthropology students worked with local cities and homeowners to build rain gardens that would clean storm water before it entered streams. Reflecting on her service-learning experience, one of my students wrote, "Visiting Japanese Gulch makes me think of Minidoka." Me, too! The revelations of my childhood had given way to repatriation as my students and I documented struggling but resurgent salmon runs in a watershed once shared with some of the same Japanese families later released as day laborers to work farms in the Snake River basin.

If we can repatriate salmon then what about other cultural and natural treasures? In recent years Angelo Baca and I have collaborated on academic articles calling for repatriation of seer stones and sacred items taken by Mormon founders from the lands of Haudenosaunee and others as well as papyri taken illegally from Egyptian tombs. While we can view Joseph Smith as a product of his settler culture, he set a regrettable example with grave consequences for successive generations of Latter-day Saints who have learned that it is okay to take sacred records, artifacts, and even remains from human graves. Mormons have searched the mountains and valleys of Utah and beyond for items that might lend credibility to the claims of scripture. While calling ourselves Saints we have stolen dozens of human remains and hundreds of grave goods from places like San Juan County, Utah, and displayed them in church museums in Salt Lake City. Church museums advertised the bodies of the dead as "Cliff Dwellers" and "mummies," adorned "Egyptian" style, and placed them in displays alongside racks of sacred artifacts taken from the Hawaiian Islands, under protests from the royal family. The people whose graves we have disturbed have great-grandchildren, still living, who want to see their ancestors rest in peace.

Members of the American Indian Movement came to Salt Lake City in April of 1974 to share their perspectives by protesting at the Latter-day Saint General Conference. Ojibwe organizer Vernon Bellecourt decried the church's Indian programs for engaging in "acts of cultural and religious genocide." A Tuscarora activist named Wallace "Mad Bear" Anderson traveled from the lands of the Haudenosaunee to Temple Square to ask for the repatriation of Indigenous ancestors on display in church museums, so that they could be given "a proper burial" and sent "back to the spirit world in a proper way." The collection of skeletons and artifacts from San Juan County were moved to the Museum of Peoples and Cultures at Brigham Young University a few years later. Mad Bear's request for repatriation was not honored until well after the passage of NAGPRA in 1990.

Two decades after federal legislation required consultation

with tribal leaders, BYU finally returned the human remains the church had once displayed as mummies, akin to those from Egypt, to their culturally affiliated relatives in Hopi, Paiute, Zuni, and Pueblo nations. We should have known better. In a much less well-known story than that of disturbing the grave of Zelph, Joseph Smith set a better example. In an act of diplomacy at Nauvoo in the 1840s the prophet made a gift of a portion of Egyptian papyri, from which he had translated the Book of Abraham, to the Potawatomi people. While from today's perspective, we might expect papyri to be repatriated to Egypt, he seems to have believed he was returning it to its rightful heirs, Indigenous people he believed had descended from Abraham. His colleagues, too, had regrets about their treatment of Zelph. Heber C. Kimball, in his journal, described having "very peculiar feelings, to see the bones of our fellow creatures scattered." Wilford Woodruff felt so ashamed of stealing Zelph's "thigh bone" that he reburied it in Clay County, Missouri, in apparent remorse.

To stop the perpetual onslaught of environmental degradation and looting of important cultural sites in San Juan County in the 2010s, the nonprofit Utah Diné Bikéyah sought the assistance of predominantly LDS elected officials in an effort to protect sacred land around Bears Ears. Disappointed by the politicians, the Diné turned to their Indigenous neighbors, some of whom were once traditional enemies, to build a coalition with Hopi, Zuni, Ute, and Ute Mountain Ute nations to advocate for a national monument at Bears Ears. Their successful efforts in the waning days of the Obama administration yielded unprecedented results: a national monument designation that paired traditional knowledge holders with scientists to collaboratively manage these important public lands. Utah's elected officials, however, lobbied the incoming Trump administration to dismember and shrink Bears Ears and Escalante National Monuments. On the same 2017 trip to Utah to celebrate the dismemberment of Bears Ears, President Trump met with LDS church leaders. My colleague, Angelo

Baca, lamented, "They have sacrificed their own Mormon values and beliefs." When asked to work together to protect lands and cultural resources of importance to tribal communities, those who call ourselves Saints have too often failed to rise to the challenge. It seems that many Latter-day Saints are more comfortable telling Native Americans about their history as imagined in scripture rather than making it anew alongside them.

As a Boy Scout at Camp Little Lemhi, I learned to value environmental service and ecological knowledge. That childhood inspired a career as an anthropologist blending traditional teachings and science together through community-based service-learning. The stories I had learned from the Book of Mormon obstructed genuine engagement with Native peoples. My callous disregard for the dead changed after I bungled the handling of someone's clavicle and then discovered that the bones of my Indigenous grandmother were missing too. I had to abandon sacrilege and historicity to change course. Revelations gave way to relations, which ultimately fostered repatriation. I invite those who share a Mormon heritage to listen to those who differ from us, restore habitat, remove dams, protect public lands, and to repatriate human remains and sacred objects taken without regard for their living descendants.

The Bears Ears Inter-Tribal Coalition would gladly welcome more Mormons as allies, or better yet, as collaborators in protecting cultural and natural treasures. "We seek help from all nations in building strong alliances and partnerships with the international community, tribal leaders, elders, traditional knowledge holders and native non-profit organizations to help Utah Diné Bikéyah and Indigenous communities restore land protections and promote healing for all," Angelo Baca wrote in 2018 to the United Nations Permanent Forum on Indigenous Issues. There is clearly room at the table for more Latter-day Saints to collaborate in the protection of lands, where we, too, share sacred places. Settler Mormons no longer need to dress and act like "Indians" or dig up the grandparents of Indigenous peoples to feel connected with the land. Instead, we can stand shoulder to shoulder with Indigenous colleagues as we work collaboratively to repatriate lost ancestors and cultural and natural treasures. Avoiding these ethical responsibilities will have grave consequences for us all.

INHERIT

Melody Newey Johnson

I Sleep Beneath a Quilt

I sleep beneath a quilt
and dream of cotton, lace, silk;
of women's hands held just-so;
the needle set, thread pulled
through beeswax, over tongue,
stitches sung while women sew

memories. I sleep beneath
music made by women's hands,
dream beneath a quilt made by
my grandmothers and while I sleep
they lay their needles down and
touch my feet. They lay their quilted

hands on my head, heart, belly
breast and bless me. What is
the garment of God's love if
not a quilt, a blanket blessing
from the hands who made it?
Who dressed us when we left the

garden? Who made the skins
we wear? I wake beneath a quilt
sung by the Mother, her music
weaving sunrise through darkness,
her visage wrapped around me in
grandmother's flower garden and stars.

Reb Cuevas

When the Ground Shakes

"Your ancestors were doing a healing dance," said Susan. And I didn't ask questions. I nodded, doubtful even as my scalp lit up at the suggestion. But I might have asked what they'd looked like to her.

She saw things sometimes when she treated me: spectators of our aromatherapy sessions, visitors. I want to describe them, and my imagination yearns toward a pre-colonial American magic; it calls on the genesis of my father's trajectory. Whatever Susan had actually pictured as the healing dance of my ancestors, I summon *la danza Azteca.*

Mi'totiliztli.

They are as brown as the soil they collected from lake bottoms and piled onto the floating gardens of Tenochtitlan, the seat of the Aztec Empire. Men and women alongside each other, vibrant in regalia glittering in precious metals, polished stone— the women in tunics and the men in chest-wear and loincloths, *maaxtlati.* Shells and seed pods tremble around their ankles, clatter in *maraca* prototypes. Pheasant and eagle feathers blossom from their headdresses like sun rays. They beat gourds tensed with animal hide, and *teponaztle,* slit-drum logs engraved with story. They wake the gods.

Susan's suggestion that otherworldly entities took notice of my pain was a boon. I sat a while in my car after such sessions, lingering in a transcendent ASMR-buzz for as long as it would last. *Autonomous Sensory Meridian Response.* Braingasms. Hybrid bursts of euphoric paresthesia and synesthesia traveling my scalp, neck, and limbs. A phenomenon of the medial prefrontal cortex, ASMR is said to be evolutionarily linked to the act of grooming in primates, a bonding instinct. The hypotheses proliferate, but I didn't have to understand it to experience it, and for these flashes of inexplicable respite, I would gratefully shelve my skepticism.

ASMR was a reminder that I could feel something other than sick, sleepless, and scared. And it was triggered so rarely that the first rash of tingles through my scalp was like the finger of god on my third eye.

~

Another time Susan said, "I felt your grandmother." Again, I didn't question her. But only one of my grandmothers was dead then. Emilia. My father's mother. A woman I was certain I mostly annoyed while she was alive. Now I imagined her sympathetic, in tune with our mutual ancestors, though I'd never learned to speak her language, not well—either Spanish or the peculiar speech of mothers. I especially never mastered the language of belief, her transplant Mormon tongue.

I crave a mystic energy beyond the dogma of still, small voices and a god of rules—his redemptive love like a promise at the end of a maze. I tired of the null repetitions, the dogged claim to morality, but something remains of my early religious training. The longing for the miraculous abides like a predisposition.

Susan deviated from our shared Mormon vernacular and told me things that brought Indigenous imagery to my mind, a bountiful call toward my unharvested roots. She made me feel that I wasn't alone with my panic and pills, alcohol and Ensure, my mantras. Together with my counselor, she made me feel, perhaps especially, that at the darkest time of my life I wasn't alone with my floundered Mormon faith, fending for myself.

I loved the smells of the oils she'd pick for me—eucalyptus and ylang-ylang, lavender and rosemary. I left her house soaked in a perfume of promised wellness. Susan knew I wasn't sick in the traditional sense, but that I came to her every Tuesday for several weeks with a need, and she believed in the power of her touch, the wellspring properties of her oils. They'd unclasp my nervous system, cleanse my fountainhead. I believed I needed *something*—a soft touch, a sweet voice, good smells, a few minutes of calm—to help me through what my counselor called a period of adjustment anxiety. What it felt like was a prolonged panic attack, a cryptic certainty that I'd shattered whatever vessel for happiness I was handed at birth.

I'd clung to, then finally severed, a toxic relationship that sent me white-knuckled into therapy. I'd quit a triggering job, but before both I'd left my childhood faith and a seven-year marriage. The emotions manifested like addiction withdrawals and PTSD. I was losing weight and sleep for no other reason, it felt, than my failure to appreciate how many people had it worse.

I felt stupid and melodramatic, helpless, and broken at an unreachable depth.

~

During my personal epoch between the chickenpox and acne, my skin color regularly rivaled my fast-tanning Mexican father's. He was in continual battle with his particular strain of Meso-american blood as every summer he tried not to get "too dark," having made a connection between the ways he was treated in both Mexico and the US, the ways he felt about himself, and the gradient of his skin tone.

Then, one summer before the seventh grade, I was the one who got too dark. And then, within the span of weeks, my face went from the darkest it could get to the whitest I'd ever seen it. An invisible threshold was crossed. I don't know how else to describe the appearance of pale spots on my otherwise chocolate forehead and cheeks. These spots spread daily into geographic patches, devouring my tan the way water travels through fabric, a percolating migration. By the end my face was ghost white. Only gradually, as I entered adulthood, could it tan again.

Lacking a dermatologist's explanation, I've decided that my sunscreen-free childhood overwhelmed my pigment's ability to tan, rebooting to a default setting as stark as printer paper. I also suspect the interference of puberty; everything about my body was subject to drastic upheaval. Now my skin fluctuates hues like a mood ring, lightening and deepening with the seasons, but the patches have never returned.

In the midst of my childhood, from the early nineties on, my dad was quietly writing a novel he would one day commission me to co-author and publish, my brother to illustrate. He began it shortly after his immigration as a way to organize his past. To wrestle it. I think even to reinvent it. It's fiction, crafted in his second language, and spans the life of Pedro, a boy of Holmesian intellect, good looks, and generous opportunity. Unlike my father, Pedro is born into wealth. He is never hungry. His father figure is present and hardworking. His adoptive mother is a scholar and devoted mentor who molds him for greatness from day one.

Though his material circumstances echo nothing from my dad's reality, apart from his place of birth in rural Mexico, Pedro's personal traits are clearly intended to mirror or amplify my father's—except for one: in my dad's earliest drafts, Pedro was criollo—Spanish-descended, the progeny of conquistadors.

Pedro was white.

~

I'm guilty of a lazy genealogical appetite. On my mother's side there are books I've never read that trace the Berrett/Gerber journey from Germany and the early British Isles to Zion. And it wasn't until researching for the rewrite of his novel that I learned about at least one centuries-old branch on my dad's side that breaks with "Indian slave—parents unknown." Andrea de la Cruz, my distant relative, lived almost as near to the reign and conquest of our Aztec progenitors as I now do to the conception of Mormonism.

Your ancestors were doing a healing dance. Andrea, my ancestors—they are my summer skin, my Sunday-skirted girl-hood twirling, myself in a club with an instinct to jump, my skin on fire. The gods have awoken and *la danza Azteca* continues.

A man leads them, the *tlayeconqui*, and their movements are prayer, a solemn flow. They step and stomp and twirl. They cry out. It is a bid for cosmic communion, elemental integration. I proxy myself to their shapes. I lift and open my palms to the sky. The drums sound; we hold our gods' attention. I listen too. There is an answer all around me. I put my hands to the soil; I crouch and turn on my heels. I rise and step. I am soaring. The grand *penacho* fixed to my head streams and floats with my movements. I cry out. The drums sound. Our feet stomp a restive rattle. Seeds and shells shiver in our hands. The drums sound. I cry out. Enter celestial vibrations—the drums guide me. I cry. I stomp. The ground shakes.

I take whatever I can.

~

By thirty years old I wanted out of Utah so badly I was willing to follow a man back to a town I'd left twenty-three years before, an objectively desolate place I never imagined I'd move back to. But my fiancé graduated in physics and made himself attractive to the hungry recruiters of the Naval Air Weapons Station in Ridgecrest, California.

Turnover is high on the base, especially for those averse to yucca- and snake-strewn landscapes and intense summer heat.

My dad worked there for eleven years until impulse prompted him to relocate his family of nine back to Utah. He had no job lined up and no real problem with the heat, but he wanted to be closer to family, and to curtail the chance that one or most of his children would sink into the local meth plague or get pregnant before graduation. For enough people there's nothing to do there but fuck and toke.

An hour and a half's drive from the hottest place on earth—Death Valley National Park—Ridgecrest attracts foreigners seeking novel experiences in the armpit of hell, or mountaineers with an eye on Mount Whitney. There is nowhere more populous for a hundred miles in every direction. Returning, sea-changed, I absolutely loved it for all the reasons I'd once hated it.

I was born in Ridgecrest Regional Hospital and for years I thrived in the lizard-brain confidence of an impetuous, largely untracked fifth child of seven. All I remember of those years are pupa scenes of desert romping, playgroup spats, and barging in on neighbors.

"Are you still writin'?" asked one such neighbor on a visit back in my early twenties.

"Was I writing back then?" I said, surprised. I was accustomed to invoking my fourth-grade teacher as the reason I started writing, years after we'd moved out of Ridgecrest.

"No, rotten!" said the neighbor, a woman whose cigarette butts my brother and I once plucked out of the gutter and put in our mouths.

I felt myself flush even as I laughed. "Was I rotten?"

She said we'd routinely tromp up her porch to ask for candy. As far as I know, though, I never entered her house leading a passel of friends to jump on her couch, as I'd done to another neighbor. I was rotten. But in Utah, after straying from a formula that had preceded me for generations, I was rotting. Ridgecrest now became a site of aggressive individuation. What remained of the rot that had soured the core of my Utah experience, the smog that had pooled in the valleys of my Wasatch life in Provo, Orem, Salt Lake City, I was eager to cleanse.

I gave the same answer to anyone who asked how I was doing in the middle of nowhere: "I love the isolation." I finished rewriting my dad's novel. Medi-Cal matched me with a physical therapist who helped me start running again without knee pain. I lived in daily range of ravens warbling in palm trees, nudging me toward romantic introspection.

When the casualties of vaping began to make headlines, I saved my toking for the weekends until one Friday morning I coughed blood into the sink. At the end of 2019, my fiancé and I moved back to Utah's air quality—some of the worst in the US— and I bought a mask to wear on my runs. Better the poison I choose than the poison chosen for me. It is now the same mask I wash and re-wear through the COVID-19 pandemic, a disease that stifles the lungs. It seems the world conspires to choke us, while the ground beneath our feet lulls us into a false sense of stability.

Ridgecrest was sabbatical. Occasionally the ground shook, but it was mostly imperceptible until July 4, 2019, when the largest earthquake to hit California in twenty years threw my haven of isolation into the national spotlight.

∼

My skin color links me to a specific history. *Indian slave—parents unknown.* But I'm not unique, and neither is Mormonism in its attempt to divine meaning from biology. A white man from the early nineteenth century claimed an answer to Indian origins, called their color a curse, and a brown girl over 150 years later was helped to understand that the lingering vestiges of that curse would be lifted once she got to heaven. Nothing I saw in Mormon depictions of heaven refuted an all-white throng of the saved. If I made it there, I would see my color dissolve into shocking whiteness, just as I had that summer before middle school, and I imagine I would feel the same mortification and regret.

I am not unique.

My experiences fizzled during a time of transition within the church, but there were those who came before me in their significant dark skin, shouldering crimes that ranged from the infuriating to the unimaginable—the Native American children rehomed during the Indian Student Placement Program of 1947 to the '90s; Jane Elizabeth Manning James, who was sealed to Joseph Smith for time and all eternity *as his servant*; Thomas Coleman, a Black church member who was murdered, brutally, in Salt Lake City for courting a white woman. Coleman's manner of death echoed the temple's "blood atonement" ritual as well as sanctions issued by Brigham Young condoning the slaying of mixed-race families.

I am not unique. And neither is the church as an enduring, sluggishly adapting institution that was founded—and for generations operated—by racists. During the '70s, parsing out eternal blessings to select bloodlines became untenable as the church's missionary efforts ventured into the racial morass of Brazil, of the world at large, and as social pressure to end its discriminatory practices intensified. By the time I was born, Black men in the church and their families had enjoyed full access to the highest tier of heaven via the priesthood for a mere nine years, while its spokespersons still preached the sin of interracial marriage.

Today the church disavows all notions of white supremacy as it scrubs existing curricula and reinterprets scripture. But my parents, both devout, married in a tunnel of progressive interpretation for their time. Certainly, the prophet of their era advised against it at the pulpit, but my father, lacking "a drop" of African blood, was still permitted access to the temple where they married. In fact, he and his children won some distinction as the descendants of Israelites-turned-Lamanites, even if his darkness still proved difference. Lamanites were cursed because of "iniquity." Until recent revisions to past prophetic discourse, the mark they bore to distinguish them from the worthy was their color.

I remember the phone call. I was in the early stages of revision, puzzling out the physical descriptions of Pedro as a young boy. I pictured him as a tiny version of my father, but where I wanted to describe his hair as "inky," my dad insisted it should be "honey." I was still learning the semantics of the time and location—of criollo versus mestizo, cholo and coyote—often antiquated or derogatory terms to delineate the variety of racial mixing between Indians and Africans, Spanish and all of the above.

I asked my dad to send me pictures of how he imagined his characters to look.

"Dad," I said. "Did you notice that only your antagonists are brown?"

I didn't doubt his surprise. He hadn't thought of it. These had not been fully conscious decisions, but something trained in him, something compelled to become instinctual.

"I want Pedro to be mestizo," I said. "I want him to look like us."

~

Andrea de la Cruz was the daughter of unknown parents, a slave of Indigenous origin, and on April 20, 1727, she married Juan Antonio de Cuebas Sossa—the criollo son of slave owners—in Jalisco, Mexico. My ancestors, all of them. Slave and master. After our conversation, my dad remembered Andrea and Juan—they became the new inspirations for Pedro's parents, and he became mestizo.

Andrea was Aztec, her own ancestors likely subjugated by Hernán Cortés during the conquest of the Aztec Empire and construction of New Spain in the 1500s. It is said that when Cortés and his men arrived at Tenochtitlan, now present-day

Mexico City, they entered in awe, thoroughly mystified by the engineering wonders of a kingdom on a lake, its floating gardens and pathways, its aqueducts and freshwater baths. The Spanish had come from scenes of billowing industry and plague—disease that would assist in wiping out at least 90 percent of the Indigenous population.

Cortés and his like led a campaign of exploitation and reaping, guided by ambition, faith, greed, fear, and whatever else propels a human body over ocean fathoms toward discovery. Each of us bears a bleak and storied inheritance. My Aztec ancestors believed that the sun would not rise if they failed to slake the thirst of their many gods. Only "precious water" would appease them, the water of life, the dearest thing a human body could give. The Aztec gods demanded blood.

I am not one-of-a-kind. And neither is a Spanish conquistador, nor an Aztec sovereign with his hand on a blade. They washed the walls of their temples in blood, sent headless bodies tumbling by the hundreds down temple steps. The Spanish claimed horror at the sight of these rituals and then set about the business of massacre and domination. Human sacrifice is by no means exclusive to "the savage," by no means relegated to the fringe of Christian civilization, and by no means over. The Mormon Church has recently changed its discourse on suicide, on the post-mortal fate of the person who takes their own life, as the bodies of its youth tumble too.

What do I do with these legacies? How do I reconcile my quest for old magic with a philosophy that does no harm? The gods aren't real and they don't want our blood. But I'm still afraid the sun won't rise.

~

It's like betrayal. When the ground beneath you undulates like water, how do you process? That was never supposed to happen under *your* feet.

Ridgecrest sits in the Eastern California Shear Zone, a convergence of fault strands that alleviate the stressors that will one day trigger the dreaded San Andreas. The July 2019 earthquakes toppled chimneys, severed highways, unseated trailer homes, and sparked fires—all totaling over one billion dollars in damages. The tremors reached Nevada and killed a man who had been working under his Jeep.

After the quake, I slept outside for several nights cuddling my border collie. Community posts on the Ridgecrest Facebook group were a study of paranoia during the series of aftershocks—*Did you feel that?* and *Get out while you can! I have a bad feeling!* I marked it as personal progress that my own anxiety was in check. Sleeping outside was a welcome novelty and even my border collie feared the persistent Fourth of July fireworks far more than the tremblors. We were lucky. Aside from a bit of shattered glassware, we were out of power for a day and work for a week. But some people had children who couldn't sleep. Others lost their homes.

It strikes me that in the wake of earthly rupture my ancestors would have sought explanation in the metaphysical, in the portent of blood and the distance of the cosmos. It makes simple sense to counter bad feelings with senseless action, but heads roll at the intersection of fear and belief, ignorance and superstition. I respect violence like I respect pollution. Like disease.

Give me barrier and intervention. Give me kind solution.

I am not unique. I take whatever I can. I am moved in the pattern of my ancestors, my cyclical migration, my star search. Eucalyptus for recovery. Lavender for calm. Ylang-ylang to jolt my child-brain to attention. Fear abated, postponed and intervened, I wake the god of my own disposition. I write and bounce my leg, put my hands to soil, to warm and loving bodies. Enter celestial vibrations.

The ground shakes. I listen.

Megan Fairbanks

Iosepa

Take the I-80 from Antelope Island,
west through barren mud flats.
Watch for telltale tire tracks on the empty plain—
the brave ones have waded out
with heavy stones in their pockets,
to spell out things like "love u Barb"
or "screw you" in slow-sucking squares
of salt sludge. Go around the mountain that,
from your home, looks blue and snow-capped
and beautiful but close-up is just like *your* mountain:
sage-brushed and sun-burnt, smelling of clay.
Pass over a cattle guard (or three) and you will find
a valley that might have been yours
before the cities were built:
waves of golden grass surrounding
a great stone plateau
that boy scouts sometimes camp around
in pale dots that could be mistaken
for the cool indifference of sheep,
on the lam from their silent owners,
seeking refuge on land that is
untouched by the order of people
who have never bothered to look across
to the cave on the other side of Ditto,
our version of Area 51,
where military doughboys poured a slab of
concrete for dancing, unaware of the cemetery

parallel to their music and headlight brights.
This valley knows to hold its secrets,
but walk the survey trenches in the July heat,
watch for the darkest strip of earth
that runs like a road through the topsoil,
and you'll see.

Once, there were green things here.

RISE

Lisa Bickmore

Vesper Sparrow on a Fence Post

made of pine, no plinth but the ground,
yarrow and balsamroot gracing the foot,
the bird of a genus the synonym,
precisely, of small bird, of common.

I think: at its divine office, the sixth
canonical hour, it sings, although
the guide to bird life suggests it sings
in the morning, too. Just now, it perches,

poised, prepared to loose, I imagine,
its psalmody, its *in adiutorium*
meum intende. Of course we're in
Idaho, and not one of those rites

is my own: only we're walking along
the Henry's Fork, the river making
its way north to the sea: a river
I've returned to nearly every year

of my life, so a language for that,
hierophantic, or at least attuned
to a sacred day's hours, is what's called for:
words that arise from the sky to the west

touching the far range. Or from an old
volcanic surge, from the birds that follow

the river as a byway. A language
that exceeds field guides and pamphlets

from the agricultural extension:
derived from my kora at the river bank,
the lengthening recitative of birds,
and their habitats, their disappearances

and returns: a language that is both
home and exile, that scatters and gathers
an antiphon in my ear: noise of water-
clatter, a dun bird on its shorn tree.

ODE

The white horses by the lake lift their heads
to see whose feet make a plodding tattoo
on the road: mine, dear white horses:
I'm advancing a hypothesis that I can run,
even as my years advance, adding
evidence to the brief against
my ineluctable decline.

White horses, gleaming across the damp,
across riparian grasses and untidy trees—
dear pearl of the sky, with belled canopy
and sheen, I stop to take a photograph
of the horses, using the rule of thirds to frame it—
more a rule of quarters, to capture more sky—
I love you more even than white horses
in the rain, constant but not somehow
insistent, beading my hair and needling

my shirt. Birds in transit, if these were my waters,
I could name you; still, I watch you move
from ground to sky, the cloudy corridors
and vestibules for your traverse, and
watching you, for once the world feels
reasonable, knit of many skeins but
of similar weights, as you purl

the cumulonimbus, drawing the sky
nearer, though only when I half-say it,
turning an idea of the unreachable
familiar. Your gray bellies mirror the crowns

of the oaks and alder, and in your unseen
fingers combing the leaves, I see
that you too are stirred by something
invisible, the only evidence being that drift,
like the little breath of cold air that seeps in
around the edges of an old window:
the soft inhalation of a mover, I think,
for no reason except I like it, a name
for that breath other than equations
someone has devised to describe it,

dear space I hold open against all evidence:
the ones who have passed before me
are nowhere to be seen, I hear no trace
of their speech, no matter how I figure
what is above me: trees not yet aflame,
your blossom just finished, I won't
be here in autumn when the cold
will set color in your leaves, fire
that burns but does not consume:
and thus I won't hear *draw not nigh hither,*
put off thy shoes, though I am always
prepared for a thing to be holy.

Julie J. Nichols

EXTINCTION ILLNESS
AND OTHER STORIES

1959, Orinda, California.

"WHOSE IS THIS?" MY FATHER BRANDISHES MY JOHNNY before my siblings and me, the teddy bear's brown coat patchy, the stitch of his nose pulled free, my furry friend left in my private sanctuary under the garage till I could get back there for another reading session. But Dad hates disorder. He's just been down to the storeroom for something else and found the doesn't-belong-there-bear. "I've told you." Dad waves the bear threateningly. "If you leave something where it doesn't belong, it gets thrown away. Say goodbye." And he whisks the bear away.

I may be young enough to love a teddy bear, but I'm not too young to recognize unfairness. My dad, who is supposed to love and protect me, is willing to toss out the things I care about if I don't do with them what he wants. I'd better toe the line—or learn to face injustice.

1967, Orinda.

Michelle and her lesbian mother; Greta and her Icelandic family; artist Bernice with her quiet wit—these people in my high school fascinate me. I fascinate them too. That I go to early morning Mormon seminary, that I talk about Jesus as if I know the One True Story, that despite these aberrations I write poems as good as theirs and sometimes better—I'm as exotic to them as they are to me. I hang out with them, buy the Grateful Dead and Steeleye Span albums they listen to, attend the Friday night Balkan folkdance class they love where the line dance "Ma Navu" has the same name as Joseph Smith's sacred city. I don't do drugs. Michelle and Greta and Bernice don't do drugs either, but they're campers in the wilderness, sisters to clever older brothers who drive their cars through the Bay Area fog over the hill to Berkeley where protests are going on, life is happening, stories are being questioned, revised, replaced. They might do drugs, as far as my father knows. It's true their difference from my sheltered Mormon life stimulates me like a drug. What they think, do, and say tempers what my dad and mother teach. I'm addicted to them. On Sundays I go to the Lafayette-Orinda Ward and raise my hand with all the right answers to Sunday school questions, but during the week, I align myself with these women so closely my dad interferes. "Your friends are *dirty*," he says. "Why don't you go to charm school? Why don't you learn to be—well, not *hippie*?"

1971, Orinda to Provo, Utah.
"I'm not paying for your college," my dad says. "If you can get a scholarship to BYU, great, I'll pay for your dorm and food. But I'm not paying tuition." I don't believe I can pay my own way anywhere else, so off I go, on a full-ride scholarship to what is arguably the most conservative, least free university in the United States. One of my favorite dorm-mates, from Orange County, has a silver tooth, lets me listen to my Joni Mitchell albums on her turntable, isn't in any sense of the word Mormon.

1976, Salt Lake City.
I live alone in a studio apartment on 1200 East while I'm doing an editing internship at the Church Office Building. On Sundays I go to a grad student branch of the University of Utah,

where my friends are refreshingly outside the box—edgy, smart, funny. One day a Sunday school teacher says, "Everything Jesus did—all the miracles, all the healing—you can do it too. All of it." He excludes the Atonement, the taking on of the sins of the world, what Rudolf Steiner calls "the miracle at Gethsemane." But everything else, the teacher says, anyone can do. I take note of this. It resonates with me, it goes on the same shelf as the meditation Michelle practices, the yoga Bernice pursues, the taking-for-granted of Norse mythology that Greta embodies. I tuck it away, keep it safe and private for some other unknown time.

1980, Provo, Utah.
For a few years now I've been married to a reformed black sheep, a dyslexic cowboy with ADD whom my father can't quite like. I have two small children. I've been in shock since we married: neither marriage in general nor this man in particular is the answer I thought it would be. And frankly, I've lost track of the question. I feel raw and scraped. Bernice and her man Yaz come to visit me and do not miss the visible manifestations of my trauma, my consternation.

"Are you happy?" they ask.

I look away, I look everywhere but at them. They see that *I* am lost, nothing that makes me *me* is here. "I don't know what to do," I tell them.

"Oh," says Yaz, understanding. "Wait, though. You do have your answers. You just have to find them." They hug me and continue on their earnest way to a yurt community in Jackson Hole.

What Yaz says burns me. The University of Utah Sunday school teacher's claim about Jesus drifts back into my mind. I reread the New Testament, asking, "How? How did Jesus do what he did? What made him who he was—was there really One True Story? If everyone can do what he did, how can I, and thereby maybe find my answers?"

I'll bet few Mormons read the New Testament the way I read it that year. I start praying for answers, even though I don't know the questions. I take my children to the Provo library and find Susan Cooper's *The Dark is Rising* series, where a Lady protects and guides the friends of Merlin and saves them in moments of despair. I write to Susan Cooper: Who is the Lady? She has the grace to write back. I could never be a Mormon, she says, but I'll tell you, you have to find the Lady yourself. She is everywhere. Read *The White Goddess*, she says, maybe that will give you some direction. I go to the BYU library—by now I'm adjunct faculty there, earning the income my husband doesn't make—and I find Robert Graves's 1948 "grammar of poetic myth" right next to Christ and Plaskow's *Womanspirit Rising: A Feminist Reader in Religion.*

During that same time, a student in a creative nonfiction class I co-teach—a fairly forward-seeing class for the 1980s—writes a paper about real magic. What she writes resonates with the books I'm finding everywhere I turn these days, titles like *Jesus the Magician* and *When God Was a Woman* and *The Chalice and the Blade.* I ask her to talk to me more about "real magic"—what does she mean? How do I—what is it I want to know?—*how do I find what you're talking about?* "You can find your way in to magic anywhere," she tells me. "Sci-fi movies—look at *Star Wars!* People are flocking to it! But so many other things—alternative medicine. Environmentalism. Great literature. Art, music—heck, you can find it *knitting* if you're going at it right. Real magic is in everything." Yaz was right. My answers are dropping into my hands.

1996, Cotati, California.
I begin a six-year-long study program with an energy healer/bodywork master, after some years' journey in which the genealogy of my reading and research expands vertically and horizontally. Myth, gender studies, feminist spirituality, goddesses

and Wicca. Tarot. Consciousness. Meditation. All more or less secretive, during a period in which I give birth to two more children—at home, with the help of herb-administering midwives—teach technical and creative writing at BYU, and earn a PhD in fiction writing at the University of Utah.

In Cotati, the teacher shows by action and example and hands-on experience, how Jesus did what he did, better than any Mormon General Conference talk ever has. He says, when I push against the differences between his studio in Cotati and my life in Provo: "Here's how you know you still have lessons to learn: you're still breathing." Oh. So *all* this is my path, is it? This *is* who I am. Oh.

Photos of me during that time show wide-open eyes, a straight back, a clear open face welcoming whatever comes. I write and publish stories of what I'm learning, fearless and fine.

1998, Provo, Utah.

The head of the English department at BYU calls me into his office and asks, "That story you just published in *Sunstone*—is the lesbian protagonist you?"

"It's fiction," I remind him. "People of all kinds experience conflict on many levels. It's a story about things I've observed to be true."

"Can you recant, though?" he asks. "It'll save your job."

"Recant fiction? Are you kidding? What is there to recant? It's a good story. The characters are authentic. The conflict is real."

He laughs ruefully. "Oh, it's a good story—almost too good. Mature and sophisticated. And unsuitable for our students. I'm afraid we're going to have to let you go."

The memory of my father throwing away my Johnny-bear floats into my body. "That's a shame," I say. I mean it. Injustice is always shameful. "This job is a lifeline for me," I tell him honestly. "It's our family's income. My son's just been called on a mission—"

"If you can't recant—"

I can't, and I don't. My job is terminated. My income is cut off, my service to bright young people (including gay BYU students who can't come out to anyone else and women who are coming into their own voice) is severed.

I'm offered a temporary position at the University of Utah, but I fail at it. When the program in Cotati ends, I set up an office in Salt Lake's hip Ninth and Ninth district from which I do energy work and lead workshops in writing as healing modality, but I make barely enough there to cover expenses. I stop writing. I'm afraid of not having an income, so I take work teaching at a rural campus where students prefer rodeo to reading, where my "real magic" is of about as much use as orchids in a cactus patch. My eyes squint. My brain is full of stress.

2016, Orem, Utah.

For a decade now I've been a tenured professor of creative writing at Utah Valley University. The stories the BYU department head asked me to recant almost twenty years ago have been published with some others as a book. One of my reviewers complains about the magical elements. "She loves nature, anyway," the reviewer says, "so I'm willing to overlook this other—"

I don't respond. What is there to say? "Real magic"—the action of energy and consciousness—*resides* in nature. Which includes, but is not limited to, human beings. Miracles, "supernatural" things, happen, and I acknowledge them, I write about them.

The book doesn't get me fired—I'm tenured already. But I don't write anything new.

2018, Provo, Utah, and Alameda and Topanga, California.

My father died eight years ago and now my mother has passed away after fourteen months in a memory care facility where I watched her decline in a downpour of guilt, sorrow, shame.

Shortly after her funeral I attend a writing retreat led by Deena Metzger, psychotherapist, environmental activist, and healer whose *Writing for Your Life* altered my teaching forever some years ago. She writes about the connections between animals and humans, overconsumption and environmental collapse, separation from nature and mental illness. She's written a widely published essay accusing the entire human race of drawing down upon ourselves what she calls "extinction illness." She makes no bones about it: we are causing the end of the world.

I weep throughout the retreat. Other attendees write moving passages about the earth, their relationships with animals, their grief over species loss and climate change and environmental collapse, while I struggle to write anything beyond my memories of my mother's last days. "Why are you crying so much?" Deena asks, but I don't have words. I came here to try to start writing again, and all I can think of is my mother's downward spiral into dementia. Deena prompts us to write how every experience—any experience—is the story of our life. Is this mine? My mother lost, my writing out of reach, the earth in its last throes?

Deena agrees to mentor me privately for a few months. I believe I just want a writing coach, but she therapizes me, digging into the stories of my father, the healer, the department head. She reads my 2016 collection, saying, "The good news is, you're a fine writer. The bad news? Well—you're not writing. Why is that? Your answers may be—everywhere."

In her view of things, my blocked throat chakra is intimately tied to the anarchy now loosed upon the world. (My 2015 sabbatical was a Yeats pilgrimage to Ireland: I know exactly what she means.) But I don't want to hear it. I don't want to think about extinction illness, either. Isn't it easier just to do what needs to be done, the daily things, the expected moves? Stop *thinking*. But she won't let me. They're the same thing. The end of *story*. Earth's soils are depleted. Noise and light pollute the planet as surely as particulate matter in the air. Violence is everywhere.

Species are dying, languages are dying, *we* are dying. When the ice caps melt, when wildfires rage, when weather turns wicked, when coronavirus shuts down the world economy one city, one region, one country at a time; when panic infects people's hearts and overtakes their rational brains, who can possibly speak? She makes me ask. I have to find my answer.

Now. Everywhere I've ever been.
I do believe in extinction illness. COVID-19 is the ultimate extinction illness, isn't it?

What spell, what charm, what magic story was it my father invoked as we knelt in family prayer, drooping our heads over the seats of the blue kitchen chairs at six every morning of my Orinda childhood? "Grant us protection from harm, evil, or accident," he would say. He knew they were there. He lost a foot in a terrible accident when I was eight. His wife survived breast cancer. He contracted Parkinson's disease. There is harm, there is evil, there is accident. My father was the oldest child of an impoverished farm family during the Depression. Of course he insisted on order, of course he became an obsessed head of household. What an unexpected truth—that his passion for order was a stay against extinction and at the same time a trap—such that when that department head fired me on the grounds that my stories were unsuitable, when he took my job away, I believed him to be right.

～

Recently I read John Crowley's novel of extinction, *Ka: Dar Oakley in the Ruins of Ymr*. Each chapter is set in a different epoch of human civilization, leading up to and through one of many extinctions, each with new instances of human arrogance and violation. Yet the eponymous crow makes friends with humans in every period, observing their efforts, their failures, their self-destructive pain, learning from them how many ways there are to approach the end. In the concluding chapter, Crowley's narrator accompanies the crow to his next death. His depiction of the process is compelling. "In dreams," the narrator says, "we traverse other geographies....We know ourselves to be there while we are there, but we don't know how we know; it's only when we wake that we know what we saw and heard and felt... And it must be the same in the sleep of death, [but] from death we will never, never ever, wake to know of it."

"Never, never ever, wake to know of it." Why does that move me so? Dreams—I take herbs to enhance mine. Yet sometimes they frighten me, their magic dark with too much truth. So this notion of death as a dream curls tight around my heart, as I think of my mother, and my father, and the many past and future who know death.

Miraculously, in the book, after Crowley's narrator and the crow pass through the final portal, the most unexpected thing happens. *I am returned. We are still here.* It's the final line in the book. Neutral. An offering. Still breathing.

I want to hope. I want to be one of the ones who announces, by action and example, that extinction is not a final or only story. The terrible news seems to be that we are coming to annihilation, ourselves and all our relations close to the brink, driven there by inaction, bad choices, inadequate or absent words. But maybe the good news is that we're still here. We're still breathing, even when the air is full of smoke from fires a thousand miles away. I will confess: I've hired a book coach. I'm seeing an energy therapist. I'm starting to write. Maybe there are answers to be found, more stories to be written. We just have to find them, while we're still here. Keep watch with me. This time let's see if we wake up.

Tyler Chadwick

GODDESS LOOKING UP

Goddess looking up, sowing mercy
in the shadow she broadcasts like seed—
left hand sifting the infinite satchel she wears
at her hip, fingers praying each grain
as she yields them to soil. On the valley's
blank page, they punctuate
the language of wind, shape its words
into clauses the trees can understand.

As she sows, first light parts the mist, whispers
her name. Right hand to cheek, she translates
the matins' caress into the psaltery
of her skin. Her body sings azure, the tone
of a mourning dove's elegy thrumming
the cosmos she hymns with her reach.

(After *Goddess Looking Up* [2012] by J. Kirk Richards)

WANDER

Matthew Pockrus

To Twist and to Turn

THE 360-MILE, SIX-HOUR DRIVE SOUTH FROM ITS POPULA-
tion center in Salt Lake City to its relatively rarely visited
southeastern corner is one of Utah's lesser-known scenic drives.
Highway 6 carries you up-and-down Spanish Fork Canyon,
through Price, past prominent bluffs and mesas to Interstate
70, which takes you east to Crescent Junction. Exiting at Crescent Junction, it's an anxious, flat forty-five minutes past several
roadside distractions—including Canyonlands National Park
and Dead Horse Point State Park—to the steep red rock walls of
the Moab Fault. Reaching the city's northern outskirts, you'll be
challenged to fend off the enticements of Arches National Park,
cross the moat-like Colorado River, and then evade the seduc-
tions of Moab's narrow streets with their restaurants, souvenir
shops, art galleries, and tour companies. If you manage to successfully navigate these obstacles, every mile south of the city's
southern edge leaves behind overeager tourists and opens up to
the rugged sand and stone and shrubbery of the Utah desert.

Even past Moab, tourists aren't completely avoidable, of
course. Less than an hour south of Moab, Hole N" the Rock
(*sic*) is a tourist trap of the obscenest variety. The five-thousand-
square-foot twentieth-century home dug out of an iron-oxide-
rich canyon wall originally served as a family's attempt to

coalesce with, rather than build upon, the landscape. Since the homeowner's death in 1976, however, it has been added upon for the express purposes of drawing in curious foreigners and drawing out their wallets. To wit: the owners of the now-vacant abode charge six-fifty a head for tours and have added a for-profit petting zoo comprised of *exotic* non-native animals meant to placate younger and more tactile visitors. The gaudy affair is rounded out by an antique-*looking* but not antique trading post, a general store, and white letters painted glaringly upon the apricot-orange sandstone advertising its presence to passersby.

Driving swiftly—as one should—past Hole N" the Rock and continuing along US-191, drivers next encounter Monticello and Blanding and towns become sparser. As signs of settler civilization fade, it's easy to become distracted by the strata to the east—dramatic cliffs, clean-shorn by the combined powers of erosion, time, and incredible geological upheaval. These cliffs are visible records of eons of change and are punctuated by wooden utility poles perched feebly like man-made trees adrift in a red-dust sea, each signifying recent attempts to bend these unyielding landscapes to the *Western* will.

We turn right just north of Mexican Hat toward Goosenecks State Park, the road narrows into a single lane, we swerve and slow the vehicle to avoid wandering free-range cattle, and several miles down the road I dig a crumpled five-dollar bill out of the center console to cover the park's per-vehicle admission fee—for which, due to the lack of cellular service and the subsequent inability to process electronic payments, my Visa is obsolete. Another quarter mile and the road opens into a generously large and nearly vacant gravel parking lot, where we settle into a dusty unmarked parking space. I engage the emergency brake and turn the key back and my ears are jarred by the sharp, penetrating—almost hostile—silence of desert isolation, replacing the dull hum of the Saturn's V-6 engine.

As we get out of the car and stretch our tired muscles, I glance quickly over the park signage—posted in 1962 when the meager ten-acre park was set aside—and spend some time with my companion out on the rocks. We climb down the sandstone path toward an overlook nearer to the San Juan River and I take pictures with my cell phone camera. We laugh, joke, she poses for photos, we record video. It's May, eighty degrees, and sunny with clear skies. It's a beautiful day for sightseeing. Despite its remote location and tiny footprint, the park boasts sixty-odd thousand visitors a year, but it's also late afternoon on a Wednesday, so this place is empty save for a small 1980s Winnebago in the parking lot whose residents don't seem to be out and about. Still, I'm uneasy playing the role of tourist. I've seen many, and perhaps unfairly, I picture them as noisy, disrespectful litterbugs. Not long ago I worked as a landscape photographer and fancied myself a serious artist-conservationist—a wilderness defender of the Edward Abbey school of thought. As such, I struggled with hordes of tourists and their sometimes noxious habits. I'm not *not* that now, and I still fight to protect—to save—those things I love most, but in this moment I'm more focused on fighting the compulsive need to set myself apart from "ordinary tourists."

I stand on a cantilevered ledge as my friend observes uneasily from what she considers a safe distance. The slab of stone on which I'm perched is perhaps eighteen to twenty-four inches thick and plenty sturdy, but that doesn't keep either of us from doing a gut check before I walk out on it with the understanding that below me is only air for nearly a thousand feet. I gaze over the twists and turns of the San Juan River and I can't help but wonder why in this particular section—aptly named the Goosenecks—the river has bent in such dramatic ways. I'm enamored by the beauty of its curves, and understand that they were carved over the course of millions or tens of millions of years, but I can't help but wonder if it wouldn't have been easier for the water to flow in a straight line.

A seasoned geologist would be able to give me a more definitive answer, but I settle for reasoning that different rocks or layers of rock had various hardnesses and that it was inevitable that the river would carve this path, even if the course was less direct, more complicated, or required more work. Logically, this isn't a major jump for me. I sympathize with the river. Like the San Juan, my life has a defined beginning and an inescapable end. I move through this world based on a number of predefined laws—physical laws, sure, but also social and cultural laws. These are sometimes enforced by governmental authority (don't kill, don't steal), but also include rules and traditions for which I will likely face judgement, ridicule, ostracism.

Like the river, I didn't have any say in how or where I came into being. The river didn't choose to originate as snowmelt in Colorado's San Juan Mountains, any more than I chose the circumstances of my origin: my parents, my birthplace, my social or economic status, my gender, my sex, or my skin color. I didn't have a lot of say in how I embraced Mormonism—my family's religion for over a century. Like the San Juan to the Colorado, I am a tributary. My path has often deviated only slightly from those from whom I originated, often because adherence was enforced—though I admit, that enforcement wasn't always necessary. Truthfully, I had a hard time accepting that there were alternative ways of acting or passing through life. This was the result not only of my parents' brand of child-rearing, but a side-effect of residing in a place that was nearly 90 percent white and Mormon. I emerged from childhood and most of my young adulthood believing that there was a prescribed way of making it from birth to death and it appeared to me to be a straight line. I looked upon people whose lives did not align with this prescription with different eyes than the ones that gazed now upon the San Juan and its Goosenecks. Nonlinear life routes were neither beautiful nor exciting. They were confusing and unnecessary deviations from the path that to me made the most sense.

With that conviction, I made life decisions based on how well they allowed me to mitigate the risk of deviation. I took jobs that were secure and reliable. I took the classes in high school that I felt best prepared me for college. I attended a moderately priced, public in-state university and based my decision to attend primarily on the amount of scholarship money I was offered, then upon relative closeness to family and friends. I sought out roommates that shared my values and religious convictions. I declared a civil engineering major because I knew it would lead me to a career that would provide me with the financial stability I would need to support a family in what felt like an already-established linear timeline toward a future that moved seamlessly from high school to college to Mormon mission to marriage to children to death.

The first time I threw myself into a situation over which I had little control was when I filled out my application to serve a two-year Mormon mission, though calling this a risk in terms of my relationship to social and cultural norms is like calling joining the police academy a risk in terms of one's relationship to governmental authority. Even so, I had no idea where I would serve or what language I would speak. I'd had friends whose missions' most serious challenges were politely accepting a *third* free Thanksgiving dinner with members of local Mormon congregations eager to serve them, and others whose missions had seemed to be twenty-four months in unbearable climates having doors slammed in their faces. I was uncertain how true any of the stories had been, and was also unsure where my own experiences would land, so I attempted to manage my expectations. Mormons often refer colloquially to missions as "the best two years," and I suppose that unnuanced phrase captures some sense of what I wanted from it. I was comforted by the idea that I might be able to affirm the sentiment.

I received an assignment to serve in Ukraine, to speak Ukrainian and Russian.

Calling my Mormon mission "the best two years" would not be an unfair characterization, but only in the way that going to prison for a DUI might be the best thing that ever happened to an alcoholic. The work was mostly tedious, the schedule unforgiving. It was emotionally and mentally draining in a way I had never before experienced. But it was eye-opening and served as a catalyst for valuable change—though maybe not the kind the Mormon Church intended.

During my missionary service, I worked alongside people who were hurt and manipulated by the organization whose call to serve they had answered zealously. I was led by people who preached love and compassion but maintained control by establishing a strong sense of supposedly righteous fear and shame. I was publicly derided for challenging church authorities whose advice was intended to be unquestionable as they endorsed patently harmful attitudes and behaviors. I watched a country fall apart as they lost faith in their political institutions and drove their president out in the night. I watched Ukrainians *and* Mormons go to war with themselves and with their closest allies. I saw people question their political, social, national, and religious identities.

At some point along the way I met Alex, a professional genealogist who was employed by families with means to track down genealogical information in the hard-to-navigate archives of Eastern Europe. He often worked in close association with the Mormon Church, which has a famous obsession with family histories and which dedicates not-insubstantial resources to free-to-the-public family historical records and genealogical libraries. My grandparents worked in one such library—one of the church's largest—on the campus of the Mormon Church–owned Brigham Young University. In their years of volunteering, one mystery that they sought but ultimately failed to solve was the mystery of our shared surname—"Pockrus"—whose origins they were never able to trace beyond the late eighteenth century in the United States. I remember hearing at one point that they thought it was Irish and then maybe not and then Greek and then maybe German and then they were uncertain again.

While I was in Ukraine, Ukrainians asked almost daily if Pockrus was a Ukrainian name—if *I* was Ukrainian. I was flattered and told myself that it was at least in part because I was speaking their language well, but I also assumed they asked because of the name's unusual transcription from English to Ukrainian on my missionary nametag. Inexplicably, the person in charge of the transcription had spelled the name so that it was pronounced "Pōck-Rūs" (Покрусь) with a *myakiy znak*—a "soft sign" (ь)—after the last letter. I had long since concluded that this combination of the "rūs" (русь) and the *myakiy znak* (ь) drew attention because its spelling was identical to the *Kyivs'ka Rus* (Київська Русь), the original settlers of what is now Ukraine and an important part of the country's history.

Despite the frequency of the comments, I brushed them aside until I met Alex. He wasn't an on-the-street Ukrainian talking about my surname—my *prizvische* (прізвище)—because it was less uncomfortable than talking about Jesus, he was a bona fide genealogical expert, and he insisted that my last name had an Eastern European origin. He asked for my email address and said he'd do some research while he was traveling around over the next couple of months. I expected detailed information on the origin of my last name from him. I was excited—I felt as though I was on the brink of solving a fifty-year-old mystery. When the email eventually came, his response was brief. He believed the last name was linked to the Russian word "покручь" (pōk-rūtch), which meant, according to him, "to twist," "to turn," or sometimes "to corrupt."

The email was decidedly less than what I had been expecting, but it also wasn't nothing. Alex's information in combination with a blog my family back home had recently discovered that documented the origins of surnames similar to ours

(Pokros, Pokriss, Pokrassa, etc.) in a region just south of Kiev was enough for me to begin defining myself a certain way to people who commented on my last name, or asked about its origins. I was, after all, a Ukrainian-speaking American living in Ukraine. Not only that, now I was an American with potentially Ukrainian heritage who had *returned* to Ukraine. In a country filled with people who, mostly for economic reasons, were anxious to leave—preferably to America—I was already an anomaly. A corruption. These facts made me eager to claim my surname's potentially Ukrainian heritage, especially as it gave me some clout with the people I spoke with and met with, who often wanted to discredit me for no other reason than that they felt I did not belong in their country.

Eventually my Ukrainian sojourn came to an end and I returned home, where I had far fewer conversations about where I was from and what the name "Pockrus" meant. But I didn't relinquish the hold that Alex's information had on me. On the rare occasion that folks asked where my last name was from, I told them it was Ukrainian. And I often thought about a last name that meant to "twist" or "turn" or "corrupt." I thought of it especially as the foundations I had laid for my safe, predictable future began to shift and change. When I realized that I was only pursuing civil engineering to satiate my parents' expectations. When I began studying art history, which I'd been assured by many was a career dead-end. When post-mission romantic relationships didn't work out. When I was denied acceptance from my second choice of schools after deciding to transfer and was forced to instead transfer to a university that I'd long looked at as a destination for those with nowhere else to go.

I considered it as my feelings toward Mormonism began to sour—beginning with the organization's overtly discriminatory policy change in 2015 that forbade children of same-sex couples from being baptized. I considered it as my faith in God—in the religion that I had been raised to believe was above reproach—

proved susceptible to questioning and began to skew. The day
that I realized I didn't believe tithing should be mandatory, or
that God was really whispering answers back during prayers, or
that reading books of scripture could magically solve my problems. I began to embrace my identity as one who twisted and
changed the day that I realized that faith wasn't—shouldn't be—
an adequate substitute for facts, and the day that the nebulous
theoretical love of a distant unknowable but supposedly perfect
god was no longer a replacement for the tangibility of family or
friend or lover—people whose fallibility didn't keep them from
caring desperately and beautifully.

I was deviating from what had been a fundamental part of
my path: my religion. I began attending meetings less frequently.
I began to neglect my responsibilities within the organization.
Not out of laziness or busyness, as many who knew me assumed,
but because it had been my job to teach gospel doctrine to the
church's youth, and I was uncomfortable teaching principles that
I didn't feel like I believed—or didn't believe clearly. I felt I was
looking through a window that had been dirtied by doubt and
nuance—by unanswerable questions and unresolved problems.
But I was being told and I was expected to teach that we could
still see clearly if we just pretended like the dirt wasn't there. I
tried to see through the cracks—to teach *around* my feelings—
but I felt like I was lying, like I was intentionally performing my
role in a way that others might find deceitful.

Road trips to pursue landscape photography became a
weekly excuse for not attending meetings. One weekend would
have me descending steeply pitched walls of Kaibab limestone,
sandstone, and shale to the base of the Grand Canyon and its
life-giving aorta: the roaring Colorado. The next weekend, I'd
be hiking by starlight beneath red rock canopies supported by
monumental sheer walls in Coyote Gulch, a tributary of the
Escalante. I wanted to explore every inch of Capitol Reef's Cathe-
dral Valley, Antelope Island, the High Uintas, or the far corners

of Utah's West Desert. I was almost always alone, ill-equipped, nervous, excitable.

By most accounts, my failure to seat myself on a padded bench each Sunday, listen to sermons, and take part in Mormon ordinances meant I was distancing myself from celestial powers, but as I stood in the brush one night photographing countless stars reaching out from billions of miles and millions of years away, I felt spiritually nourished. The arch of the Milky Way established an angelic halo over Mount Nebo, the tallest peak in the Wasatch Range. My mind drew instantaneous connections, curated by years of religious training: this Nebo is named after *Jabal Nībū* in Jordan, where Moses saw the promised land after forty years in the wilderness. The word bears close resemblance to the Ukrainian n-/e/-bō (небо): "heaven." I'm taken back in my mind's eye to my mission: a late-night train from Kolomia to Ivano-Frankivsk, faint lights of remote villages scurrying by; boundless golden wheat fields beneath azure skies on the road from Khmelnitsky to Kodoma, imitating the blue and yellow color-fields of the Ukrainian flag. These landscapes once inexplicably brought me to tears; their remembrance is nothing if not sacred. I consider this host of connections and feel they are almost too serendipitous. I am embraced by the shadow of 11,933 feet of sedimentary stone—balm of Gilead to my aching soul. At once, I am seen; my experiences affirmed.

I could have attempted to explain my qualms with the church, hoping that others would trust me and feel my actions were warranted, dealing with whatever consequences followed. But taking this alternative path—less direct, more complicated, and requiring more work—felt like the only way to avoid fallout within a community which, in my life, had been nearly all-consuming. The changes I underwent were slow—almost imperceptible—but the consequences those changes yielded were unquestionably dramatic.

My path began to circumvent the authorities to whom I had

traditionally turned. I was veering around strict rules—commandments—that I'd spent my entire life trusting. I twisted away—in conversation and action—from those friends, family members, colleagues, and coworkers who failed to understand why my priorities had changed—who failed to consider my perspectives because they were locked in a closed relationship with an organization that taught them that the slightest deviation meant apostasy, that alteration or adaptation were terms synonymous only with perversion, and not with growth or development. In the New Testament, Christ says "strait is the gate, and narrow is the way, that leadeth unto life" (Matthew 7:13-14). In the Book of Mormon, the Mormon prophet Nephi begs God to "make [his] path straight" (2 Nephi 4:33). I'd been told that "straight-and-narrow" was the goal, but experience had taught me that divergence from that path could not only be functional, but *beautiful.*

~

I can sympathize with the Goosenecks.

I'm still not a geologist but I know now that the bends in the San Juan River at the Goosenecks are called *meanders* and that the area is unique for the way these meanders cut deep into the bedrock. Experts have theorized that these deep incisions are possible only because of flaws in the underlying strata—flaws ultimately exposed by the river's relentless tenacity.

I can't speak for the relative extremes of my departure from the conventions of my upbringing, nor can I fully grasp the extent of my own imperfect foundations, but I understand this: the current of the San Juan's life, though much longer and arguably more complex than mine, shares with mine common characteristics. Our paths have not been straight; we both were destined to twist and to turn.

I stepped back from the edge of the stone precipice on which I'd been perched and my companion and I walked and climbed our way back through dirt and gravel and up rust-orange ledges, past the perfunctory-seeming park signs finally approaching the Saturn—its windows coated in a thin layer of sediment. Shadows crept down through the valley as the sun moved toward the horizon, blackbrush and sage trembled in the evening breeze. The sky's docile blue began to give way to a rebellious cacophony of yellows, oranges, reds, and pinks. I paused for a moment and allowed myself to be washed over by the sky, the sounds, the dry air. The Navajo Nation calls this area *Tse'Bii'Ndzisgaii*: "the Valley of the Rocks." For generations they've associated these red deserts and the sandstone monoliths that speckle them—as much a part of my heritage and upbringing as Mormonism—with spirituality. I am as close to God in these moments and in these places as I have ever been.

I turn the key in the ignition, open up the Spotify app on my phone, and listen to Johnny Cash, one of the American West's holy men. His words are mine:

> *Lord, I've never lived where churches grow,*
> *I loved creation better as it stood*
> *That day you finished it so long ago*
> *And looked upon your work and called it good*
> *I know that others find you in the light*
> *That sifted down through tinted window panes*
> *And yet I seem to feel you near tonight*
> *In this dim, quiet starlight on the plains.*

It's about thirty minutes to the small hotel where we'll hole up for the night. I throw the transmission into reverse and ease off the brake. I can't see the mirrors through the dust on the driver's-side and passenger's-side windows so I roll them down. From there, I begin to see more clearly.

David G. Pace

Freedom Ruts

I T'S 2010, THE END OF THE FIRST DECADE OF THE NEW MIL-
lennium, and the world seems not only sharply divided
between the political right and left, rich and poor, east and west
but falling apart at the seams. How did I not see this coming?

Maybe it's because for twenty years as a flight attendant I
have been seeing America from forty thousand feet up—from
sea to rising sea. Now, unable to get on a flight out of Boston
to return home after Christmas vacation, I and my little family
set out to (almost) cross the continent in a rental along Interstate 80. Suddenly, this is an America from just under six feet
up—fomenting, poisoned by talk show hosts and the rising "Tea
Party," awash in the Great Recession and its aftermath.

Interstate 80 is the frozen winter road, the straight shot and
plumbed chalk-line, snapped to the frozen ground, that will take
us effortlessly the way west. The road upon which we don't have
to think about anything other than...everything.

But at Des Moines, Iowa, I-80 is closed due to the weather,
and we detour from there toward Kansas City. My wife—
Cheryl—scrambles for the map. About twenty miles later is our
exit, which she ingeniously figures out in time for us to take.
Route 92 runs parallel with I-80, our narrow home-away-from-
home. It is a quiet, snow-blown, two-lane path that stair-steps

down in elevation as it glides west toward Omaha. We pass through Winterset, birthplace of the actor John Wayne—and appropriately named on this icy day—then Greenfield, then Griswold on the Nishnabotna River.

Griswold lies at the western end of a series of terraced fields now vacant and forlorn, rimmed with the shaggy mop of hair-like growth—flaxen-colored and stiff—that tumbles over their edges. There is pleasure taken in the contours of this remarkably busy-in-an-agricultural-way land, the violent gray sky behind it the perfect complement to its heavy earthen load. It is also very near the old pioneer trail. This fact is impossible for anyone to ignore as my people, ever industrious, have made sure that the way of our seventy-thousand-plus forefathers not only be clearly marked but that long portions of the Oregon Trail be named "The Mormon Trail."

Five miles from where we currently find ourselves, my triple-great grandfather John Lowe Butler and a Brother Cummings were sitting in a wigwam getting their asses saved by Wacaka-suck, who, along with others in his Pottawatomie band, qualified with the Mormons as refugees. April in Iowa, apparently, wasn't much better in 1845 than December is now in the Hawkeye State. The weather sucked—rain, hail, and ice so thick that it coats trees and grass in seeming crystal. Complicated by Gramps's "ruma-tism" the two "Mormonites" were not doing too well, wending their way through the grass and chasing a wild pony to replace John's, which had fallen and died earlier in their journey. The Indian led them to a small village where they were served baked cornbread, a wood duck (which Gramps had shot en route) and strong coffee with maple syrup, which, according to Cummings, the scribe in all of this and with a thing for misspelled intensifiers, "went verry well…a verry good breakfast." After dining with the Pottawatomie village headman, whom Cummings made some effort to record was "a good looking fellow," the now not-so-bedraggled pair headed off, "feeling verry blessed."

Before all of this, in Missouri where the Mormons had settled after leaving Ohio, Butler made his name roughing up some locals in the town of Gallatin at a poll where his folk were being disinvited to vote. One of the candidates stood up on the head of a whiskey barrel and stated "that he did not consider the 'Mormons' had any more right to vote than the n-----s." Pates were broken and Missourians scattered in part by the brawn and bravery of my six-foot-two, sturdily built ancestor, who in the "affray" found an oak stick: "[T]hough rather large," he recalled later in his autobiography, "…I thought I could handle [it] with ease and convenience…tapping them as though light, but they fell as dead men, their heads often striking the ground first."

He continues:

> I know that I knocked them right and left every one that came in my reach, and I know that there were over eight or ten. There was one fellow commenced bawling when he saw one of his companions lye Motionless on the sod. He said that they had kill'd poor bill. And a brother hearing the poor fellow wailing for his companion thought that he would give him something els to cry for.…He up with a rock and threw at him and struck him right in the mouthe. He bah hoo'd and cry'd out "what *d n nd* hard licks those *d m d* Mormons do hit."

It's hard really to know what my triple-great grandfather thought of all this back in the mid-1800s, if he thought about it at all. I say that because as a relatively new convert to a new religion that was decidedly unpopular both on the frontier and in the nation's capital, Butler's decision to become a Latter-day Saint, made early on in Kentucky with his wife, Caroline, had, from there on out, pretty much owned him.

John Lowe Butler's story is told with immense pride even today in family circles and local history-relating outings. Latter-day Saints weren't just the chosen people being driven out from state to state, our tails between our Mormon legs. No, occasionally, we fought back. And at the polls on Election Day no less. Whatever you say about the people of my birth whose DNA still stubbornly informs my current worldview, Mormons can hold their own. They also know the value of how the story gets told later. Today, it seems, the only thing that really matters in our media-saturated age is co-opting the narrative, the staid old vocabularies, theological and otherwise, and insisting that what those words mean are something now quite different. To wit: the Great Basin became "the promised land." With apologies to "New Englandly" Emily Dickinson, it's about seeing all things "Mormonly."

For nearly two and a half years after leaving Nauvoo, Illinois—the jumping-off point for the first companies of Saints—Gramps, who was a personal bodyguard first to church founder Joseph Smith, and after Smith's murder to Brigham Young, was sent on wild errands, mostly to corral the scattered Latter-day Saints into organized groups that would eventually end up at the shores of the Great Salt Lake.

In the migration of the first-wave Mormons over grasslands and mountains with precious little provenance for the oxen that pulled those wagons, an infrastructure was needed. These hearty and obedient souls were tasked with growing and cultivating crops that would be harvested by those to come later. It was a vast cooperative, very much unlike the more solitary bands gunning for Oregon and California, not bound spiritually to a collective burned from within by religious quest. As author Rinker Buck has intoned in his 2011 trail reenactment titled *The Oregon Trail*, the much touted "[r]ugged individualism" of the migrants "was wrapped in an envelope of group enterprise." That isn't surprising about the Latter-day Saints, led by Young, who Mormons like to refer to as "The American Moses." What is surprising is how reliant the Saints were on the federal government, which they resented terribly because the Feds didn't protect them from being driven west. The resentment exists even (or especially) today. Like Gramps, the "State of Deseret," as configured in the stubborn mind of Brother Brigham, was audacious. It consisted of one-fifth of what was considered at the time to be the Western Territories, from the Rockies west to San Bernardino and from Cardston, Alberta, to the dusty Mormon colonies in the Mexican states of Chihuahua and Sonora.

Back on the prairie, Gramps was sent by Brother Brigham to crisscross the Iowa Territory, bringing messages, reading letters, fording rivers, and eating boiled corn and roast duck the size of quail. So while the first company left for what would become Utah, Gramps stayed behind. Even when the second train left the following spring, he was asked to stay on at Winter Quarters, a gathering place on the bluffs of the Missouri near present-day Omaha, where transient pioneers readied for the trek.

The Mormon story is about how refugees, driven west by "mobs," learned that the best revenge was to beat Americans at their own game—not by beating the shit out of bigots at the voting polls, but by acquiring land. And my ancestors felt entitled to "bleed the beast" in the process. Right out of the gate, shortly after leaving Nauvoo in 1846, about 550 men, in a battalion led by Mormon company officers and commanded by regular US Army officers, were mustered into volunteer service in the war on Mexico—including another ancestor of mine, "Captain" James Pace and his seventeen-year-old son William. In true Brigham Young fashion, "Moses" collected the uniform allowances of his followers, paid up front for the year, along with, presumably, the thirty thousand dollars in wages after the battalion arrived in San Diego following what has been called the *longest* infantry *march* in history: approximately 1,850 miles.

What we now call "entrepreneurship" continued in what would become Utah, where Mormons functioned as mid-trail outfitters—an occupation nefarious at best—to those bound for the West Coast on the California Trail. There was more money to be made in cash-strapped, barter-based Utah at the Green River, where Butler and his colleagues returned to set up river ferries, charging a handsome fee of those who followed in the largest land migration in American history. In 1862, Congress passed the Pacific Railway Act, which authorized the construction of a transcontinental railroad, largely made possible through land grants. The Mormons were the first in line. Like other frontier folk they did not hesitate to feed at the trough of Washington, laying the rails for Union Pacific Railroad through Echo and Weber Canyons just east of Ogden. The promised land, as the Saints referred to it, was their land, their "Zion."

~

Here at the end of the first decade of the new millennium, as with the United States, Mormonism, despite its wealth and breadth of influence, feels like a chimera to me. Now traversing the old trail, it seems like it was a journey out of moribund religion back east via the ecstasy of a mystic to another moribund faith 180 years later made material by the settling of land. To wit: we became the very thing we thought we were fleeing when we left New York State and later the Midwest: intolerant, moralistic, suffering from a surfeit of stuffy mores. Ideologues.

And yet despite this bile of which post-Mormons like me can't seem to rid themselves, I am moved as we approach Council Bluffs overlooking the mighty Missouri, and I "ponder anew what the Almighty can do," to quote from the hymn, or what something seemingly almighty did. There in the river bottoms now cluttered with interstate exchanges sits a history that defined a people, a land, and generations that followed. John Lowe Butler was held captive by something bigger than himself and in a country that despite shitting on his people he nevertheless believed was the "city set on a hill," where God's kingdom would be established. A holy land.

Even so, Latter-day Saints had an ambivalent if not outright oppositional stance to the US that could not keep its promise of liberty to everyone. "We want to take you to a land where a white man's foot never trod," the people were told by one of many they esteemed as prophets and apostles. Why? Because "we are not accounted as white people and I don't want to live with the white people." And so we were not accounted, and not, I might add, in terms of the royal "we," but in the parlance of belonging to a group that seems in some ways now, like the Jews, to have become ethnic.

Persecution complexes abound in Zion.

And so "we" put our money where our mouths were. We gave the finger to the East, shouted "damn the torpedoes," married as many times as we were commanded, crossed the Missouri, survived the Sweetwater in the high plains of Wyoming… made the desert "blossom as a rose."

~

Entering the on-ramp, we pick up speed, and America piles up fast and furious.

"Donate your pop cans to the new Library," beams a road sign.

"Unwanted Pregnancy?" (On a black-and-white billboard, a close-up of a youngish woman looking into the camera with a slightly quizzical look.)

"Get out of Debt Today!" (Something called Credit Advisors fronted by a grinning woman—brunette—in a bright blue blouse. All teeth. A phone number below inviting YOU to "become a C.A. Success Story!")

Brookside Church, slouching toward the freeway. Huge. Sprawling. A "mega" church where a muscle-bound Jesus really packs a punch.

The stretch between Omaha and Lincoln and beyond is one I've traveled before exclusively in service of my first marriage back in the late '80s. My first wife—a Nebraskan—and I used to fly into either Omaha or Denver and then motor out to McCook, four hours away from either end for family occasions. The ill-fated marriage was a testament to just how intractable Mormon indoctrination is, not so much my wife's who was a convert, but mine. It's a disease in Mormonland that Latter-day Saints will do almost anything to be able to claim to themselves, internally, that they are not "a typical Mormon." This was true of me, and wedding a convert who had a degree *cum laude* in physics and had grown up Catholic was about as far as I would go to prove it to my community, and most importantly to myself that I wasn't "typical." But the ideology of being a Mormon first and everything else second—including American—was forever imbedded in me.

Why am I thinking about this now, twenty-one years after my first marriage ended in divorce? Because the fusion of individual, family, and institutional church—what I call the Mormon glueball—has such a powerful gravitational pull, that few who grow up in the faith with two practicing parents can ever really leave it behind: families are forever and forever and…

This is how it works for *my* tribe. In terms of sociology, we're not a cult, but we do believe in the cult of the family. And America, which in 2010 seems to be regressing into some kind of ideological funk, is about family. Who's going to argue that?

So we are heading towards Kearney, and I have faint stirrings of regret for this first marriage. In the end what my ex, estranged from her own family of birth, wanted was what my faith was selling: family as an *idée fixé*, the irreducibly fundamental social unit with overtones of eternal life. And that other little thing, the Kingdom of God established in "the tops of the mountains," according to the Old Testament. It's what we all want. Family and a Kingdom, geographically rooted.

What's odd is that from the moment we left Farmington, Maine, four days previous, before we found out that we would not be catching a flight out of Boston, there has been something familiar and off-putting about the people, places, and things we've experienced along the frozen way west of I-80. There are flaring fundamentalisms everywhere, in the Jesus memorabilia in truck stops to the glorification of guns, to quotes about freedom, liberty, and traditional family values, to Old Glory on everything from bandanas to underwear. And there are conspiracies promulgated every night on television, from Obama's birth certificate to his alleged "racism," and always there is the federal government waiting in the wings to destroy America through secular humanism, socialism, and the seizure of land and guns. Public lands, even or especially those with a strong and historical Native American presence, should be managed (and exploited) by private companies deputized by western state legislatures.

When we get to Kearney on New Year's Eve we are a day and a half away from home and it is *verry* cold. It's time to EconoLodge.

~

Since leaving Maine, everyone we meet along the way, in gas stations and diners, seems either exhausted or unhinged, or both. Here at the end of the first decade of the new millennium the country seems riven by economic collapse, authoritarian impulses, and anti-Enlightenment sentiments. Western Pennsylvania feels like Utah County all over again: *Get us out of the United Nations!* What counts as national discourse is starting to feel very Mormon, as in my hometown of Provo where the electorate is now fused to "the Party of No." Always, how the story is getting told, ever-so-sincerely and simplistically, reigns supreme: the real America is under attack; our freedoms are being systematically taken away; all of government is the problem, never the solution. In this grim time, with Fox the most-watched cable news network for nine years running, what will the new decade bring?

The national narrative is epitomized by yet another influential Latter-day Saint: Tea Party enthusiast and performance artist Glenn Beck of Fox News. The country, apparently, has an appetite for not only conspiracy theories, but racism, and the oxymoron of unrestrained "freedom." It's seductive to believe in the myth of the rugged individualism of pioneers like Grandpa Butler, transferred to all Americans as if it were a national trait, but the fact is that Americans are "socialists" all, from the Homestead Act and permission to displace and kill Native Americans wholesale in the 1800s to the GI Bill after World War II, and from building the national freeway system during the '50s and '60s to off-loading multimillion-dollar grazing permits for ranchers, pennies on the dollar. Corporate welfare doesn't fold very well into the rugged anything.

Disregarding all of that, Beck and his ilk have convinced most that as anti-taxer Grover Norquist put it, "I'm not in favor of abolishing the government. I just want to shrink it down to the size where we can *drown it* in the bathtub." This is a Republican meme, and little more, designed to rally the vote. Which government are you willing to drown? Whose entitlements are you ready to water board? What will be your democracy-based rationale, your justification, for doing so?

The analogue of fundamentalism in the Church of Jesus Christ of Latter-day Saints is ideological America at the end of the first decade of the first millennium: a Black man in the White House with an opposition party whose leadership and base are less about principle-based thinking and action and more about maintaining cultural beliefs that justify particular social arrangements, including patterns of inequality at any cost. And what are those ideologies? Abortion is about killing babies, guns are an extension of the collective American penis, and American lands are here principally to be exploited for financial gain. Again, it's all summed up for the American ideologue, on the Right and, it can be presumed, more and more on the Left, in the term *freedom*, or God-given *free agency*, which happens to be the relentless warrant Latter-day Saints use to craft their Mormonly narrative of life as it should be, for all Americans.

But freedom from what? Or to what? You can't have a subject like "freedom" without an object in that sentence. You can only have a justification, something that keeps you in your wagon trail rut. What can we expect starting tomorrow, January 1, 2011, when "freedom," defined perilously as *freedom from all restraint*, is the quotidian Kool-Aid we drink? How can something as foundational to the health of our country, and the world, as public lands, or the effects of global warming, or endangered species win any arm wrestle when the individual feels—no, "knows"—that he or she is entitled to freedom from all restraint, including those founded on empirical facts, of the rule of law, of the fallibility of the strong man?

~

By the time Cheryl and I head up over Elk Mountain in Wyoming, and across the Continental Divide; by the time we go whizzing past Fort Bridger where the main ruts of the Oregon Trail shoot north but we go southwest, down past Wanship on Interstate 80; by the time we pass the buzzing ski slopes of Park City where most of my pilot and flight attendant friends domiciled in Salt Lake live and where they can conveniently ignore "Zion" as they flee down the interstate to fly away into the unreal America at an improbable but seductive height; by the time we roll into our Ninth and Ninth Salt Lake neighborhood—by that time, I will thoroughly be of the opinion that Americans are not keeping wise dominion of the earth, as the Bible commands us, "and the inhabitants therein."

Our little family parks in the driveway. The engine of the rental Toyota Corolla quiets. And we just sit there for a minute, sort of stunned from the five-day drive home through an America I don't think we really knew existed, not here on 8th East and driving around Salt Lake City in our hybrid while listening to National Public Radio.

~

Mitt Romney lost the 2012 election to Barack Obama. The election cycle was termed by some the "Mormon Moment," with the former governor of Massachusetts pitching himself headlong into the GOP base with nary a sliver of his former Beacon Hill governance that was moderate, even progressive. And now in 2020 we are knee-high in the nightmare of Donald Trump. The flight vector for his arrival was set as early as 2010, the year we crossed (nearly) the continent, if not earlier, and while Republican Utah seemed to balk at Trump's populist and more importantly immoral mien, my Mormon brethren and sisters, marinated in ideological thinking and behavior, have since been won over. With the election just months away, Trump's approval rating with Utahns, the super-majority of which identify as Latter-day Saint, is 57 percent, his highest rating so far this year. (That figure soars to 82 percent among Republicans, with half saying they strongly approve.)

And yet Mitt Romney, now a Utah senator, despite several stakes through his heart by constituents, his Republican colleagues, and even his own niece (Republican Party chair) continues to angle for a fight against the greatest threat to our democracy in our lifetimes.

Someone here recently proffered, ironically: Is America becoming more Mormon?

At this juncture, I have to say, I hope not, and I hope so.

Theric Jepson

Zzyzx Road

i have driven down zzyzx road
to the oasis hidden behind a rise
off the fifteen.

after hours in the mojave,
the green is less a surprise
than a mirage i cannot believe in.

the absence of humanity doesn't help—
once upon a time this was a destination
for glamorous angelenos;

now it's owned by the c.s.u.s,
a home for science,
but maybe science alone

because no one is here,
no one.
we wander around palms and water, outside open labs—

we've seen no civilization
since whiskey pete's, so,
for all we know, zzyzx road is all that's left of humanity—

no more people—
just fronds and frogs, empty labs
and a sign, welcoming us.

we walk in circles, breathing
the afternoon air, cooler near this water,
but hear no footfalls, no voices—

the end of our world might as well
wake up green,
surrounded by mojave brown and freeway black,

but we, we choose to leave this invisible garden
and return to that black line and its
promised humanity: just three hundred miles away.

Theric Jepson

(THE BEES OF COURSE DON'T KNOW IT)

The bees of course don't know it, but they keep us alive.
Their white box houses move from field to field that they
    the bees
may fertilize oranges and strawberries and almonds
and — so many things.
                            Fields like these: lying on either side
of four lanes of 85mileperhour impatience from San Francisco
    to L.A.
(or L.A. to San Francisco). We're fast, like dragonflies over
    a pond.
Much faster, that is, than bees.
                            Focused as they are on bundling
gold dust
into pollen baskets, bees might not notice their sister tempted
by other ultraviolet promises far across the concrete river.
Brave in the certainty of new nectar, she'll cross, only to
    become a
bright yellow bullet hole on our windshield as we rush
    Angelenoward,
suddenly sad.
                    We'll mourn bravely looking upon
the funeral procession of fluid and wipers, pushing her out
    of sight,
out of the hive, forever.
                            As we drive on,
                                    all we'll want
                                            is not
to see what we have done.

Jack Garcia

Sojourn

Permanence. That's what the Wasatch Mountains say to me as they sit cross-legged and constant, their rocky fingers interlaced in their laps, the igneous mass of their shoulders supporting the weight of that heavy blue blanket we call the Utah sky. They sit as a close-knit circle of giants surrounding Provo—granite heads bowed in reverence, Douglas fir and quaking aspen embedded in their stony scalps, perpetually fixed as a symbol of stability.

I see them through my window, those magnificent gathered mountains, as I rip off another strip of packing tape, fold down another cardboard flap, prepare to relocate once again.

Home Number One—*August 1986*
I've moved thirty-nine times in my life. Well, forty if you count the day I emerged from the womb, eyes clenched shut against the blinding world. My mother had labored all through the night, sweat matting her red hair to her forehead—my father slipping ice cubes into her mouth with nervous fingers. Something for her to bite on. Something to cool her down from the August heat.

But I don't count that move from abstract to concrete—from mother's hope to actual breathing flesh. I was brought home, swaddled and big-eyed, to a small apartment in Upland,

California. We'll call this home number one, where two newly-weds fretted about rent checks and diapers, each determined to make something of their doubt. Home number one was my mother, Kathi, a twenty-two-year-old fair-skinned ginger with a short "Pat Benatar" cut, balancing me on one knee as she smiles, brace-faced, for a photo. Home number one was also my father, Jack, a twenty-four-year-old brown-skinned Latino with shaggy black hair, glasses, and a Def Leppard tee as he lies on a brown floral couch, also brace-faced and smiling, as he lifts me over his head like I'm flying.

Home Number Three—*February 1987*
After a failed two-month stint in Washington, my parents found themselves seeking temporary refuge in the home of my father's parents in Baldwin Park, California. I remember the smell of Pond's face cream as my grandma Jessie held me close to her bosom, the sound of *telenovelas* playing in the background. Little glass tchotchkes—that she was afraid I'd break—adorned the tabletops, glittering in my peripheral vision as she nuzzled in close and pinched my cheeks. The world was all color and motion.

Many years prior, on a hot afternoon, Jessie had opened the door to two young Mormon missionaries. Always the polite hostess, she offered cold Coca-Colas to the sweating boys and invited them inside. A Catholic, she had no initial interest in changing religions, but she soon became fascinated by the Word of Wisdom. At the time, her husband was an abusive alcoholic and she had been praying for a way to change him. This new religion offered solutions, so she pragmatically accepted an invitation for baptism.

Home Number Twenty-Nine—*September 2008*
I feel that Mormons have always been a people in search of home. From the religion's inception at the Sacred Grove, their history

has been one of westward pilgrimage, desperately seeking community in Zion. One of my mother's ancestors, Sarah Loader, traveled from England on the ship *Horizon* and joined other pioneers on their way to Utah by handcart. Her group, the Martin Company, met their bleak fate in the winter of 1856, gutted by the cold and left to die in the plains of Wyoming, shrouded in snow. Sarah's sister married Thomas E. Ricks who eventually settled in Rexburg, Idaho, forming Ricks College. In modern-day Salt Lake City, Utah, at the This Is The Place Monument, you can find the name of another ancestor, John Greenleaf Holman, who arrived with Brigham Young's group to the Salt Lake Valley in 1847. Over 160 years later, I would make a similar trek.

In an old junker filled to the brim with boxes of clothes, neckties and Converse sneakers, bedding and a marked-up set of dog-eared scriptures, I traveled westward from a dusty corner of Colorado to Provo, Utah. I, too, was in search of home—determined to leave behind a series of harsh winters and relentless persecution—but these tribulations were of my own making, the foreordained punishments for my own wantonness. I needed to be amongst the Saints for fortification and hive-mindedness. I needed to be reborn. With a pair of cheap drugstore sunglasses on my face, I headed towards the setting sun, winding my way through the Colorado Rockies until I emerged, just after nightfall, among those resting giants, the Wasatch Mountains, waiting to embrace me like the prodigal son.

Home Number Five (or Three, Revisited)—*February 1988*
Jack and Kathi once again sought shelter with my paternal grandparents. My father, struggling to provide for his new family, followed the job leads. Swing shifts delivering office supplies. Throwing papers. Working a lunch truck. Jobs weren't permanent. Apartments weren't permanent. The San Gabriel Valley, however, was permanent, and both sets of grandparents lived in Baldwin Park, California, for many years on the same street.

In 1954, Grandpa Blair, originally from Sugar City, Idaho, met his wife, Myrna, while stationed in the army at Fort Lewis near her birthplace of Olympia, Washington. A few years later, following a job offer, they planted their roots in Baldwin Park. The Holmans had found their home, nestled in the lush San Gabriel Valley. With the San Gabriel Mountains to the north and the San Rafael Hills to the west, this region of California was long ago populated by the Tongva people before the arrival of the Spanish. The San Gabriel Mission, founded by Father Junipero Serra in 1771, brought farming and cattle ranching to the area and was a hub of Spanish colonial society, baptizing the area's first Mexican settlers. The city of Baldwin Park was built on what was once cattle-grazing land owned by the mission.

Like these early California colonizers, my dad's ancestry is Spanish. Grandpa Jack's bloodline traces back eleven generations to José Ulibarri, who came to settle in New Spain sometime around 1644, an area that included what is now México and the western United States. Centuries later, Elvira Balbina Ulibarri Cordova married a García and gave birth to my grandfather in Denver, Colorado. Rumor has it some distant relative traveled back to Spain and is now in possession of the Ulibarri crest.

Ulibarri is a Basque last name meaning "new village." With every move, I live up to expectations.

Grandma Jessie was Southern California–born, but her father was born in Aguas Calientes, México, a town named for its many hot springs. Her mother, a healer and witch, was born and raised in the city of Chihuahua. Seeking a better life, Jessie's parents immigrated to Los Angeles, California, where Jessie eventually met Grandpa Jack, who had left Colorado after getting into some trouble with the law. A friend of Jessie's brother, Jack asked her to marry him one night on a whim, and she said yes, having never gone on a single date. Stealing her brother's car, the two escaped immediately under a full moon to elope, traveling across three states to do so. How could she have known the drinking and heartache that would lie ahead?

Her mother, the *curandera*, mixing her poultices and lighting her candles, could have warned her, but she wasn't consulted. Instead, Jessie would look to a new sort of magic—the kind that came with a prophet and a vision.

Home Number Nine—*February 1992*

Kathi, feeling unattractive and unwanted, lay in bed alone crying softly to herself. Bands of streetlight ran across the bedding, caging her in prison-like bars. My parents were separated for the first time. My brother and I were living with my mother in Vista, California, but five-year-old me had recently thrown a fit, demanding to go to Daddy's house. My father had come to fetch me late in the night.

Sojourn.

It's fitting that my parents' story begins with a move. It was the summer of '78, eight years before my home number one, in Baldwin Park, California. Kathi Holman, the second oldest of five, was turning fourteen that July, pretty, yet hiding her face behind long red hair. Her father, Blair, was a banker by profession and served as stake president in their Mormon congregation. Her mother, Myrna, was the ward chorister. Jack Garcia, almost sixteen, short and skinny with his shoulder-length black hair, had just moved into the neighborhood with his family—his father, also Jack, mother Jesús de la Natividad (or Jessie, for short), and three siblings. His father had been a truck driver for many years, but had moved his family from Hawthorne to Baldwin Park in order to take a job as a U-Haul manager. The Holmans came over to welcome and fellowship the new neighbors, and Jack and Kathi saw each other for the first time. I imagine my father's sweaty palms as he fumbles with a moving box, his wide smile and a nod the only greeting he can muster while carrying such weight. I imagine my mother, looking down at her Converse sneakers, pushing her hair behind her ears as she quickly glances up—just once—standing safely on the sidewalk with her sisters.

Kathi didn't know it yet, but she was about to have her first kiss that summer.

After that first kiss, Jack continued to kiss every girl in the ward congregation. He played bass guitar in a cover band with his brothers, which made him undeniably cool. Two years later, when Kathi was of dating age, they went out a few times, but it didn't amount to much. After my father returned from his pros-elyting mission to Sweden, they tried it again, but it still didn't feel right. However, after making some sordid confessions to his bishop, Jack was advised to get married as quickly as possible. Jack asked Kathi, and just like Jessie, despite "promptings from the Spirit" urging her to say otherwise, she agreed. This impul-sivity—this hope that dogma will provide the answers—tied both women to two generations of Jacks.

The mission didn't fix him, and neither did his marriage. A rash decision, made permanent by sacred temple covenants and the breathing, squirming flesh that was me. Decades later, I would also go on a mission, hoping to be fixed. Like my father, I came home just as weak, just as sinful, just as human. I turned to the mountains for solace.

Home Number Twelve—*July 1993*

My mother, pregnant, my father, determined, decided a change of scenery held the answer. My grandfather owned a home—square with a pointed roof, painted bright mustard yellow by my uncle Valentin—in the small town of Rocky Ford, Colorado, where the Colorado Rockies were but a distant fingernail on the western horizon. The house sat alongside the highway entering the town, a giant pine tree in the front yard, the air smelling faintly of cow manure from a nearby feedlot when the wind blew northward. When renters moved out, my dad saw it as an opportunity to start anew.

Ulibarri.

New village.

To repair their rocky marriage, my father also resolved to be a better Mormon, hoping to reap the promised blessings for his family. For a few years things appeared to be going well; my father was a member of the bishopric, held a good job, and our wandering seemed to have stopped. But soon he became restless. His feet carried him away to unknown beds. His hands traveled over foreign terrain.

My grandma Jessie, who had traded rosary beads for CTR rings in hopes of a miracle, knew all too well that Mormonism didn't fix my grandfather either. It did, however, help to scrub away all traces of our Latino heritage. Mormonism, in many ways, is the new colonizer of the old *conquistadores*—why be a Lamanite when you can be "white and delightsome" before the Lord? My grandpa didn't teach any of his children Spanish; they never spoke it in the home. He wanted his children to assimilate, to blend in with the other families in those Sunday school pews. This is even evident in the naming of their children. Gabriel became Gabe. Carlos was only ever called Charlie. Rachel was never Raquel.

When I was seven years old, Grandma Jessie passed away. As we put her body to rest, I remembered how she used to call me *mijo*, slang for "my son." This is the only Spanish I can recall being spoken to me—this one small term of endearment. Not knowing what it meant, I started referring to her as Grandma *Mijo*. There's a photograph of me, as a toddler, asleep on the couch, clutching one of her bright red pumps as if it were a teddy bear. Seemingly any part of her was enough to soothe me—even her shoe.

Grandma Jessie is buried in Rocky Ford, Colorado, miles away from the place where she lived and died, trading palm trees for prairie grasslands because that's what my grandpa wanted. One last pilgrimage, even in death—forever following that man, saying "I do" a thousand times over in a stolen car.

Home Number Seventeen—*October 1999*

When I think of permanence, I think of roots, deeply embedded into the rich soil like the aspen, fir, and spruce that dot the Colorado Rockies so far and unreachable in the distance.

But I was a seed, blown about, never taking root.

My parents eventually divorced and more moves in Colorado's Arkansas Valley followed. Cheraw. La Junta. Ordway. Each move came out of avoidance, a sort of running away from things. Perhaps if we move, things will be better. Things will be cheaper. We'll love each other more. I'll hate you less. Nobody will know us. We'll be closer to work. There will be less traffic. I won't cheat. I can change.

It'll be different.

Home number seventeen was purchased, not rented. It took Mom's second husband, Steve, to make this historic first for us. He was a schoolteacher who Mom met at church—a sci-fi nerd with novelty ties. His idea of courtship was to come over every day after work and eat my mother's cooking. He made himself permanent.

It was here, in a red ranch-style house—three bedrooms, one bathroom—that life started to settle. During this time, I tried my best to nurture the things I wanted to take root, and uproot those that I was afraid would take hold. There were thoughts that I prayed were temporary, and others I hoped would last forever. These high school years had me digging, planting, grafting, trimming, and replanting, taking small saplings from one pot to another until my hands were caked in dirt and my knees were filthy.

One thing I wanted to cultivate, which had never been cultivated before, was a sense of Latino heritage that had always been denied me by the whitewashing of my family. My aunt jokes that she's a coconut—brown on the outside, white on the inside. My dad says culture doesn't really matter because we're all God's children in the end. My grandfather, perhaps realizing the damage he has caused, said to me, "You white people don't know your family."

All I heard was "You white," told to me by my light-skinned Spanish-American *abuelo*. In the summer, my face tans just as almond-colored as his. My hair is as dark and waved as his was before it frosted over. Our eyes are both brown like coffee beans, wide and sparkling in the sun, but the way he saw it, we were simply not the same.

One summer, a few years prior, that same grandfather came to visit with his foster kids: five Latino siblings. Being around them was the closest thing I ever had to a Latino childhood, and it was only in doses; and those doses did nothing more than to "other" me. One day, we drove down to Trinidad, Colorado, where Grandpa Jack said we had some relatives. To this day I can't remember who those relatives are. One of his brothers, perhaps. Everyone spoke Spanish while I sat not understanding a thing, looking blankly at framed snapshots on the walls, crosses, virgins, and candles that meant nothing to me. The house was adobe, out in the middle of some rocky landscape, with prairie brush and cacti and cattle. We ran out from the house, kicking up dirt, the girls laughing and throwing insults at each other in Spanish, and me, just worried and insecure. I wanted to go home.

When we got to the gates, there was a cow hanging, ready to be butchered. The man who might have been my grandpa's brother slit its throat. A horrible sound reverberated through the canyons, a splatter of blood rained near our shoes.

The ghost of my great-grandmother, the *curandera*, traveled within that echo. *There are folk remedies to be made with the sangre. Escúchame, mijo. Listen. The dirt under your fingernails is a brown crescent moon. See how it smiles?*

Home Number Thirty-Nine—*October 2017*

My aunt once told me I'd marry a white girl. She was half right; I married a white man.

Five years later, we were separated and I moved into a studio apartment in Provo, Utah, in the historic downtown area on Center Street. In an old, brick building called Harman House, the apartment was pleasant with lots of natural light, even if it did lack square footage. It also came furnished, which was a plus as I had abandoned most of my things with my estranged husband. Through the blinds, I had a great view of the mountains and the downtown Provo temple. Mormonism, no matter how much I tried to uproot it, would never seem to let me go; its roots held tightly to my heart.

My mother, shortly after I moved to Utah and came out of the closet, left her second husband. She gathered what little money she had, signed a lease to an apartment without seeing it, and drove to Washington. When we were each at our lowest point, we decided to make that pilgrimage westward. My mother needed a coastline and I needed mountains.

She remarried for a third time and moved to Idaho—returning to the same state that brought her father to life. The same state that was once populated by her Mormon pioneer ancestors, presided over by Two Point Mountain and the Sawtooth Range, lifting their jagged faces towards God. After all of her journeying, my mother has finally broken free of temporality.

My father's journey was similar, coming home to roost with his third red-headed wife, content in Colorado—the land of Ulibarri and Cordova and García. Land of Pikes Peak and *conquistadores* long ago. His feet are no longer restless; his hands no longer wandering.

A Jack had found his home.

Home Number Twenty-Three—*October 2006*

Among the vineyards with their rows of *uvas*, in the sliver of fertile soil between the Andes and the Southern Pacific Ocean, I found myself in white shirt and tie, alongside my Peruvian companion, Elder Auccapuclla, in Molina, Chile. I was now proficient in Spanish, and my surname and suntanned coloring convinced many that I was Chilean. I loved it there. The small, brightly painted cement homes with their wrought-iron gates and shared walls. The people greeting one another with *besos* in the street. The hot summers and rainy winters.

I came there with a lot of expectations. I wanted to learn Spanish—connect with my heritage in some way—although my personality never fully came through in this foreign tongue. Even at my most bilingual, I still felt like a visitor in that vocabulary; the words weren't mine. It was also more and more evident that I was, indeed, gay. It was proving to be something I couldn't run away from or uproot, despite my best efforts. Like my father before me, I hoped that a mission would make me better somehow. More righteous. But it didn't.

I returned home a year later, feeling neither Mormon nor Latino.

Home Number Forty—*January 2019*
Once again, I find myself journeying, but this time I'm headed east. East to Baltimore, Maryland, where my new boyfriend has a job offer. A rowhome apartment is waiting for us in Fells Point, nestled atop a bright pink boutique. Vines grow along the courtyard wall where I'll sit in the summer with my man, sipping boxed wine while we talk about politics and literature and gossip. The humidity will glue my T-shirt to my body as we take a walk along the pier overlooking the Patapsco River and the Domino salt factory, the lapping water reflecting my new thirst—not for permanence like the mountains of the West, but for the undulations of a life unexpected. For *sangre*. For *vida*. For the magic of my great-grandmother and the gambles of my grandma Jessie, manipulating their fates for better or for worse.

For the first time, I'm not moving to run away from something, but *towards* something.

My sister has come along for the ride, occupying the passenger seat that could be filled with the box of kitchen supplies that I opted to leave behind, but her company is more precious cargo to me than a blender I can easily replace from Goodwill. Something I've learned through my many moves is that most stuff we accumulate is just extra baggage; the sooner we get rid of it the better. Sure the Spanish came in ships, but the pioneers came in handcarts, so I can come in a Kia Forte filled with knickknacks and books, sneakers and clothes, bedding and a coffeemaker.

At thirty-two, I've learned that home isn't a destination. My life has been filled with a series of temporary stays, identities that didn't stick, and more cardboard boxes than I'd like to admit, but for me, that's home. Home is in those boxes. The boxes I leave behind and the boxes I take with me.

I'm meant to sojourn—to roam free from place to place like my ancestors before me.

This is the place, they'll say. *For now.*

And do you see the crescent moon? See how it's smiling.

Danielle Beazer Dubrasky

Southern Utah Wind Gap

I fly over arteries of lights in a Brasilia,
tilt to one side along the Buckhorn Flats.
Home is scattered: red cliffs to the east,
a dry sea to the west, and in between,

a town of three exits where I have lived out
the same day for 30 years. A glossy magazine
promises vacations to Denmark, Bali, Alaska,

where oceans beat the shores with breakers
from our first breaths before our lidless eyes
could no longer see through water.

At the wind gap, symbols on rock tell of the equinox,
tell of rain, a journey, a woman giving birth.
Flat clouds signal a storm building in Nevada
that will reach us by tomorrow night.

But this afternoon, the wind blowing across
sandstone reminds me how long I have been held
by this land, unable to swim away through invisible seas.

Winter Solstice in the Gorge

Our myths turn long nights into cut evergreen
on grocery store parking lots, a continent away
from reindeer starving as the Arctic ice dissolves.
Only one star guides the way for miles of commerce

that thread the Mojave—diesels lit like Christmas.
The longest night spills from a cup of tears I drink
through this highway that weaves between monoliths
of an American Stonehenge along the Virgin River's winding
course.

At the hour's cusp I see her face in the rock—
Freya who carries the sun in antlers. She spins a wheel
around our breath, seeds the earth with bits of amber.

At dawn the sun stands still on a plateau of Kaibab sediment,
reaches its rays down gypsum layers, touches sandstone
near big horn sheep who step out of shadow.

UNVEIL

Kumen Baldwin Louis

Hózhó Náhásdlíí

THERE HE STOOD ON TOP OF THE MOUNTAIN GETTING blessed by his uncle. The small cabin belonged to his uncle's wife. It was good area, not too far off the main road. The cabin was built at the edge of the west tree line and overlooked a small opening to the east. In the breeze the sound of nature carried over the tops of rocks, fallen logs, ditches and gullies. Roy, the uncle, held four eagle feathers in his hand. Tied together it mimicked a fan. Roy hunched over the fire and used the feathers to guide smoke to the feet of his nephew.

Bless yourself with the smoke, he said to his nephew. Begin with your feet, using the smoke to cover your entire body, ending at your head.

The nephew had an experience he felt would be unbelievable to anyone he told. He trusted his uncle and knew he had the gift of healing. But also knew that he could get some guidance and direction.

~

It was early, one spring morning, and snow had fallen during the night. The snow was deep, and it covered the earth. It made everything look soft and silent. Yahashke walked over to the wood pile, each step he took the snow recorded his footprint.

He grabbed an armload of wood and turned to go back into the house. He was startled to find Coyote standing in his tracks as if he earned the right. They looked and observed one another. Coyote finally broke his gaze and checked his surroundings, then looked back at Yahashke.

I have something to tell you, said Coyote. Will you hear it?

Confused, scared, and instinctively getting ready for a fight, Yahashke stood his ground.

~

Putting some more wood into the fire, Yahashke reflected on what just happened. He never experienced anything like it. He did not know how to process what he was told and the fact that an animal had talked to him. He sat there thinking of what was said to him by Coyote. Thoughts like *who would believe me if I told them*, and *what if people think I am crazy*, or worse, *what if people think I am cursed or the cause of curses*, all stockpiled in his mind. He contemplated just letting the experience melt away like the snow. If he did not share it with anyone, no one would be the wiser, and he could carry on like nothing took place. But this was a moment of significance, a moment that should not be forgotten. Yahashke stood up and grabbed his coat, rifle, and sidearm. He stepped out into the snow once more and walked over to the horse corral. He threw his saddle over the back of his horse, Eber. Cinched him up, got in the saddle, twirled Eber around and nudged his side, and rode out into the country.

Lord, Yahashke said. Thou knowest my heart and soul. I am not sure what thou would have me do. I know thou created the world and all the creatures in it. Why this has happened to me, I know not. My heart is telling me I should seek the answers, only I don't know where to begin. Help me to work this out, is my prayer, amen.

~

Alden and John were cousins of Yahashke. They too were on horseback and riding in the country.

Hey, good morning, said Alden. Nice bit of snowfall, huh?

Yeah, not too bad, said Yahashke.

John asked, Did you hear about Ernest?

No.

We went over to his place, Wednesday. Because he needed some help. Anyway, we took some hay and water to his cows and he started to tell us that he saw something in his field.

What?

Yeah, he said he was doing the same thing, going about his normal routine. When he got to his field and started to open his gate, he saw the back of some person in the middle of his field. He said he thought it was someone up to no good, so he started to walk toward the person quickly. As he got closer, he noticed that it wasn't a person at all, and thought it might have been a bear standing up. So he stopped and yelled at the thing. He said it turned and looked at him, and it wasn't a bear. It was Bigfoot.

Really?

Crazy thing, huh?

What else did he say?

He said, when it turned to look at him, it had a humanlike face—only with thick facial hair. And that creeped him out.

Yeah, that'd be pretty scary.

So, our dad wanted us to go check up on him and make sure he's doing okay. What you up to?

Just going on a ride.

You can come with us, if you like.

Yeah.

Let's go then.

~

When they got to Ernest's place he was outside working on a flat tire. That old Ford pickup truck was something he enjoyed working on. He was always tinkering. Ernest heard his dogs begin to bark as the guys rode up on their horses.

John said, How's it going?

Oh, just changing this tire, must've gone flat some time during the night. Colder temp.

Dad wanted us to stop by to see if you needed help with anything.

That's nice of him. I think I'm good, just going to run into town today and pick up some things. A couple days from now I'll have to fix some fencing.

Yeah, let us know.

Actually, could I get you to split some wood for me, since you're here?

The guys jumped off their mounts and tied them up. Both Alden and John went to splitting wood, and Yahashke started to help Ernest with changing his flat.

Anything new happening these days? said Yahashke.

Not much, just staying busy. I'm sure your cousins told you what I saw up here the other day. Nice of them to come by to check up on me.

Yeah, they mentioned it.

Was a strange thing. Still taking some time to process what I saw. I keep thinking that my mind was playing tricks on me. I've heard of people seeing things like that but never thought it'd happen to me.

I can imagine.

I really thought it was a bear because that's what made sense to me.

Yes.

But when it turned, and I saw that it wasn't, I just kind of froze. I could not believe what I was looking at. I was filled with fear.

I'd be afraid, also.

No, I wasn't afraid. I was filled with fear. I mean, when I think of being afraid, it's something you can handle. But, I was in fear of something that I couldn't control. I don't know if that makes any sense. But I wouldn't use afraid to explain what I felt because it was so much more.

Yeah, that must have been something.

It happened and now I am trying to just get on with my life. Whatever it was I saw, I think I witnessed on mistake. I don't think I was meant to see that thing. People in this life have some great things happen to them. Spiritual things that help to uplift and give hope. What I saw didn't do that for me. I wasn't in awe. All it did was confuse me and caused me to feel something I don't much like.

Well, let us know if we can help with anything. I'm not sure what we can do for you to help with that thing you saw, but we're here.

Thanks, I may just go visit your uncle, he seems to know what to do with such things. He has that gift.

Yeah, that's a good idea. I didn't think of that.

I know, I did, said Ernest with a bit of a chuckle.

They both tightened the lug nuts, lowered the jack, and put the tools away. The morning snow might have been an added obstacle to some, but to these country boys, it was just a part of life, nothing to complain about or wish for warmer mornings. They all knew things like that were out of their control, and all they could do was just get on with living.

~

Standing in the horse corral, Yahashke unsaddled his horse and replayed in his mind what he experienced that morning.

Looking straight into the gem-colored eyes of the coyote as the last bits of snow fell to the earth, Yahashke dropped his pile of wood. He slowly reached for his knife fastened to his belt.

You don't have to do that, said Coyote.

Yahashke did not trust Coyote, and for that reason was not certain if he could trust what he was hearing. Was Coyote really speaking to him?

I have something to tell you, will you hear it? said Coyote for a second time.

I'm not sure, said Yahashke.

Well, I am going to say what I have to anyway, said Coyote.

Okay.

Prepare your mind—know harmony comes after disharmony in some instances. Try to be unafraid because everything has purpose, said Coyote before walking off.

Yahashke thought on those words told to him. He collected his gear and locked them up in the shed. He wanted answers so he decided to go and see his uncle.

~

After being blessed, Yahashke sat beside the fire. The smell of cedar still lingering. His uncle Roy said to him, There are many things in this world that still do not make sense to any of us. I have people from all over the world come to me for prayers and blessings. Some things they tell me are hard to believe. But, what I do for them is all I know how to do. I can't explain everything that goes on. I just stick to the things I was taught. There is healing in the songs and prayers because they have been passed down for generations. In our history, people used to talk to animals because we were all equal. We all inherited or were given this world and somewhere along the way we lost our ability to communicate. What you experienced is a marvel. What was said, I can't say for sure what it means. But I get the impression that soon you'll find out for yourself. I know also, that you and your family are Christians. And there are parallels to what you believe and what I do. I think you should talk with your church leaders and seek blessings from them also. We all occupy this country and we need to learn how to bring back the harmony in all things.

Yeah, I had thought of discussing this with them, said Yahashke. But, wasn't sure when would be a good time. I mean, I'm still trying to process what happened.

Speaking to them as you have spoken to me is the process.

Yahashke stood up, shook his uncle's hand, and gave him some money for having performed the blessing.

Thank you, Son, his uncle said to him.

Thanks for the blessing. Can I help you with anything around here?

We're fine. Your brothers chopped wood for me yesterday, and my water pail is filled, so we're good.

Okay. I'll see you later.

~

Yahashke made his way back to his place. Grabbed his guitar and fiddled with it. Sat down and started strumming a tune he had written. He did this sort of thing to help clear his mind. As he sat holding his guitar, he thought of the significance of the prayer his uncle performed for him. The sacredness of the fire, smoke, eagle feathers, and songs.

A rapping at the door interrupted his thoughts. He got up and answered. Standing outside the door was one of his church leaders.

Hey, thanks for coming, said Yahashke.

Not a problem, said Damon. I don't mind driving around in the mud. The snow this time of year never makes it through the day.

Come on in.

How's everything going?

Not too bad.

Yahashke offered him a seat. They discussed other small matters about one another's families and property. They began to sip on some tea harvested from local plants and dipped old pieces of tortillas into their beverages before eating.

This morning, when the snow fell fresh, I had an experience, said Yahashke. This coyote spoke to me.

Really. The coyote actually spoke?

Yes.

I don't know what to say.

I told my uncle Roy about it.

What did he have to say?

Told me that I should talk with you also.

What did the coyote say?

It said that I should prepare. Not be afraid. And that disharmony brings harmony in some cases.

What? I wouldn't know how to interpret that.

I just thought I would tell you and see what impressions you might have.

You know, it reminds me of when the donkey started talking to Balaam in the Bible. In that story, the Lord gave Balaam's donkey the ability to speak, only because Balaam was blinded by his own greed and was unaware of the presence of an angel sent to keep Balaam from making a mistake and going against the Lord's promised people. So, as I hear your story, and although it's hard to believe that coyote spoke to you, it is not unlike God to communicate in this way. He uses all mediums to communicate to his children. I know that you're a person who loves being in nature, that you're a respecter of all life, and so I think for whatever reason, this experience you had is one way of getting you to understand.

Understand, what?

That God uses our own understanding to communicate. You said that this happened this morning?

Yes, around 6:45ish.

And it's only been a day. I think there is more to come. I mean, I think that what you were told will have significant meaning to you, and when whatever happens, you'll have had a foreknowledge of those things as or before they happen.

Yahashke was still a little confused as he tried to work out all of what happened and what he heard from his spiritual advisors. He asked for a blessing before Damon would leave. Damon obliged his request and laid his hands upon Yahashke's head and blessed him. As the weight of hands were upon his head, Yahashke thought about how the two blessings had different approaches to the same God or Creator. His uncle told him to start sweeping smoke over his body beginning at his feet and ending at his head. Here, the blessing was beginning at his head. The prayer conducted by his uncle taught him that we are all connected to this earth and the beginning of prayers acknowledge that fact. But on the other hand, the blessing he currently received began at his head, as if coming from above, or in other words, heaven. The two prayers, in his mind, demonstrated balance. Something he had never thought of before.

He thanked Damon for coming by and listening to him.

~

A week or so passed and Yahashke was on his horse riding up to check on Ernest. Yahashke's cousins said they were up there a few days ago and helped him with his fencing. They also said they drug off a dead horse. Yahashke was on his way up to speak with Ernest and tell him of his experience with the coyote.

As the horse stepped rhythmically on the trail, its hooves pressed down onto the earth and the leather straps bounced off the saddle; it all created the sounds of a person riding horseback to visit a friend. Both horse and rider were getting close to Ernest's place when Eber stopped. Eber sensed something and began to nervously stomp his hooves. Eber snorted.

Easy, boy, said Yahashke, rubbing Eber's neck and holding tightly to the reins.

Yahashke scanned the country, leaning back into his saddle as an indication of him trying to see past the trees and undergrowth. He did not notice anything out of the ordinary. He waited to see if Eber sensed anything more. Nothing. Yahashke made a clicking sound with his mouth and Eber moved forward. Then, Yahashke pulled on the reins. There about sixty yards out he saw what he thought to be a tall person. It was looking straight at him and then it turned and started to run off. Yahashke took seconds to think, clasped the reins in his right hand, and grabbed the saddle horn with his left. Pressed Eber's side with his legs, and said, Let's go boy!

At a full gallop, through the trees, Yahashke was determined to discover what that thing was. He had a good eye on where it was running and kept on its trail. Up the side of a little hill, on a deer trail, that thing ran. Yahashke knew where that trail led and he knew where he could cut that thing off. It was a gamble, but he decided to take it. He got to the place where the trail opened up into a small meadow. He halted, and grabbed and readied his pistol. Looking out in front of him he saw what he guessed was the thing he followed into the trees. It was hunched over and looking back at him. Yahashke moved closer. He saw the thing stand and come forward a little. Yahashke stopped his horse. Eber was fully alert and stared right at that thing. It was tall, walked on two legs, had long hair, its face was dark, and its eyes were very large and round. Holding on to his pistol, Yahashke lowered it, and rested it at his side. The thing moved steps closer. Its arms were a little longer than a human arm and its hands were hard to see with the hair that dangled from its wrists. It moved in long motions with a rhythm that was somewhere in between smooth and edgy. It stepped into the afternoon sun and exposed its tannish color, deepened in soot, mud, or darker earth-toned soil. Yahashke could see its chest moving. It matched the deep breaths Eber was taking from the run, and it reminded Yahashke that he needed to take a breath. All three creatures, man, horse, and what appeared to be Bigfoot, all shared this moment in time together. On a hidden meadow, beneath a sun well past its zenith, in northern New Mexico, on a country filled with traditionalist medicine men, healers, and Christians.

Nothing was said, no sounds were made, and all things just stood and studied each other. Finally, that thing moved, and it caused Eber to shift footing.

Whoa, boy, said Yahashke.

The thing was standing more at an angle now, and Yahashke commanded, Go, be on your way.

Yahashke holstered his pistol, pulled the reins, and backed up. The thing stood its ground and made some aggressive steps towards them. Yahashke halted. Looked that thing straight on and rode toward it with equal aggression. The thing stopped. Lifted its head as if to smell the air. Turned and walked away. Yahashke saw it disappear into the trees.

He continued his ride to Ernest's place. On the back of a horse, high in the country, the breath of the earth moving through the pine trees, and now he saw what few others have witnessed. He thought about his experience with the coyote, the prayer and blessing given to him by his uncle Roy and Damon. He thought on words spoken to him from his grandmother years ago before she passed.

She said to him, The Navajos end their prayers with the phrase *hózhó náhásdlíí*, meaning that all things will return to beauty again.

His mind recalled passages in the book of Isaiah that beauty would come from ashes. He sat upon his horse comfortably, knowing that all things would return to beauty.

Christopher Nelson

BLUE FLAGS
—for Charlotte

A meadow in May, driving home from
their first camp together, the lovers, still
pungent from each other, stop

to take them in, walk out among them
in the boggy ground, their papery and delicate
blooms unavoidably signifying

celebration, never mind their poisonous
root, which centuries ago the herbalists
employed for syphilis and strangeness

of the gallbladder and had their own names for
though most agreed to call it *fleur
de Louis,* after the king, but we know

what becomes of kings, so they called it
fleur de luce, but we know the implications
of praising light, so they called it *fleur*

de lys, and it stuck because no one knew
what it meant, which seemed appropriate
for a flower of such beauty, for what

really can beauty ever mean? The lovers
are kneeling beside them, getting muddy,

as if the whole show is for them,

which it is—that's the first purpose
of desire, its bridge the color between
spirit and matter. Named after

the god's messenger, Iris, who brought
to us fleeting beings the words of the divine,
and harkening to the iris of the eye,

tiny circle of the body's wildest color
that opens and opens in the presence
of the lover, and not even in their absence

can it close. They've returned to the car,
she with a handful of them, emblems
of no country but kingdom without boundary.

On Eden

Picking apples from the seven old trees—
six since the spring ice storm—trees we've neglected,
twigs and branches jutting vertical and downward.
Two wheelbarrows full, and three times that
on the ground that we've let rot and squish
under foot and attract wasps
ants, gnats, butterflies, beetles, and all manner
of critters I can't identify. From the playpen, our son
sings, screams, cries, sings again—
waving the toy ukulele like a flaming towel
before settling down to try carefulness
and the single pluck. Early fall, a break in the rain,
the groundhog has taken over the woodshed again,
the bats the crawlspace. Asters, so many blooms
they're collapsing, purple as mythology,
purple as the robe on the picture-book Jesus.
In my future when (as the painters and
carpenters say) a man past 40 starts to fall
from ladders, that future, when my backwards
descent shows me the fatigueless blue sky
then my upside-down house, then my wife,
her twelve-foot apple fork aloft, lost
to ancient industry and song. When I land
in the fetid mush, may the bees not scatter,
may their feast continue, may they care
nothing of me, may they keep the truer way.

POSTLUDE

Karin Anderson

TURN

I N MY EARLY THIRTIES: I HAVE THREE SMALL CHILDREN, A HUS-
band committed to art and faith. We live in Utah—my hometown no less, a place that looks deceptively like Eden to comers
like my husband. Everything complicates everything: I work
ever-inadequate hours as chair of a growth-pained college department. I spend whole nights on campus, kids dreaming in their
little sleeping bags on my office floor. When I'm home I want to
forget the pressures of work and just be a mother, but I can't keep
my mind off unwritten memos, marital strain, icky local politics.

We live in a storybook house created by my talented husband. Our second-level bedroom window contains the breadth
and height of the Lone Peak Wilderness: monument to the best
meanings of *home*, but I'm walled away.

My husband and I launched our union from divergent
points on the religious map; it's an *a priori* fact of our marriage.
But by now our differences are seeping beyond our pink stucco
walls. The neighborhood can't not be concerned. It's clear I'm
not devout enough to be assigned a real congregational job—a
"calling"—but as summer approaches, the bishop drops by to
ask brightly if I'll help supervise the teen girls' camp. My oldest
child—my up-for-anything daughter—is six. I say I'll help with
girls' camp if she can come with me.

It's hard to leave the boys for a week; I reach from all the places I have to be, trying to hold my children close as they shimmer into new figures, voices, and visions. But I'm also stunned by the grace of precious time with my little girl—my big girl? Who is this wide-eyed person, strapped tight in the seat beside me, hair flying in the jeepy breeze, gulping in air and panorama? We rise and twist by Daniel's Summit, catch wet smells of Strawberry Reservoir, jam east through Tabiona's badlands. Blue Uinta mystery to our left, mile after mile. The wind is fast and hot, too loud for talk but no matter: little passenger has fixed her gaze on hill and horizon, desert gray and blue-brown, orange flash on azure. She engulfs and is engulfed. She's spent good hours in outside places, but now with no near-twin brother to consult, no toddler up-and-comer to instruct, too much blowing for crayons, it's only this kid and the planet.

In the methane mirage of Vernal, a shape-shifting city at the base of Uinta upturn, we stop for soda and French fries. From the parking lot of a run-down strip mall, a clean window beams from the sparsely occupied storefronts. Somebody's go at a bookstore, a dimensional crack in an obscure corner of Drill-Baby-Drill town. We can't stay long; I've been assigned to pass as a righteous role model in Zion for a pack of girls who want nothing less than a week in the woods with role models. In the bookstore, my daughter and I linger and scan, touch the spines, breathe scents of candles and paper.

Little one makes off with a pocket-sized book of dinosaurs. I emerge with a book written by some woman I've never heard of, who purports to love nature. I suspect I'm in for a sentimental gush on timeless stars and self-knowledge, divine design and the answering harmonies of the soul, maybe some forced rhyme.

I think in camp we're all really trying. The women are blandly nice and the husbands jovial. The girls are mostly preoccupied in their huddles. We learn how to make campfires with teepee-shaped kindling. We herd the whole group on a hike to the ice caves. The camp leader wakes us up every morning at six with what has apparently become the new national anthem, blasted from the speakers of her husband's decked-out truck: I'M PROUD TO BE AN AMERICAN / WHERE AT LEAST I KNOW I'M FREE!

I offer to help cook, but the leaders have got it covered. But thanks. I could be a chat-worthy resource for older girls who want to talk about their plans for college? It doesn't seem I've spoken audibly. I brought my guitar—anyone wants to play it, here it is in the portal of my tent—where it remains untouched all week. It turns out I *am* useful for letting the two surliest girls—hair dyed black, goth makeup—ride with my daughter and me on the way home from rafting at Flaming Gorge. They blink, and chew gum.

These really are my people. I grew up with muscular trucks and big-griddle breakfasts and faith-promoting stories at the campfire, overbearing mother-stand-in camp leaders in familiar family campsites and beloved hunting grounds. But here the instructive testimonials never drop a key into earthy cowboy jokes, shoulder-to-shoulder feminine repartee, tonal complexity, double entendre. The girls go to bed on time and stay there: we do not once awaken to bras waving from the flagpole, plastic wrap stretched across porta-potty seats, or labels peeled off identical silver pantry cans. I feel like *we're* wrapped in plastic, though. I don't understand what's happening, or not happening, here. If I could see myself from outside my own eyes—from inside of theirs—I'd look pathetic, prickly, mildly dangerous to impressionable girls even at arm's length.

Maybe I'm inventing everything. I have no access of what any human being in this camp feels, thinks, believes, or desires. This is seismically disconcerting. I have, in my home places among my home people, believed I had some capacity for reading hearts, for touching the singular, for unearthing affinity.

Now I feel like Temple Grandin—an anthropologist on Mars—but when did my familiar Earth transform into Mars?

Tonight, the penultimate evening of camp, is the all-important Testimony Meeting, soaring emotion facilitated by a blazing fire, dropping to reverent embers under alpine starlight. I help clean up dinner and retreat with my daughter to our tent, leaving the faithful to close the circuit of safe communion. I finger a few familiar songs. She drifts to sleep, so sweet in her flannel bedroll she almost makes me weep. I place my camp chair just outside, light the lantern, and give my bookstore find a proper examination.

Raven's Exile.

Ellen Meloy.

I read the first chapter.

. . .

What the *hell.*

My first people are down at the fire, bearing witness of what they know *without a shadow of a doubt.* I know that the ceremony will permit inscrutable countenances to break into sobs, tumbling words through streaming tears. Down there at the bonfire, my first people unite in an ecstasy of religious emotion, touch something raw and holy that only arises precisely here: words that mean something transcendent beyond their recitations. I know this because they are, beyond the heaves of national transformation, my tribe, and I will claim them.

But never again my only people.

And, my God. This woman here.

Word by word, image by image, she takes me in. Stops my breathing. Un-ticks each clotted nerve. Returns something to me I was about to lose forever, gives me something I can barely allow myself to claim. Embraces my sleeping daughter as I read out loud to all of us, my also-people, my future people, my uncanny people, here under the stars, flat on the ground.

I feel the continent roll, and the century turn, beneath us.

About the Contributors

Poetry

Tacey M. Atsitty, Diné (Navajo), is Tsénahabiłnii (Sleep Rock People) and born for Ta'neeszahnii (Tangle People). Her first book is *Rain Scald* (University of New Mexico Press, 2018), and she is a PhD student at Florida State University.

Matthew James Babcock is professor of English at BYU-Idaho in Rexburg. His books include *Points of Reference* (Folded Word), *Strange Terrain* (Mad Hat Press), *Heterodoxologies* (Educe Press). His debut fiction collection, *Four Tales of Troubled Love* (Harvard Square Editions), won first place in the 2020 Next Generation Indie Book Awards. His follow-up fiction collection, *Future Perfect*, was a finalist for the 2020 BOA Editions Short Fiction Prize and is forthcoming from Engine Books.

Lisa Bickmore is the author of three books of poems, most recently *Ephemerist* (Red Mountain Press, 2017). Her work has been recognized with the Antivenom Prize from Elixir Press, the Salt Lake Mayor's Artist Award, and the Ballymaloe International Poetry Prize. She is a professor at Salt Lake Community College, where she teaches writing of all kinds.

Scott Cameron is an associate professor of English at BYU-Idaho. His poetry has appeared in *Ruminate*, *Dialogue*, *Ascent*, and *Fire in the Pasture*. When he isn't teaching or writing, his first choice is to be out on a trail with his family.

Tyler Chadwick is an award-winning writer, editor, and teacher. He has three books to his name: two anthologies, *Fire in the Pasture: 21st Century Mormon Poets* (Peculiar Pages, 2011) and *Dove Song: Heavenly Mother in Mormon Poetry* (Peculiar Pages, 2018), and a collection of poetry and essays, *Field Notes on Language* *and Kinship* (Mormon Artists Group, 2013). He lives in Ogden, Utah, with his wife, Jess, and their four daughters.

Star Coulbrooke is the Inaugural Poet Laureate of Logan City, Utah. Her most recent poetry collections are *Thin Spines of Memory*, *Both Sides from the Middle*, and *City of Poetry*.

Kathryn Cowles's book of poems, *Maps and Transcripts of the Ordinary World*, was published by Milkweed Editions in March 2020; her first book, *Eleanor, Eleanor, not your real name*, won the Dorothy Brunsman Poetry Prize. She earned her doctorate from the University of Utah and is an associate professor of English at Hobart and William Smith Colleges in the Finger Lakes region of New York, where she co-edits the poetry and multi-media sections of *Seneca Review*.

Stacie Denetsosie is a Diné (Navajo) poet and writer. She is currently an MFA candidate at the Institute of American Indian Arts.

Danielle Beazer Dubrasky's poems have been published in *Chiron Review*, *South Dakota Review*, *Ninth Letter*, *Pilgrimage*, *saltfront*, *Sugar House Review*, *Under a Warm Green Linden*, *Mississippi Review* and *Terrain.org*. She is the director of the Eco-poetry and the Essay Conference at Southern Utah University.

Megan Fairbanks is a poet, writer, and current graduate student in the Ancient Languages and Cultures program at Utah State University. She spent her childhood in the Tooele Valley desert and made frequent summer drives to visit Iosepa, which helped foster her long-standing interest in history and archaeology. When not writing or studying, Megan enjoys finding new places to explore and searching for wayward plants in need of adoption.

Theric Jepson (@thmazing) lives in El Cerrito, California, with his wife and children. He is past-president of the Association for Mormon Letters and author of the novels *Byuck* and *Just Julie's Fine*.

Kimberly Johnson is the author of three books of poetry, including most recently *Uncommon Prayer* (Persea, 2014), as well as of book-length translations of Virgil and Hesiod. With Jay Hopler, she edited *Before the Door of God: An Anthology of Devotional Poetry*. She lives in Salt Lake City and spends as much time as possible in Utah's open spaces.

Melody Newey Johnson is poetry editor for *Segullah* journal. She earns a living as a registered nurse and grows a respectable garden in the American West, where she lives with her spouse, Jeff. Her first full-length poetry manuscript, *An Imperfect Roundness*, was published in 2020 by BCC Press.

Dr. Farina King, a citizen of the Navajo Nation, is an assistant professor of history and an affiliate of Cherokee and Indigenous studies at Northeastern State University in Tahlequah, Oklahoma. Her first book, *The Earth Memory Compass: Diné Landscapes and Education in the Twentieth Century*, was published by the University Press of Kansas in 2018.

Lance Larsen has published five poetry collections, most recently *What the Body Knows* (Tampa 2018). He's won a number of awards, including a Pushcart Prize and a fellowship from the National Endowment for the Arts. A professor at BYU, he completed a five-year appointment as Utah's poet laureate in 2017.

Christopher Nelson is the author of *Blood Aria* (University of Wisconsin Press, 2021) and three chapbooks: *Blue House* (Poetry Society of America, 2009), *Capital City at Midnight*, recipient of the 2014 *BLOOM* Chapbook Prize; and *Love Song for the*

New World (Seven Kitchens Press, 2019). He is the founder and editor of Green Linden Press and the journal *Under a Warm Green Linden*.

Twila Newey grew up Mormon in Provo, Utah. In mid-life she converted to poetry, gardening and California. Her poems can be found at *Radar Poetry*, *JuxtaProse*, *Green Mountains Review*, as well as other journals. Twila lives, writes, and plants with the help of her husband Jon and their four children in the San Francisco Bay Area.

Dayna Patterson is the author of *Titania in Yellow* (Porkbelly Press, 2019) and *If Mother Braids a Waterfall* (Signature Books, 2020). Her creative work and poembroideries have appeared recently in *AGNI*, *Irreantum*, *The Maynard*, and *Tahoma Literary Review*. She is the founding editor-in-chief of *Psaltery & Lyre* and a co-editor of *Dove Song: Heavenly Mother in Mormon Poetry*. daynapatterson.com

Lisa Madsen Rubilar is a writer and editor whose work has appeared in literary journals such as *The Fredericksburg Literary & Arts Review*, *The Carolina Quarterly*, *Dialogue: A Journal of Mormon Thought*, *Irreantum*, and the anthology *Dispensation: Latter-Day Fiction*. A mother of four and grandmother of six, she and her husband, Roberto, live near the Peaks of Otter in central Virginia. To reach her, visit her website at www.lisarubilar.com.

Kathryn Knight Sonntag is the author of *The Tree at the Center* (By Common Consent Press, 2019). Her creative works appear in *Psaltery & Lyre*, *Dialogue: A Journal of Mormon Thought*, *Segullah*, *Exponent II*, www.visitutah.com/she, *Amethyst Review*, *The Inflectionist Review*, and others. She holds an MLA from Utah State University and works as a landscape designer and land planner in Salt Lake City, Utah. KathrynKnightSonntag.com

Laura Stott is the author of two books of poetry, *Blue Nude Migration* (Lynx House Press, 2020) and *In the Museum of Coming and Going* (New Issues, 2014). She holds an MFA from Eastern Washington University and is an instructor of English at Weber State University. She lives with her husband and daughters in northern Utah where they garden and enjoy the outdoors as much as possible.

Nano Taggart is a founding editor of *Sugar House Review* and is a co-recipient of a grant from the Utah Division of Arts and Museums. You can see some more of his writing in places like *Terrain. org*, *Weber—The Contemporary West*, and *Verse Daily*.

Robert Terashima lives with his wife Karen in South Jordan, Utah. He is a retired pediatrician.

Laura Walker holds an MFA from Northern Arizona University, and currently teaches writing classes at Southern Utah University in Cedar City, where she lives with her wife. From Southern California by way of Flagstaff, Arizona, she always finds herself wishing for a little more snow and a little less sun. Her work is featured or forthcoming in *Roanoke Review*, *Sugar House Review*, *The Horror is Us* anthology from Mason Jar Press, and elsewhere.

Darlene Young's collection, *Homespun and Angel Feathers* (BCC Press 2019) won the 2019 award for poetry from the Association for Mormon Letters. She teaches at Brigham Young University and has served as the poetry editor for *Dialogue: A Journal of Mormon Thought* and for *Segullah*, and as secretary for the Association for Mormon Letters. She lives in South Jordan, Utah, with her husband and sons.

Natalie Young's poetry has been published in the *Los Angeles Times*, *Rattle*, *Tampa Review*, *Green Mountains Review*,

Tar River Review, South Dakota Review, Terrain.org, and others. She is a founding and managing editor for *Sugar House Review*. Natalie is half Puerto Rican and half Brigham Young. NatalieYoungArts.com

Prose

Karin Anderson is a crabby not-grandmother who lives in Salt Lake City.

Phyllis Barber is the award-winning author of nine books, the latest being *The Desert Between Us*, a novel, listed as one of the ten best reads of the month by *The Chicago Review of Books*. She has published fiction and nonfiction in many literary magazines (AGNI, *The Missouri Review*, and *Kenyon Review*, among others), won the AWP Creative Nonfiction Prize for *How I Got Cultured: A Nevada Memoir*, and has been listed as notable in *Best American Essays* and *Best American Travel Writing*.

A native of the Utah desert, **John Bennion** writes personal and historical essays and fiction about people struggling with that forbidding landscape. He has published a collection of short fiction, *Breeding Leah and other Stories* (Signature Books, 1991), and three novels—*Falling Toward Heaven* (Signature Books, 2000), *An Unarmed Woman* (Signature Books, 2019), and *Ezekiel's Third Wife* (Roundfire Books, 2019). He has published short stories and essays in *Interdisciplinary Studies in Literature and Environment, Hotel Amerika, Southwest Review, Utah Historical Quarterly, High Country News, Journal of Mormon History*, and others. He teaches creative writing at Brigham Young University.

Jennifer Champoux lives in Colorado with her husband and three children. She holds an MA in art history from Boston University, has taught art history as adjunct faculty at several universities, and is past-vice president of Mormon Scholars in the

Humanities. Her writing on religious art has appeared in *BYU Studies*, *Dialogue*, and *LDS Living*.

Despite decades of opportunity, **Reb Cuevas** remains a Utahan who's never been skiing. She blames her bad knees, but really, she knows she wouldn't be good at it and she'd rather fail at summer sports. Her work has appeared in *peculiar*, a Utah-based queer-lit journal, and *Aesthetica Creative Writing Annual*, in which she was one of 60 international finalists for her poem "dry erase." Find more of her writing at www.rebcuevas.com.

Amelia England was deemed Master of Romantic British poetry at Oregon State University, and currently self-proclaims as Master of French macarons in Salt Lake City. She writes endless freelance content. She and her husband live in South Salt Lake with their dogs, chickens, bunnies, and fish.

Jack Garcia is the co-founder and co-editor-in-chief of *peculiar*, a queer literary journal based in Provo, Utah. He has had poetry and prose published in journals such as *Touchstones*, *Essais*, *Orogeny*, *Inscape*, and *The Matador Review*. When not teaching teens how to analyze and respond to literature, he enjoys binge-watching reruns of *The Golden Girls* with his boyfriend and walking their Parson Russell terrier in their new home: Baltimore, Maryland.

George B. Handley is professor of interdisciplinary humanities at BYU where he has taught since 1998. His creative writing includes the environmental memoir, *Home Waters: A Year of Recompenses on the Provo River* and the novel, *American Fork*. He also recently published a collection of essays on Latter-day Saint environmental values, entitled *The Hope of Nature: Our Care for God's Creation*.

A native of southeastern Illinois, **Jack Harrell** has published on topics ranging from Mormon literary theory to the aesthetics of death metal music. His most recent book is the novel *Caldera Ridge*. Harrell teaches writing at Brigham Young University-Idaho.

Heather Holland is an instructor of English and creative writing at Snow College whose poetry and essays have appeared in *Sunstone, saltfront, The Found Poetry Review, Segullah, Exponent II,* and in her chapbook *Mastering the Art of Joy*. She lives in the foothills of Provo, Utah, where she loves to hike and explore with her partner, children, and their neurotic rescue dog, Millie.

Tamara Johnson lives in San Diego, California. Her work has been published by Greenhaven Press, City Works Press, and Manic D Press.

Kumen Louis was born into the Honey-Combed Rock People clan (Tsé níjíkiní). Being Diné, he was heavily influenced by stories told to him by his grandparents, parents, and many other family/tribal members.

Lyn McCarter is a Utah native whose writing is rooted in the cultures and landscapes of the American West where she is most at home. She lives in Summit County, Utah, with her grandson and other animals.

Michael McLane is author of the chapbook *Trace Elements* and is an editor with both *saltfront: studies in human habit(at)* and *Sugar House Review*. His work has appeared in numerous journals, including *Dark Mountain, Colorado Review, South Dakota Review, Utah Historical Quarterly, High Country News* and *Laurel Review*. He is from Salt Lake City and currently lives in Wellington, New Zealand.

Dr. Thomas W Murphy is professor of anthropology at Edmonds College in Lynnwood, Washington. Washington Association of Conservation Districts selected him as the 2011 Washington State Educator of the Year and Puget Sound Regional Council awarded Edmonds College a VISION 2040 award in 2012 for Dr. Murphy's collaboration with the City of Mukilteo and Snohomish County on the Japanese Gulch Fish Passage Project.

Lee Ann Mortensen is a professor of English at Utah Valley University, where she teaches fiction, playwriting, and literary theory.

Sarah Newcomb is Tsimshian of the First Nations from Metlakatla, Alaska. Sarah is a freelance editor, writer, and blogger. She is creator of the blog *Lamanite Truth*, which explores Native American history, experiences, and current issues as they intersect with colonization and Mormonism. Sarah currently resides in Garland, Texas, with her husband and four children.

Julie J. Nichols teaches at Utah Valley University in Orem, Utah. She's at work on her second novel.

Salt Lake City-based **David G. Pace** is the author of the novel *Dream House on Golan Drive* (Signature Books, 2015) and former literary editor of 15 Bytes. "Freedom Ruts" is excerpted from his narrative nonfiction book-length work *Cold Desert*, second-place winner in the Utah Original Writing Competition.

Michael William Palmer's first book, *Baptizing the Dead and Other Jobs*, won the 2019 Monadnock Prize and was published by Bauhan Press. His nonfiction has appeared in *Bellingham Review*, *Terrain.org*, *West Texas Literary Review*, and numerous other publications. He grew up in Utah County and currently lives in Forest Park, Illinois.

Matthew Pockrus has degrees in art history and English literature from Utah Valley University, where he also helped author, edit, and design three award-winning books in collaboration with the University's Fine Arts Department. He is an accomplished landscape photographer, amateur woodworker, and an aspiring educator. Though he calls Utah home, he currently resides in Minneapolis, where he is pursuing an MFA in creative writing at the University of Minnesota. He is working on a memoir about his tenure as a Mormon missionary in Ukraine during Ukraine's 2013/2014 EuroMaidan revolution.

Ronda Walker Weaver was reared in Rigby, Idaho, although she didn't claim her Idaho heritage until her mid-adulthood. Recently retired from teaching Folklore and Composition at Utah Valley University, she is now a chaplain for Intermountain Healthcare. She enjoys traveling, listening, and creating, as well as "thinking out loud" at folkladysadventures.blogspot.com. She and her husband, Scott, have six children, and twenty grandchildren.

ACKOWLEDGEMENTS

Barber, Phyllis. "The Desert: Waiting." *Upstreet*, no. sixteen, July 2020.

Bickmore, Lisa. "Vesper Sparrow on a Fence Post." *The Moth*. Issue 20, Spring 2015

Chadwick, Tyler. "Goddess Looking Up." *BYU Studies Quarterly*, vol. 56, no. 1, 2017.

Coulbrooke, Star. "Overlook." *Tertulia Magazine*, Oct. 2003. *Thin Spines of Memory*. Helicon West Press, Logan, Utah, 2017.

Cowles, Kathryn. "Hymn." *Maps and Transcripts of the Ordinary World*. Milkweed Editions: Minneapolis, MN, 2020.

Dubrasky, Danielle. "Winter Solstice in the Gorge." *Terrain.org*. July 2017. (Originally published as "Winter Solstice in the Gorge, 2016.")

Johnson, Kimberly. "Goodfriday," "Voluptuary." *A Metaphorical God*. Persea Books: New York, NY, 2008.

Johnson, Melody Newey. "I Sleep Beneath a Quilt." *An Imperfect Roundness*. By Common Consent Press: Evansville, IN, 2020.

Larsen, Lance. "Nest." *Erasable Walls*. New Issues Press: Kalamazoo, MI, 1998.

Patterson, Dayna. "Breathe In." *River Mouth Review*. May 2020.

Sonntag, Kathryn Knight. "The Older Covenant." *The Tree at the Center*. By Common Consent Press: Evansville, IN, 2019.

Taggart, Nano. "Mojave Dirge." *The American Journal of Poetry*, Vol. 4, 2018.

Terashima, Robert. "Snow Canyon." *Hanging Loose Magazine* #105.

Young, Darlene. "Utah Mormon." *Homespun and Angel Feathers*. By Common Consent Press: Evansville, IN, 2019.

Young, Natalie. "Utah Complications." *Dark Mountain Project*. Issue 13, 2018.

TORREY HOUSE PRESS

Voices for the Land

The economy is a wholly owned subsidiary of the environment, not the other way around.
> —Senator Gaylord Nelson, founder of Earth Day

Torrey House Press publishes books at the intersection of the literary arts and environmental advocacy. THP authors explore the diversity of human experiences with the environment and engage community in conversations about landscape, literature, and the future of our ever-changing planet, inspiring action toward a more just world. We believe that lively, contemporary literature is at the cutting edge of social change. We seek to inform, expand, and reshape the dialogue on environmental justice and stewardship for the human and more-than-human world by elevating literary excellence from diverse voices.

Visit www.torreyhouse.org for reading group discussion guides, author interviews, and more.

As a 501(c)(3) nonprofit publisher, our work is made possible by generous donations from readers like you.

Torrey House Press is supported by Back of Beyond Books, the King's English Bookshop, Maria's Bookshop, the Jeffrey S. and Helen H. Cardon Foundation, The Sam and Diane Stewart Family Foundation, the Barker Foundation, Diana Allison, Klaus Bielefeldt, Patrick de Freitas, Laurie Hilyer, Shelby Tisdale, Kirtly Parker Jones, Robert Aagard and Camille Bailey Aagard, Kif Augustine Adams and Stirling Adams, Rose Chilcoat and Mark Franklin, Jerome Cooney and Laura Storjohann, Linc Cornell and Lois Cornell, Susan Cushman and Charlie Quimby, Betsy Folland and David Folland, the Utah Division of Arts & Museums, Utah Humanities, the National Endowment for the Humanities, the National Endowment for the Arts, and Salt Lake County Zoo, Arts & Parks. Our thanks to individual donors, subscribers, and the Torrey House Press board of directors for their valued support.

Join the Torrey House Press family and give today at
www.torreyhouse.org/give.